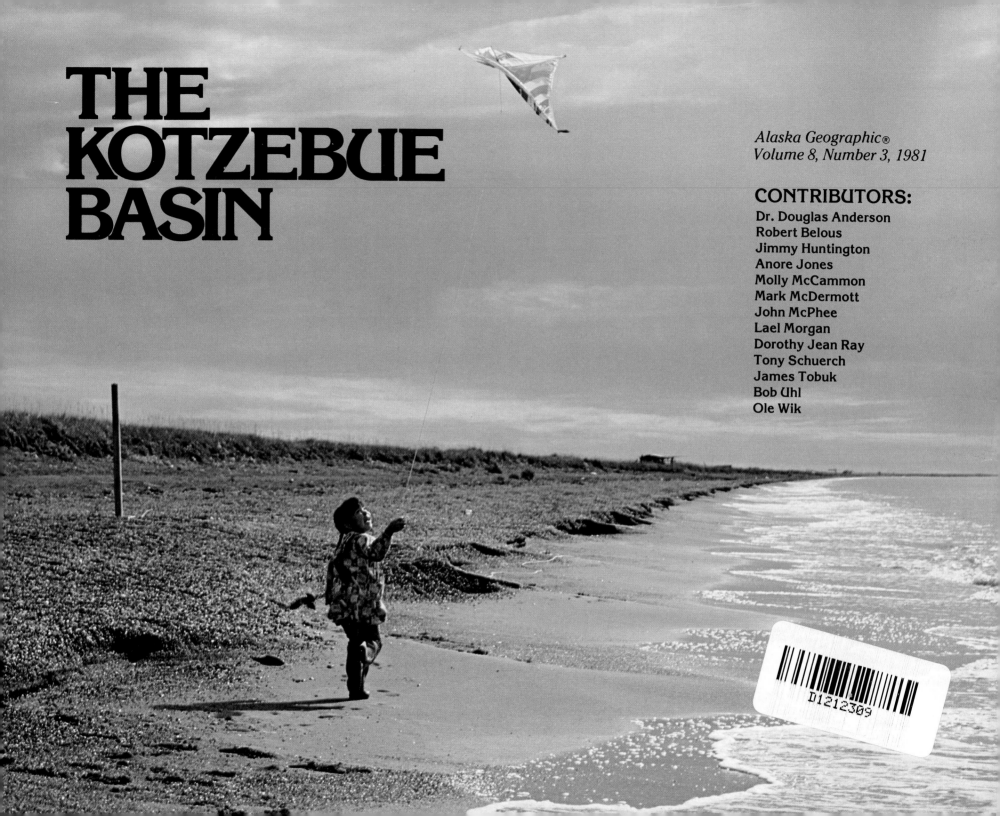

THE KOTZEBUE BASIN

Alaska Geographic®
Volume 8, Number 3, 1981

CONTRIBUTORS:

Dr. Douglas Anderson
Robert Belous
Jimmy Huntington
Anore Jones
Molly McCammon
Mark McDermott
John McPhee
Lael Morgan
Dorothy Jean Ray
Tony Schuerch
James Tobuk
Bob Uhl
Ole Wik

The Alaska Geographic Society

To teach many more to better know and use our natural resources

---

About This Issue: We are grateful to the many contributors who, with *Lael Morgan*, roving editor of *ALASKA®* magazine, put together this picture of the Kotzebue Basin. Special thanks go to northwest Alaska residents *Bob Uhl*, who covered the coast, and *Ole Wik*, who covered the interior, for their contribution on the countryside, birds, fish, and subsistence living; to *Robert Belous*, special assistant to the director of the Alaska Region for the National Park Service for material on parklands; to northwest Alaska resident *Molly McCammon* for sharing her impressions of the Noatak and Ambler rivers; to *Anore Jones*, plant expert, and *Tony Schuerch*, impetus behind the innovative gardening efforts taking place in the region, for contributing knowledge gleaned from many years in the Kotzebue Basin. In addition, we appreciate the help of *Mark McDermott*, formerly with U.S. Bureau of Mines and now with Anaconda, for his contribution on contemporary mining; *Dorothy Jean Ray*, an authority on Alaska Native art, for her piece on arts and crafts; *Dr. Douglas Anderson* for sharing his knowledge of the region's early peoples; and the cooperation of *Daniel Gibson* of the University Museum, University of Alaska, Fairbanks, in reviewing portions of the manuscript.

We acknowledge the assistance of *Mrs. Rachael Craig*, Northwest Arctic School District; *Russell Dale Guthrie*, Department of Biological Sciences, University of Alaska; *John Cross*, retired pilot, Kotzebue; *Mrs. Edith Kennedy* and *Mrs. Mildred Sage*, Kivalina; *Mrs. Edith Bullock*, *Mable Walsh*, and *Laura Beltz Crockett*, all formerly of Kotzebue; *A. George Francis*, magistrate, Kotzebue; The National Bilingual Materials Development Center, Anchorage; *Tom Richards Sr.*, Wien Air Alaska; *Ray Skin*, Selawik weatherman; *Mrs. Clara Lee*, Ambler; *Doug Sheldon* and family of Candle; *Lona Wood* of Selawik; the Friends Alaska Mission; *Frank Whaley*, miner and retired Wien pilot; and the many from NANA Regional Corporation for their help and cooperation.

We thank the many fine photographers who shared their material with us and we are grateful to the publishers who allowed us to reprint selections from their publications in this issue.

ALASKA GEOGRAPHIC®, ISSN 0361-1353, is published quarterly by The Alaska Geographic Society, Anchorage, Alaska 99509. Second-class postage paid in Edmonds, Washington 98020. Printed in U.S.A.

THE ALASKA GEOGRAPHIC SOCIETY is a nonprofit organization exploring new frontiers of knowledge across the lands of the polar rim, learning how other men and other countries live in their Norths, putting the geography book back in the classroom, exploring new methods of teaching and learning — sharing in the excitement of discovery in man's wonderful new world north of 51°16′.

MEMBERS OF THE SOCIETY RECEIVE *Alaska Geographic®*, a quality magazine in color which devotes each quarterly issue to monographic in-depth coverage of a northern geographic region or resource-oriented subject.

MEMBERSHIP DUES in The Alaska Geographic Society are $30 per year; $34 to non-U.S. addresses. (Eighty percent of each year's dues is for a one-year subscription to *Alaska Geographic®*.) Order from The Alaska Geographic Society, Box 4-EEE, Anchorage, Alaska 99509; (907) 274-0521.

MATERIAL SOUGHT: The editors of *Alaska Geographic®* seek a wide variety of informative material on the lands north of 51°16′ on geographic subjects — anything to do with resources and their uses (with heavy emphasis on quality color photography) — from Alaska, Northern Canada, Siberia, Japan — all geographic areas that have a relationship to Alaska in a physical or economic sense. In late 1981 editors were seeking material on the following geographic regions and subjects: Alaska fish and fisheries, the Seward Peninsula, Canada's Northwest Territories, and mining in Alaska. We do not want material done in excessive scientific terminology. A query to the editors is suggested. Payments are made for all material upon publication.

CHANGE OF ADDRESS: The post office does not automatically forward *Alaska Geographic®* when you move. To insure continuous service, notify us six weeks before moving. Send us your new address and zip code (and moving date), your old address and zip code, and if possible send a mailing label from a copy of *Alaska Geographic®*. Send this information to *Alaska Geographic®* Mailing Offices, 130 Second Avenue South, Edmonds, Washington 98020.

MAILING LISTS: We have begun making our members' names and addresses available to carefully screened publications and companies whose products and activities might be of interest to you. If you would prefer not to receive such mailings, please so advise us, and include your mailing label (or your name and address if label is not available).

Editors: *Robert A. Henning, Barbara Olds, Lael Morgan, Penny Rennick*
Editorial Assistant: *Kathy Doogan*
Designer: *Dianne Hofbeck*
Cartographer: *Jon Hersh*

THE COVER — *Eli Williams (left) and Wally Williams cross dangerous ice on the Chukchi Sea just off Kotzebue Sound while hauling an oogruk, or bearded seal, to their camp at Sealing Point, Cape Krusenstern. Both men are of the Williams clan, but not brothers. On this day Wally is the hunter and Eli was giving him a hand.* Robert Belous, National Park Service

TITLE PAGE — *Arunya Jones flies her kite along Sisualik Spit. The flat, six-mile-long spit points to Kotzebue, nine miles away, and for centuries the spit has been known to Eskimos as the place of white whales.* Peter Connors

Library of Congress cataloging in publication data:
Main entry under title:
The Kotzebue Basin.
    (Alaska geographic, ISSN 0361-1353; v. 8, no. 3)
    1. Kotzebue Sound region (Alaska)—Description and travel—Addresses, essays, lectures. 2. Kotzebue Sound region (Alaska)—History—Addresses, essays, lectures. 3. Natural history—Alaska—Kotzebue Sound region—Addresses, essays, lectures. I. Henning, Robert A. II. Alaska Geographic Society. III. Series: Alaska geographic; v. 8, no. 3.
F901.A266 vol. 8, no. 3 [F912.K66] 917.98s 81-7910
ISBN 0-88240-157-2   [979.8′7] AACR2

CONTENTS

Ice fishermen on Kotzebue Sound in front of Kotzebue have built partial walls of snow and ice surrounding their fishing holes.
Frank Bird

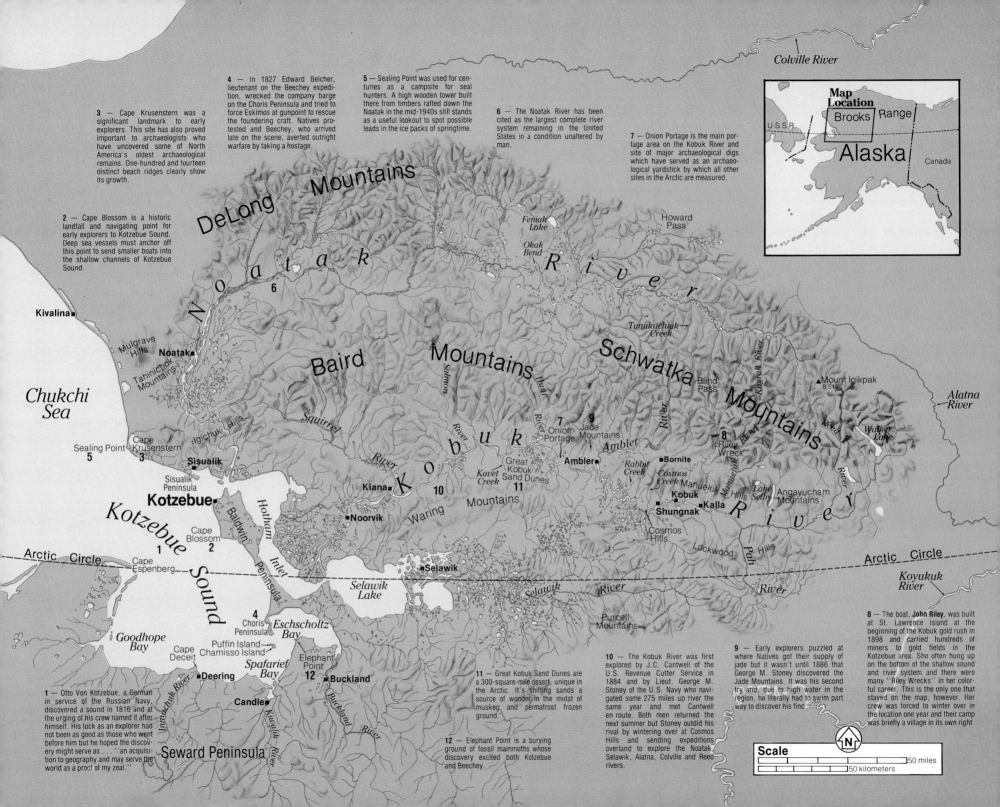

Map Location — Brooks Range — Alaska — U.S.S.R. — Canada

3 — Cape Krusenstern was a significant landmark to early explorers. This site has also proved important to archaeologists who have uncovered some of North America's oldest archaeological remains. One-hundred and fourteen distinct beach ridges clearly show its growth.

4 — In 1827 Edward Belcher, lieutenant on the Beechey expedition, wrecked the company barge on the Choris Peninsula and tried to force Eskimos at gunpoint to rescue the foundering craft. Natives protested and Beechey, who arrived late on the scene, averted outright warfare by taking a hostage.

5 — Sealing Point was used for centuries as a campsite for seal hunters. A high wooden tower built there from timbers rafted down the Noatak in the mid-1940s still stands as a useful lookout to spot possible leads in the ice packs of springtime.

6 — The Noatak River has been cited as the largest complete river system remaining in the United States in a condition unaltered by man.

7 — Onion Portage is the main portage area on the Kobuk River and site of major archaeological digs which have served as an archaeological yardstick by which all other sites in the Arctic are measured.

2 — Cape Blossom is a historic landfall and navigating point for early explorers to Kotzebue Sound. Deep sea vessels must anchor off this point to send smaller boats into the shallow channels of Kotzebue Sound.

1 — Otto Von Kotzebue, a German in service of the Russian Navy, discovered a sound in 1816 and at the urging of his crew named it after himself. His luck as an explorer had not been as good as those who went before him but he hoped the discovery might serve as . . . "an acquisition to geography and may serve the world as a proof of my zeal."

8 — The boat, **John Riley**, was built at St. Lawrence Island at the beginning of the Kobuk gold rush in 1898 and carried hundreds of miners to gold fields in the Kotzebue area. She often hung up on the bottom of the shallow sound and river system and there were many "Riley Wrecks" in her colorful career. This is the only one that stayed on the map, however. Her crew was forced to winter over in the location one year and their camp was briefly a village in its own right.

9 — Early explorers puzzled at where Natives got their supply of jade but it wasn't until 1886 that George M. Stoney discovered the Jade Mountains. It was his second try and, due to high water in the region, he literally had to swim part way to discover his find.

10 — The Kobuk River was first explored by J.C. Cantwell of the U.S. Revenue Cutter Service in 1884 and by Lieut. George M. Stoney of the U.S. Navy who navigated some 275 miles up river the same year and met Cantwell en route. Both men returned the next summer but Stoney outdid his rival by wintering over at Cosmos Hills and sending expeditions overland to explore the Noatak, Selawik, Alatna, Colville and Reed rivers.

11 — Great Kobuk Sand Dunes are a 300-square-mile desert, unique in the Arctic. It's shifting sands a source of wonder in the midst of muskeg and permafrost frozen ground.

12 — Elephant Point is a burying ground of fossil mammoths whose discovery excited both Kotzebue and Beechey.

Colville River

DeLong Mountains

Noatak

Feniak Lake

Okak Bend

Howard Pass

River

Baird Mountains

Schwatka Mountains

Mount Igikpak 8,510

Alatna River

Walker Lake

Reed River

Blind Pass

Tunukuchiok Creek

Chukchi Sea

Kivalina

Mulgrave Hills

Noatak

Tahinichok Mountains

Sealing Point
5

Cape Krusenstern
3

Igichuk Hills

Sisualik

Sisualik Peninsula

Kotzebue

Squirrel

River

Kobuk

Salmon River

Hunt River

Onion Portage
7

Jade Mountains
9

Ambler

Kiana

Kavet Creek

Great Kobuk Sand Dunes
11

Ambler

Rabbit Creek

Bornite

Cosmos Creek

Manueluk

Manueluk Hills

Kugrak River

Ambler River

Lake Selby

Angayucham Mountains

Riley Wreck
8

Kobuk

Kalla

Shungnak

Cosmos Hills

Kotzebue Sound

Cape Blossom
2

Baldwin Peninsula

Hotham Inlet

Noorvik

Waring Mountains

Selawik

Selawik Lake

Selawik River

Lockwood

Pah Hills

River

Arctic Circle

Koyukuk River

Cape Espenberg

Goodhope Bay

Choris Peninsula
4

Eschscholtz Bay

Puffin Island

Cape Deceit

Chamisso Island

Spafarief Bay

Elephant Point
12

Buckland

Purcell Mountains

Deering

Candle

Inmachuk River

Buckland River

Kiwalik River

Seward Peninsula

Scale — 50 miles — 50 kilometers

INTRODUCTION

The Kotzebue Basin region of northwest Alaska is bisected by the arctic circle, and within the region lie the extreme northern and western borders of North America's boreal forests. Deep woods of birch and spruce contrast with tundra steppes.

Much of the ground is laced with permafrost, but some is free of it and suitable for gardening. Fair-sized mountains can be seen on the region's horizons; some of the region's rivers cut through steep canyon walls, while in other areas habitable land is just barely far enough above sea level to keep tidewater from the door.

Temperatures as low as -68° have been recorded at Kobuk in March and as high as 100° in the Jade Mountains in July. There are rocky highlands where only lichens grow; swampy, pond-pocked, river-braided lowlands of muskeg; and bonafide deserts of shifting sand which are particularly astonishing because they lie within the Arctic.

Yet few areas of Alaska are more homogeneous when it comes to people. Almost the last place on the map to be explored, the region was among the first to encourage tourism and development, yet — surprisingly — its cultural integrity has been maintained. A full 85% of the residents are Eskimo — Inupiat all — who speak the same language, share the same broad philosophy and customs, and who function rather like one large, extended family.

Nor do latecomers differ greatly, for if they like the country, it is natural for them to become a family member regardless of background or race.

Decked out in fine fur parkas, Clara Jackson (left) and Susie Barr take five on a grassy bank at Kiana during Fourth of July festivities.
Lorry Schuerch

THE COAST
— Bob Uhl

Coastal geography of the Kotzebue Sound region explains to a large degree the ancient and modern living patterns of the area's changing human populations. Different fish, mammal, bird, and plant populations that have sustained these people seem inexorably tied to diverse coastal geography. This diversity includes large river estuaries; huge brackish-water inlets; smaller fresh- and brackish-water coastal lagoons; open-ocean beaches with chronologically exposed ancient sand-gravel beach ridges; coastal mountains of 2,000 feet elevation; and vertical, rocky bluffs in isolated locations of otherwise narrow, low, sand-gravel beaches.

Mountain ranges terminating at the coast divert those inland animal species such as caribou, bear, and sheep, that might not otherwise come within reach of coastal-dwelling people. Low, marshy tundra which predominates behind the beaches provides nesting, feeding, and staging areas for a multitude of waterfowl, shorebirds, and other avian species that prefer wide open spaces. Jutting spits and capes that extend into the Chukchi Sea provide access to deeper-water, ice-dwelling mammals such as bowhead whale, walrus, and polar bear.

Much of the spring harvest in Kotzebue Sound, focusing on bearded seal and common ringed seal, takes place in waters off Cape Krusenstern and Cape Espenberg. Arctic char and chum salmon, important food species

which spend part of their life cycles in large rivers and part in sea waters, are abundant here because of the existence of those geographic features necessary to their survival.

Hotham Inlet, or Kobuk Lake as it is named locally, is a relatively shallow, brackish inlet fed fresh water by the large Kobuk and smaller Selawik river systems. This continual mixing of fresh and salt water in the inlet creates ideal habitat for sheefish, which probably reaches its peak of perfection as a species here. The deep, narrow, half-mile-wide channel at Kotzebue townsite carries nearly all the fresh-water runoff from the great watershed of the Noatak, Kobuk and Selawik rivers.

In a different drainage system to the north, the village of Kivalina lies at the lagoon outlet of two small but important arctic char streams; Wulik and Kivalina rivers.

Buckland, to the south of the Kotzebue area drainages, is located in the lower reaches of the other large river of the region. Buckland River is the spawning ground for a multitude of rainbow smelt, and the noteworthy Elephant Point beluga hunting ground is not far from its mouth.

Choris Peninsula and adjacent Chamisso Island, a national wildlife refuge, add to the diversity with ancient beach ridge archaeological sites on the peninsula and seabird nesting cliffs on the island. A long stretch of shallow water lies between the villages of

OPPOSITE — *Thirty-five miles northwest of Kotzebue Cape Krusenstern curls into the Chukchi Sea. A significant landmark to early explorers, the cape is proving even more important to archaeologists who have uncovered some of North America's oldest archaeological remains on this site.*
Carolyn Connors

ABOVE — *A hunter crawls toward his prey, seals, on ice floes off Cape Krusenstern. The white snow shirt helps to blend the hunter's image with surrounding ice floes.*
Robert Belous, National Park Service

Deering, Candle, and Kiwalik and the next inhabited point at Cape Espenberg, where icepack marine mammals again become primary food staples.

Point Hope with its present and ancient bowhead whale hunting tradition is the northern limit of this spectrum of species, people, and geography. Espenberg will be the southern limit of this geographical sketch of northwest Alaska's arctic coast.

It is apparent that changes in geographical patterns are part of the explanation for why people, living renewable resources, and related activities occur as they do. The idea of

LEFT — Buffeted by winds, colorful laundry brightens this beach scene at Kivalina, population 208, 47 miles northwest of Cape Krusenstern. Lael Morgan, staff

BELOW — Clinton Swan's whaling camp on the ice near Kivalina serves as a reminder of a long tradition. Every year hunters of Kivalina go out, and only one in seven to ten years do they get a bowhead whale. Kivalina is the only village in the region that hunts the bowhead. Mary Couche

any of this section being termed barren arctic coastal tundra is preposterous, yet this is most often the first impression of the casual traveler. A journey south from Point Hope along the coast reveals the diversity and active ecosystems of the region.

The DeLong Mountains run to salt water at Cape Thompson where rocky sea walls provide nesting sites for murres, puffins, and other seabirds, which in turn supply large quantities of fresh eggs in season for people of Point Hope and Kivalina. The ridge spines of the DeLongs run more or less continuously to meld into Brooks Range proper which shelters caribou, bear, wolf, wolverine, and arctic ground squirrels, which in turn, are utilized by the residents.

At Kivalina, two large coastal streams provide winter homes for large numbers of arctic char, which probably reach their species peak of perfection here, and become preferred food for the people of Kivalina. This, however, is not the residents' only food, as their location permits easy access to open water leads in the winter icepack which produce seal, oogruk (bearded seal), beluga whale, arctic fox, and occasionally bowhead whale and polar bear.

The mountains upriver provide caribou, red fox, wolverine, and wolf.

A series of large lagoons in which the salinity of the water varies much from season to season begin just south of Kivalina and continue to a point 15 miles north of Kotzebue. Every few miles the continuity of the ocean beach is cut by an outflowing channel of some small watershed that often terminates in a seaside lagoon. These become in some years large, natural fish traps as several species of whitefish move into them during spring snow runoff, and are trapped later in the summer as huge ocean swells move a coarse gravel dam across the outlet. This situation has been exploited by Eskimo fishermen in the fall for many centuries, and is still utilized in the large system just south of Cape Krusenstern.

Midway between Kivalina and Krusenstern a short but abruptly rising mountain range gives the inland horizon a file-toothed skyline when viewed from the proper angle. This range is drained by several small and one large, clear-water stream called Rabbit Creek on the map. This is translated properly from the Eskimo place name *Ukalliksuk*. File Mountains would be the map name of the range if the process was consistent. *Agaigrauq* range becomes, on the map, the Mulgrave Hills. This area is known as good winter caribou range because sharp peaks close to feeding areas provide protection from wolves and snow machines. It is also nesting territory for golden eagle and rock ptarmigan. This area has considerable archaeological potential, as it seems to have been a site for flint and chert gathering in a time when those materials were necessary for hunting tools. Shallow, unvegetated topsoil also provides a potential for paleontological studies in an area that was presumably mountain landfall across the plains when the Bering land bridge existed. Outcrops of lead, zinc, and silver ore indicate at least some mineralization. Sport fishing for char by small aircraft is a relatively new use of this drainage.

Moving on south, a large lagoon called Killiqmaiq fronts a backdrop of low hills between the Mulgrave Hills and the next small cluster of coastal mountains. This low, lake-covered area formerly was much used by Noatak River people as a low portage for travel toward coastal spring marine mammal harvesting camps. Many families would camp together on the southwest end of the lagoon during May and June, then return by skin boat through Kotzebue and up the Noatak River to their wintering areas by late August.

A famous bedrock headland called *Uqsruraq* rises from waters' edge a short distance along the beach. It is the first headland since leaving Cape Thompson and the only exposed ocean beach outcrop of bedrock between Cape Thompson and the Choris Peninsula. The headland was made famous by ancient men who battled there. Evidence of this was later discovered by J. Louis Giddings in his years of archaeological exploration at Cape Krusenstern. This site was named Battle Rock by him in his book *Ancient Men of the Arctic* (1967).

Moving past this ancient battle site, yet another lagoon lies at the base of another group of coastal hills, the tops of which were used in the 1950s by the U.S. Army as a coastal communications site. This lagoon fills quickly with snowmelt runoff in May because of abrupt, steep terrain, and is one of the first places usable by migrating waterfowl.

A small creek, called *Aitiliguaraq* in Inupiat, beside a 40-year-old Alaska Road Commission cabin made of halved logs, empties into the

Waves lap at the flanks of Battle Rock, the only exposed ocean beach outcrop of bedrock between Cape Thompson and the Choris Peninsula. Archaeologist J. Louis Giddings found evidence of ancient battles here and named the site Battle Rock.
Robert Belous, National Park Service

10

ocean through a miniature grand canyon cut through a tableland of tundra tussocks.

A few miles farther along the beach, this tableland ends abruptly as the extensive beach ridge section of Cape Krusenstern comes into view. The importance of this area as a horizontally laid out record of man's history in the Arctic (especially in conjunction with the vertical midden at Onion Portage on the Kobuk River) has been described by archaeologist J. Louis Giddings in his book. Meat racks and tent stakes of a more recent group of marine mammal seekers remain at the narrow strip of land separating the huge lagoon from the ocean. One reason for the positioning of this camp called *Itiptigvik* is the portage potential

when seal harvesting is over. Heavily loaded boats can cover half the homeward journey to Sisualik in an inland sheltered waterway while surf pounds the exposed ocean beach for days at a time. Sealing Point has become the English name for this important site, and it is still used intermittently as a marine mammal harvesting campsite.

The high wooden tower at the point of the cape was constructed of spliced spruce timbers rafted down the Noatak River in the mid-1940s by a group of Eskimos needing a higher vantage point to locate possible open leads in the pack ice for seal hunting. Since then the U.S. Coast and Geodetic Survey, and the U.S. Coast Guard have used the tower for a benchmark and to support a navigation light.

This flat area in the central beach ridge complex has unique flora, examples of a sea level-alpine plant community, and avifauna. This seemingly ambiguous sea level-alpine condition is brought about in part by the character of the soil. Beach gravel and sand make a dry, well-drained surface unlike the soggy mud and peat permafrost more com-

mon in the Arctic. Mountain and ridgetop conditions are brought down to a few feet above sea level. Alpine azalea, moss campion, and pink plumes are gaudy, if miniature, flower examples. Golden plovers, whimbrels, cranes, and jaegers, birds that prefer dry nesting sites, are found here.

A few miles on toward Kotzebue the major salmonberry or cloudberry *(Rubus chamaemorus)* harvesting area in the region begins. In a good year, many tons can be picked in late August. This berry is the largest and most citruslike fruit the Arctic affords.

The outlet of Sealing Point lagoon lies several miles inland from this area, and the network of lakes and connecting sloughs makes the dry land areas between a preferred nesting and rearing site for several species of birds. Large colonies of glaucous gulls and arctic and aleutian terns follow their natural colonial nesting tendencies here; joined by cranes, pintails, western and semi-palmated sandpipers, lapland longspurs and savannah sparrows, all of which prefer more privacy for nesting and rearing of their young.

ABOVE — *An arctic tern hovers over its nest in the coastal tundra. Each year the terns make a round trip from high latitudes of the southern hemisphere to nest and raise their chicks in the far north.*
Peter Connors

RIGHT — *This glacial esker near Cape Krusenstern dates from the Illinoisan age approximately 200,000 years ago.*
Robert Belous, National Park Service

All of this inland waterway comes to a terminus a few miles down the beach at the very end of the beach ridge area. This terminating point, a 50-yard-wide slough flowing into the ocean against a high mud-and-peat cutbank, is probably the most valuable point in the entire Kotzebue Sound coastline from the local subsistence user's viewpoint.

Each fall this slough becomes a major whitefish harvesting site. Each spring, as the winter accumulation of snow melts, a great flush occurs in the Kotzebue Sound area as it does in all waterways of the North. Large numbers of several species of whitefish leave their wintering grounds with this flood. As they move down into salt water, they spread out into what is for them now brackish water, their summer forage grounds. This same spring flush leaves a fine, deep channel in the outlet mentioned above. Many tons of Noatak and Kobuk whitefish, flushed out from the main systems, go up into sloughs, lakes, and the major lagoon of the Krusenstern flats. Here they find good forage and tend to remain through July. Early in August through September, the fish would normally work their way back out of the Krusenstern system into the sea and then on up their respective river systems to spawn or overwinter. However most years, sometime in late July or early August, large ground swells on the ocean side of the outlet made by strong winds, combine with a lessening of fresh-water outflow because of disappearing snowmelt to cause coarse beach gravel and sand to be thrown across this outlet, completely damming it. This traps the whitefish, yet allows underground seepage enough to keep the water from backing up, overflowing, and breaking the dam. Thus the stage is set for a multi-ton harvest of high-quality whitefish, a goodly number heavy with roe ready for fall spawning. As soon as September temperatures approach freezing, many residents gather to fill 50-pound burlap sacks with these fish to be eaten frozen with seal oil through the coming winter.

A few miles farther on, a large lagoon called Aculaq traps fish the same way though less extensively. This lagoon is guarded on the east end by an old-style Eskimo, "teepeelike" pole grave. It is placed on the beginning point of a willow-carved mud bank that faces the ocean for several miles, a few feet behind the rye-grass-topped present beach line. The mud bank terminates where the flat land of Sisualik peninsula hints at coming lowlands of the Noatak River delta.

As the high bank drops away, ahead lies the most dramatic coastal geography change in a southward sweep of Kotzebue Sound's shoreline. Six miles of flat, back-bent-fishhook-shaped peninsula, composed of ancient beach ridges, form a low, rye-grass-covered finger pointing at the town of Kotzebue nine miles away; this is Sisualik — place of white whales.

Sisualik is the traditional beluga whale hunting area of the Noatak River people. It is also, now, the first year-round residential homesite area on the coast south of Kivalina. Though a few clan families now stay through the winter, Sisualik is mostly a spring and summer place. Most of the land above high water line is taken up by historic clan families through Native allotments. Summer sees entire families back on the land from which they have been absent for nine months of every year. Summer in Sisualik is really a joyous time of fishing, hunting, berry picking, and beach-oriented fun.

Carrie Uhl and her young helper Arunya Jones prepare beluga meat and muktuk *(skin and blubber) to be rendered into oil at Sisualik.*   Anore Jones

A boater speeds by floats marking salmon fishing nets in Kotzebue Sound.

John and Margaret Ibbotson

Here, too, lie the boundaries of the Kotzebue Sound commercial chum salmon fishery, farthest north extension of that important state industry. For a number of local people income from various parts of this million-dollar fishery satisfy the bulk of their monetary needs for supplies and equipment to maintain their subsistence life style.

The southward coastal journey moves from the fishhook tip of Sisualik Spit in a more-or-less direct, nine-mile crossing to Kotzebue, largest community in the region. East of this direct line of travel lies the Noatak delta, Hotham Inlet and the Kobuk and Selawik drainage mouths: all areas of brackish water, relatively shallow (2 to 3 fathoms) except for narrow, deep channels, and extensive mud flats. This habitat has its own complex ecological characteristics different from the salt-water arctic coast. This is the water habitat dominated by shee, great northern pike, and multitudes of several species of whitefish. It is probably the area in which the shee reaches its species apex of quality and numbers. Plants, animals, and birds found here often belong either in more inland areas or more coastal habitat, and the region is therefore a transition zone between aquatic and terrestrial environs . . . a mixture of freshwater drainages and the salt water of Kotzebue Sound.

The Arctic Ocean coast and inland freshwater drainages require different techniques and natural history knowledge to be exploited by people of the land. Thus, historically, resident indigenous people divide here. To some extent these distinctions remain. There are salt-water people, Kobuk Lake people, and river people. Representative families from these groups now make their homes in Kotzebue.

The high ground ending in a beach-front cutbank a short distance south of Kotzebue, that was in times past the site of a community permafrost cold storage, is now a man-made landmark of electronic discs, towers, and other military and communications paraphernalia.

Cape Blossom, the next rise from flatlands beyond Sadie Creek, was the historic landfall and navigating point for early explorers to Kotzebue Sound. Old journals of whalers, missionaries, gold seekers, and visiting ornithologists mention Cape Blossom anchorage because off this cape sea-traveling vessels must anchor to send smaller boats into shallow channels that permit access to Kotzebue. This nearly ten-mile distance between ocean-going vessel anchorage and Kotzebue business interests has been an obstacle over the years, and has provided many adventures for those involved in transferring goods or people under adverse summer or fall weather conditions.

From Cape Blossom south the region might be termed "Inner Kotzebue Sound," as waters in this area are relatively unaffected by the huge river systems in the Kotzebue area. Some beach camping sites are used seasonally. One outstanding use of Baldwin Peninsula, as this long, narrow stretch of land is called, has been for reindeer grazing. Herding began in 1901, and is presently actively pursued by NANA, the area's Native regional corporation. Because of geography, topography, and caribou migration routes, wild herds of caribou and domestic herds of reindeer can more easily be kept from intermingling, a problem in other grazing areas. In those areas where the animals cannot be kept separated, both populations suffer. History of the reindeer industry in Alaska has proved the two species incompatible on the same range at the same time. Baldwin Peninsula, being the isolated handle leading into Seward Peninsula, and being separated from inland mountains where caribou range, is a natural area in which to develop a moderately large reindeer industry.

Choris Peninsula and adjacent rocky bluffs of Chamisso Island, a national wildlife refuge, provide the first sea-cliff bird nesting site south of Cape Thompson. Murres, black-legged kitti-

wakes, and horned and tufted puffins, choose this site as a place to procreate, and have, in turn, constituted a seasonal food source for adventuresome men for ages. Fall sealing is sometimes done in waters off Choris Peninsula where young bearded seal, beautifully spotted larga seal, and ringed seal often abound.

These marine mammals have attracted Natives to Choris since ancient times. J. Louis Giddings, early in his archaeological work in the NANA area, discovered a new village site that dated between Norton and Old Whaling cultures in arctic archaeological time sequences. Choris People were typified by an exceedingly large, peculiarly shaped, oval

Youngsters jig for smelt in the ice in front of Kotzebue. Holly Odd

ABOVE — *Puffin Island rises near the tip of Chamisso Island in Kotzebue Sound. Both islands as well as nearby islets comprise Chamisso National Wildlife Refuge, an important seabird nesting site and now part of Alaska Maritime National Wildlife Refuge.* Mark McDermott

OVERLEAF — *Tents of beluga whale hunters line the beach at Elephant Point on Eschscholtz Bay.* Russ Dixon

Beluga whale bodies line the shore at Elephant Point near Buckland. Traditional beluga hunting is in jeopardy because wealthier Eskimos from villages beyond Buckland come to the hunt in power boats, and the noise from their engines scares the animals away. Russ Dixon

house discovered on old Choris Peninsula beach ridges. These ancient people, a pre-Eskimo culture, were potters, and left hints of also being reindeer herders 1,000 years before Christ. If this is so, reindeer husbandry on the Baldwin Peninsula does indeed have some very old roots.

Visitors to Choris Peninsula have entered the orbit of Buckland village people. Regional residents know this as the coastal area where beluga whale delicacies and sun-dried rainbow smelt are harvested, and preserved in such large quantities that most local families have a continuous year-round supply. Elephant Point on Eschscholtz Bay is the scene of a geographical trap for beluga whales that has for ages been exploited by indigenous people. Rainbow smelt travel up the Buckland River on a spring spawning run in such numbers at such an early date (latter part of May) that they can be spread out on the gravel to dry. Cool, dry air of this early breakup at Buckland makes this unique process of handling smelt possible. Insect activity and too-high air temperatures prevent this method of handling the same fish in more inland areas at a later date.

Next comes the very base of Seward Peninsula, an area probably best known in this century as a gold-producing drainage, and the only area important for this reason within the boundaries of this coastal geography sketch. Kiwalik, Candle, and Deering were active early-20th-century mining communities. People of the century before found other values in this deep pocket of Kotzebue Sound and on around to open sea at Cape Espenberg. Egg-gathering, cod-hooking at river outlets, and spearing or netting of overwintering seals at their breathing holes provided year-round sustenance for an older technology. Many people of the NANA region trace their ancestry to beginnings in this *Kuguruq* area.

The west shore of this lower sound is known mostly for its treacherous boating conditions. Shallow water many miles out from shore makes casual traveling tedious and dangerous. It is an area much used by waterfowl and shorebirds, both as nesting grounds and as twice-yearly staging areas for south and north migrants.

This geographical sketch ends with Cape Espenberg, on the more open ocean but with some very basic differences from its northern counterpart, Cape Krusenstern, across the mouth of Kotzebue Sound. Sand is the chief difference. While Krusenstern beach ridges are made up of gravel and coarse sand, un-movable by wind action and therefore well vegetated, Espenberg's back shore country is often wind-blown sand dunes. Several families may or may not be living at this salt-water hunting location in any given year, as some families move back and forth to Shishmaref.

———————

On a map of Alaska the sketch has covered less than 300 miles of arctic coastal beach line, some just above the arctic circle, some just below. What great diversity! How many different habitats for how many different species of plants, animals, birds, and fish. The people? Yes, very different too! Each Eskimo place name and traditional campsite is different from every other. Some of the same people may use different places at different times, but the place where they are living at the time will determine to a very great extent what they do, what they eat, how they keep warm, what they learn, and where they might go next. □

KOBUK COUNTRY

— Ole Wik

The Kobuk, Alaska's ninth largest river, rises in southward drainages of the Brooks Range in northwest Alaska. The river flows for 347 miles, always north of the arctic circle, before emptying into Hotham Inlet, an embayment off Kotzebue Sound.

The Kobuk drains some 11,980 square miles of mountains, hills, tundras, and lowlands. Mean annual rainfall ranges from 10 inches near the delta to a bit less than 20 inches in the headwaters, for an average of 14 inches over the entire basin. Total flow is thus on the order of nine million acre-feet annually, an output which also ranks ninth in the state.

The river gathers its water from five distinct physiographic zones. To the northeast stand the Schwatka Mountains, whose rugged, glaciated summits culminate in Mount Igikpak, at 8,510 feet the highest point in the central Brooks Range.

Adjacent to the Schwatkas on the west are the lower, moderately rugged Baird Mountains. Both systems show such effects of glaciation as U-shaped valleys and piedmont lakes (the largest of which is 14-square-mile Walker Lake), but only a few cirque glaciers survive in the shadows of the taller peaks.

Dominating the skyline near the headwaters of the Kobuk and Noatak is 8,510-foot Mount Igikpak, highest peak in the central Brooks Range. John and Margaret Ibbotson

19

BELOW — *Walker Lake, near the headwaters of both the Kobuk and Noatak rivers, is the largest piedmont lake in the region.*
John and Margaret Ibbotson

RIGHT — *Named for pioneer American naturalist Spencer Fullerton Baird, the Baird Mountains extend east and west for 120 miles at the southwest end of the Brooks Range.* Mark McDermott

20

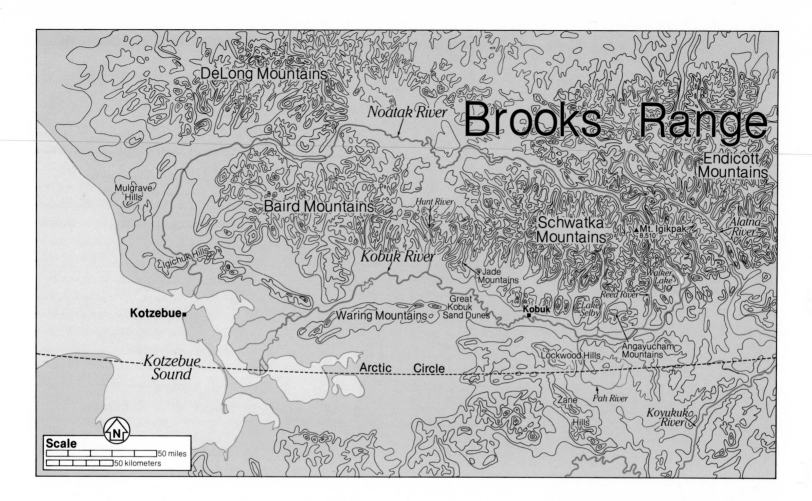

Between the Kobuk and the abrupt front of the Brooks Range stands a group of hills and ridges that physiographers recognize as part of the Ambler-Chandalar Ridge. Selby Lake, the region's second largest, lies in a deep cleft in the ridge's steep, eastern section, where the taller summits of the Angayucham Mountains exceed 4,000 feet. Rich copper deposits have been discovered beneath the gentler western portion of the ridge near Bornite.

Hills, low mountains, rolling plateaus, and lowland flats speckled with lakes and ponds characterize the Pah River country southeast of the upper Kobuk. In its northward flow the Pah passes through a narrow canyon across the Lockwood Hills.

And finally, the Kobuk Lowlands include most of the areas that are actively used by man — river floodplain, patchy forests, wind-swept tundras, a brushy delta.

Rising to the south of the river, the Waring Mountains face the Jade Mountains to the north, forming a kind of broad gateway spanning the scenic central Kobuk valley. At the foot of the Warings lie the splendid Kobuk sand dunes, which include not only the actively moving sands but also at least 300 square miles of dormant dunes now covered by a sparse mantle of vegetation.

In its westerly flow the Kobuk crosses the imaginary boundary between the sub-arctic and the arctic climatic zones. In the river's upper reaches the severe, continental climate, characterized by great extremes of temperature, predominates. At Kotzebue, on the coast, the climate is moderated by the sea.

21

Dating from Pleistocene times, the sand dunes of the Kobuk valley cover at least 300 square miles of surrounding lowlands.   Manya Wik

Kobuk valley winters are long. The river typically freezes by the middle of October, and remains frozen until the third week in May. But in an extreme fall, under the influence of high pressures and clear skies, freezeup might come as early as the third week in September. Similarly, if the skies are cloudy in spring, the river could remain frozen until the very end of May. Either way, the sudden breakup of seven or eight months' worth of ice is always exciting.

Really big weather in Kobuk country, both winter and summer, is associated with storms that track northward through Bering Strait. In

ABOVE — *Many species of wildlife inhabit Kotzebue Basin including the lynx, shown here swimming the Kobuk River.*   Frank Bird

RIGHT — *Winters are long in Kobuk country where temperatures can plunge to -52°F.*   Mark Ocker

May and June this storm track shifts eastward into the Interior, and the Kobuk valley enjoys some of its finest weather of the year. But in August, some storms that would otherwise track through the Gulf of Alaska join those that turn northward through the strait, often bringing prolonged rains and high water.

The Kobuk is free of rapids for most of its length, and is navigable by tug and barge as far as the village of Kobuk. But commercial use comes to a standstill during periods of drought — especially in mid-summer after mountain snowbanks have melted but before the usual autumn rains have come. At such times shippers and customers alike simply have to wait, hoping that there will be enough rain to lift the water level before ice claims the river for another seven months. Skiffs can navigate as far as the Reed River confluence in periods of high water, but rapids of lower Kobuk Canyon are ordinarily traversed only by kayakers making the trip downstream from Walker Lake.

Permafrost is extensive throughout northwest Alaska, where the mean annual temperature is 22.5 °F, and a visitor traveling by plane might get the impression that the Kobuk valley offers little more than barren tundra. But bands of spruce, as well as stands of birch, cottonwood, and aspen grow here. Well-drained hummocky areas of stabilized sand dunes are particularly interesting, as they support open stands of birch that contrast strongly with brushy, sometimes scarcely penetrable spruce forests.

The mountains, rivers, wet and dry tundras, forests, and active and stabilized sand dunes all come together in the central Kobuk valley near the Hunt River confluence. This area, representative of so much of the best of Kobuk country, was set aside by President Carter in December 1978 as the 1.7-million-acre Kobuk Valley National Monument. With passage of the Alaska lands bill in 1980, this area became Kobuk Valley National Park. ☐

PARKLANDS IN NORTHWEST ALASKA

— Robert Belous,
National Park Service

E ven in the Jet Age, it is a long way from Kotzebue Sound to Yellowstone National Park in Wyoming. Yet the two areas have something very special in common. In 1872 our young nation gave birth to an idea that would one day affect the steaming geysers and bison of Yellowstone and the tundra-clad hills, caribou herds, and people of northwest Alaska. This new idea held that some of our most outstanding landscapes and historic places were special, above the marketplace, and that they best served the American people by remaining in their natural, unaltered state. Since Yellowstone became the world's first national park, this distinctively American concept has spread across the nation to include over 300 separate areas, and to more than 30 countries around the world. And now it has come to northwest Alaska.

But is there anything special or unique about the Kotzebue Sound area? Are there any undiscovered Grand Canyons, Yosemites, Mount McKinleys, Everglades? The opportunity to see if such wonders existed in this

The Noatak, 20 miles from its headwaters, meanders through a tundra-covered valley, part of the Noatak National Preserve.
John and Margaret Ibbotson

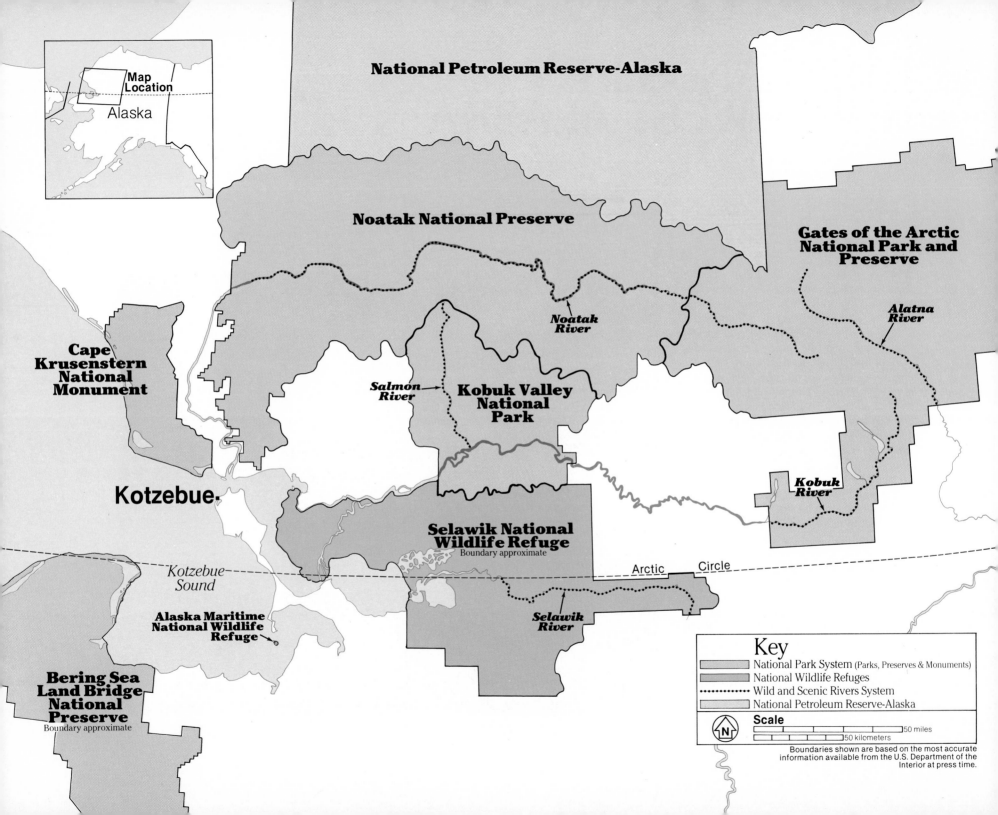

National Petroleum Reserve-Alaska

Map Location

Alaska

Noatak National Preserve

Gates of the Arctic National Park and Preserve

Alatna River

Noatak River

Cape Krusenstern National Monument

Salmon River

Kobuk Valley National Park

Kobuk River

Kotzebue.

Selawik National Wildlife Refuge
Boundary approximate

Arctic Circle

Kotzebue Sound

Kotzebue ---

Alaska Maritime National Wildlife Refuge

Selawik River

Bering Sea Land Bridge National Preserve
Boundary approximate

Key
National Park System (Parks, Preserves & Monuments)
National Wildlife Refuges
Wild and Scenic Rivers System
National Petroleum Reserve-Alaska

Scale
50 miles
50 kilometers

Boundaries shown are based on the most accurate information available from the U.S. Department of the Interior at press time.

detailed picture of early man's environs. They tell us that spruce trees (now common along the river) first appeared a scant 7,000 years ago, and alder about 1,000 years later.

Even the meandering edge of the forest offered something unusual. While elsewhere on our continent this so-called tree line is an abrupt interface between the boreal forest and tundra, here in the Kobuk valley the transition zone is miles wide, north to south. This represents a zone of climatic tension between

LEFT — *A dog musher and his team head across a crumbling snow crust in Kobuk Valley National Park in May.*

BELOW — *Entrance to an Eskimo house at Onion Portage on the Kobuk River, one of the most important archaeological sites in Alaska. Two faces are barely discernible in the dimly lit interior.* Both by Anore Jones

region came with passage of the Alaska Native Claims Settlement Act of 1971. Section 17(d)(2) of the act called for publicly owned lands to be studied for possible inclusion in our system of national parks, wildlife refuges, forests, and wild and scenic rivers. And so in the spring of 1972 a team of Park Service planners and specialists began a search which would ultimately bring to light a bevy of remarkable natural and cultural resources, all radiating out around Kotzebue Sound like spokes on a great wheel.

Some of the region's special qualities were already well known. In the Kobuk Valley, some 100 miles east of Kotzebue, the rich cultural heritage of the *Kuuvangmiit* Eskimos ("People of the Kobuk River") enjoys a hallowed place in scientific annals. At a river bend and caribou crossing known as Onion Portage, for example, archaeological excavations uncovered delicate stratified layers of earth containing the hearths and stone tools and artifacts that established human occupa-

tion for at least 12,500 years. And slightly downriver, at *Ahteut*, an extensive series of old housepits form the pivotal dating and description for the direct forebears of today's *Kuuvangmiit*, the Woodland or Neo-Eskimo people of 1,250 A.D.

But there were values along the Kobuk less easily grasped. The cold and dry climate of this mountain-rimmed valley continues to approximate conditions of Glacial Age Alaska and Siberia. Sagebrush, grasses and sedges of the ancient arctic steppe tundra flourish here like an island out of the distant past. Among its communities of flora there survives a unique and colorful legume of the peavine family, *Oxytropis kobukensis* — a plant named for the Kobuk Valley and found nowhere else. Thus the region comprises a living relict environment of late Pleistocene times when long-horned bison and woolly mammoths roamed the valley floor.

Microscopic pollen grains from deep under the Kobuk's riverbanks brought to light a

LEFT — *Across Kavet Creek a stand of arctic spruce faces the 100-foot-high sand dunes more akin to the Sahara Desert than to an area 35 miles north of the arctic circle.*
Robert Belous, National Park Service

competing forces of global proportion. Like a tilting scale measuring subtle shifts in climate, the Kobuk's gentle lichen woodland is a quiet battleground where one system inches forward against the other as favorable conditions dictate; the tough, squat plants of the tundra winning during cold periods, losing ground to spruce, birch and alder when warmer cycles prevail. If the earth is developing a greenhouse effect due to airborne pollutants, the Kobuk valley will plainly show the change.

Add to this rich mosaic the Great Kobuk Sand Dunes, a sprawling Saharalike desert of 25 square miles where shifting dunes reach a height of 100 feet and summer temperatures can soar to 100°F. The scene has already attracted highly refined scientific opportunities. An unmanned telemetry station has been considered by the National Atmospheric and Space Administration for location on the dunes. This small black box would beam to an information satellite miles above the earth continuous readings on moisture, evaporation rates, and the crystalline structure of snow. NASA believes such data can be helpful in preparing for future landings on Mars, where polar conditions are estimated to be roughly similar to those on the Kobuk sand dunes.

BELOW — *Caribou bulls swim the Kobuk River following migration paths this species has used for centuries.*

RIGHT — *Alaska Department of Fish and Game personnel lasso cow and young caribou as they swim the Kobuk.*
Both by David Fritts

The Noatak River has been cited as the largest complete river system remaining in the United States in a condition unaltered by modern man. That comes as both a plaudit as well as sad commentary on past stewardship of our nation's priceless waterways. With its headwaters astride the jagged summit of Mount Igikpak, the highest peak in the central Brooks Range, the 360 miles of the Noatak under Park Service administration is unsurpassed as a recreational river. Textbook examples of geological succession line its picturesque banks. And its communities of arctic flora match in number of species those of the entire Brooks Range. The Noatak is thought to be a gateway or migration path into the New World for plantlife with origins in eastern Asia.

The Noatak corridor seems to have been a gateway for human migration as well. The very old Inupiat word *Noataq* roughly translates to mean a path inward, or "way into the interior." Recent discovery of a stratified archaeological site along the northern rim of the watershed near Howard Pass marks the area's importance as an early hunting and trade route in the Arctic. Future discoveries may well tie the area to the epic migration of Eskimo people during the Western Thule period of 1,000 years ago which extended their language and culture across the top of North America and on to Greenland.

Combined, the rich and varied qualities of the Noatak have led to both national and international recognition and the area's designation as a Biosphere Reserve, a part of the United Nations' Man and the Biosphere Program of exemplary worldwide reserves.

LEFT — *Low light illuminates the shoreline of Okak Bend along the Noatak about 15 miles southwest of Feniak Lake in Noatak National Preserve. A U.S. Geological Survey explorer noted an abandoned Eskimo village along the bend's north shore in the early part of this century.* Saro Arno

The Noatak watershed and its major tributaries, the Kelly, Cutler and Nimiuktuk, are well known to local hunters, trappers and fishermen. But living memories, even cultural memories, are comparatively short. No one could have remembered when the Noatak did not flow along its present course, but instead turned abruptly westward just south of the present-day village of Noatak, from there flowing not into Kotzebue Sound but directly into the Chukchi Sea. That was more than 100,000 years ago, and long before man walked in this part of the world. But the knowledge of that event, and the known location of the old glacier bed that was the former river corridor, has led to still further inquiry and to a startling discovery.

Exact dating of the old glacier bed, lying between the Igichuk Hills and the Tahinichok Mountains at nearby Cape Krusenstern, could provide a firm benchmark in time. This would add measureably to the overall picture for northwest Alaska and its evolving landscapes, and give clues to how they got the way they

ABOVE — *Low water after an abnormally dry summer forces kayakers to push kayaks down the Noatak River near Tunukuchiak Creek, 25 miles southeast of Howard Pass.* Saro Arno

OVERLEAF — *This photo of the Noatak valley near the entrance of Kavachurak Creek captures the essence of a nearly untouched watershed which meanders more than 400 miles from the central Brooks Range to the Chukchi Sea.* Wilbur Mills

are. The windy stretch of tussock tundra along the old glacier bed has attracted little recent attention, except as a trail for Eskimo seal hunters on their way from Noatak to traditional coastal camps in spring. But detailed inspection of aerial photos revealed an odd-shaped mound about the length of a football field. On-the-ground tests showed it to be a glacial esker. Such gravel formations are created by a glacier's internal rivers which force the gravel into discrete channels that mold their shapes and leave behind these

LEFT — *This ivory doll discovered along ancient beach ridges of Cape Krusenstern dates back to 1,200 A.D. and the Western Thule period. During this period Eskimo culture and language spread across the top of North America all the way to Greenland.*

curious serpentine land forms. Since this tundra plain is known to have escaped the scouring action of subsequent glaciers of the Wisconsin period, the esker was verified to date back to the Illinoisan period, some 200,000 years ago. It is the only one of this age ever discovered in Alaska.

This discovery also helped to close the circle of geological history for the neighboring Cape Krusenstern area, already world-renowned as an archaeological site. The seaward face of the old Illinoisan glacier bed forms a major source of the beach gravel shuttled by wave action down to the cape. Once accumulated in offshore reservoirs, the gravel awaits the 50-to-75-year periods of south and southwesterly storm fronts that drive the gravel high and dry to form a new beach front. Thus a pebble tossed into the sea by a youngster at one of the cape's sealing camps could well have come from the lofty slopes of Mount Igikpak over 200 miles away.

The beach-building process at Cape Krusenstern continues today as it has for the past 5,000 years. In its day, each of the cape's 114 distinct beach ridges was the ocean front and camp site for early Eskimo hunters. Each ridge forms a repository for the tools, pottery, hearths and artwork of its period, like pages of an unbroken chronicle of human survival and cultural evolution in the Arctic. Cape Krusenstern and Onion Portage on the Kobuk River comprise an archaeological yardstick by which all other sites in the Arctic are measured.

But how do such places find their way into the National Park System? The most important test is based on national significance. The question to be asked is: Can the resource's natural, historic, or scientific importance be held to be of nationwide value and public interest? If the resource in question does not meet this test, then it should be addressed on the state or local level. Or perhaps not at all. But if, like Grand Canyon, it is unduplicated,

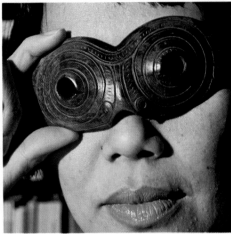

LEFT — *Very much like today's* ulu, *or woman's knife, this early equivalent dates back to the Ipiutak period of 100 to 300 A.D.*

ABOVE — *Ornate carving of these snow goggles identifies them as part of the Eskimo cultural period known as Ipiutak dating from 100 to 300 A.D.*   Both by Robert Belous, National Park Service

unique, or of singular scientific or inspirational stature, it then would qualify as part of our National Park System. The three areas in northwest Alaska unquestionably meet or exceed this test.

Accordingly, recommendations were made to Congress in 1973 to include the three candidate areas in the park system. But Congress failed to act within its self-imposed deadline in December 1978, and the protective land status afforded under the Alaska Native Claims Settlement Act was due to lapse. As a means of affording continuing protection for these prized resources, Presidential Proclamations were invoked establishing the areas as national monuments under authority of the Antiquities Act of 1906. But near the close of the 96th Congress, the Alaska National Interest Lands Conservation Act was passed and signed into law by President Carter on December 2, 1980. The act included establishment of Cape Krusenstern National Monument (560,000 acres); Kobuk Valley National Park (1.7 million acres); and Noatak National

Preserve (6.5 million acres). The entire process establishing the areas took just short of nine years.

The size and shape of the areas reflect careful evaluation of resource character and natural integrity. Hydrographic systems have been followed whenever possible, so that important watersheds will be wholly protected. The containment of self-sustaining ecosystems was the goal rather than acreage alone. Biological support systems in arctic latitudes are spread far and thin. It takes more than 100 square miles to sustain a single brown/grizzly bear, and many times that amount of habitat for herds of caribou. Comparisons with dimensions of national parks outside of Alaska, therefore, can be deceptive.

Also, many of our well known parks and monuments in the lower-49 states were formed out of remnant lands that were left

after all other uses had taken their toll — railroads, highways, agriculture, mining, and industrial and townsite development (both planned and ill-planned). In many cases a patchwork of private and state lands left little opportunity to design stable and self-sustaining parklands from the outset. In certain cases we must now go back and repair such areas little by little, and at considerable cost to the taxpayer. But the cost of land acquisition for parks established under the Alaska lands bill was zero. The lands were still in public ownership, and still in pristine condition, unmarred by roads or development.

Modes of protection for a park's wildlife and landscapes and historic objects basically harken back to the establishing act for the National Park Service in 1916. With the exception of sport fishing, parks are to be used and enjoyed in such a way that leaves them *unimpaired* — which traditionally means no hunting, logging, or mining. But the methods of planning today's parks and preserves in Alaska are somewhat different. The Noatak, for example, was recognized as an important sport hunting area which was also large enough to accommodate non-consumptive uses without serious conflict. And so the area was planned not as a park but as a preserve. This relatively new status allows sport hunting, but is otherwise managed as a park.

Similarly, subsistence hunting, fishing, and gathering were also recognized as important sources of community well-being and traditional activities at the very core of the region's cultural character. Therefore subsistence was built in as part of the management scheme, and is specifically provided for in legislation creating the new parklands in northwest Alaska. Subsistence is given priority use in preserves where sport hunting might become a competing harvest activity. Yet subsistence must strike a balance with other uses and purposes for which the park or preserve was created.

There were several considerations underlying the inclusion of subsistence uses in Alaska's new parklands. One is that the landscapes and fish and wildlife in the new areas had been intensively used for thousands of years, yet the resources were found to be in an unspoiled condition that qualified for our nation's highest protective status, that of our National Park System. With centuries of use the impact was light.

Also, the longstanding interplay between people and the natural resources that sustain them forges a unique bond. From this elemental relationship there springs techniques and adaptations for survival in one of the earth's most unforgiving environments. Largely undocumented, these techniques can serve to enrich our understanding of the past, and heighten our appreciation for today's cultural diversity that still marks our collective American heritage.

Lastly, there exists no easy replacement for caribou, moose, sheefish, salmon, whitefish, waterfowl, seal, beluga whale, and a remarkably long menu of wild greens and berries. These are foods with a long-ingrained cultural preference built in. They are a continuing tie to the land, and offer a very special fulfillment that comes with successfully harvesting one's sustenance in tough surroundings.

Assuring the opportunity for subsistence uses also echoes the declarations of the U.S. Congress in the Historic Preservation Act of 1966. It states in part that "the historic and cultural foundations of our nation should be preserved as a living part of our community life and development in order to give a sense of orientation to the American people." For those in generations to come who seek to learn of the cultural heritage of northwest Alaska, there should be more than books and diagrams and artifacts to turn to. Held in trust as part of the National Park System, at least some of the important landscapes, hallowed places, fishing and hunting sites — as well as

BELOW — On ice floes off Cape Krusenstern, Eskimo seal hunters labor toward shore with their hard-won catch, an oogruk *or bearded seal more than nine feet long and weighing more than 600 pounds. This long-standing food source has helped sustain Eskimos for thousands of years, and still plays an important role in their diet.*

RIGHT — Underneath the seal hunters' snow shirt, or kattikning, *a small tool called a* kookik, *or scratching tool, is carried. This tool makes the same scratching sound one seal makes when close to another seal. The hunters use the tool to calm the seals, and thus gain closer access to their prey before making the kill. The opposite end of the tool forms a plug which is used to close the hole made in the seal's neck into which the hunters blow air to ensure the animal floats during the return trip to shore. The* kookik's *claws come from* oogruk.   Both by Robert Belous, National Park Service

the fish and wildlife — will be there intact as a *living* part of the reference.

A crucial part in achieving these ends comes through close involvement with local people. Their guidance has already come to mark in a very positive way the design of the new northwest parklands. At important fish harvest locations, such as *Anyiaak* at Cape Krusenstern, it was essential that the seasonal sensitivity of the area be gleaned from local people well versed in its use. As the sole outlet for the inland waters of the cape, *Anyiaak* becomes an immense fish trap each fall when wind and wave action block the outflow with beach gravel. Thousands of pounds of whitefish teem just behind the barrier in search of a way out to sea. Highly skitterish, the swarm can be driven back into the inner lagoon by a child running along the beach.

When local Eskimo people come for the serious business of harvesting this resource, they leave the kids back at camp. A shallow trench, or *kargisaak*, is dug in the gravel so that a low flow of water is just enough to get the whitefish swarming through the bogus outlet. The fish wind up flopping high and dry

as the water quickly disappears into the gravel before reaching the sea. Without hook, line or net, the trick has worked for generations. And there have been no handbooks describing the process.

To head off the problem of visitors inadvertently blundering into such a sensitive setting, a system of "time zoning" has been conceived. Critical subsistence areas would be off-limits to visitor use while harvest is under way. This approach would also apply to critical caribou hunting locations along major rivers, and seal hunting camps at Krusenstern's *Itiptigvik.* Close cooperation and rapport with local people will make the difference.

A prime example of the value of local input is the case of the former Caribou Lake in the Kobuk valley. During the National Park Service's early planning phase in 1973, a sizeable tundra lake near the Jade Mountains was noted as a possible floatplane landing site for access into the Baird Mountains. It was far enough from the main river and local routes of travel to have little or no impact on day-to-day activities of local village people. But in discussing the prospect with the people of nearby Ambler, the question was gently raised as to why the Park Service had chosen the name "Caribou Lake."

Our only answer was that none of the available maps showed the lake to have a name, and so we picked Caribou because it was not far from well known migration trails. Following a long and respectful pause (and some lengthy exchanges in Inupiat), one of the elder hunters delivered the news: The lake has had a name for as long as there have been Eskimo people in the Kobuk valley. And the name has nothing whatever to do with caribou. That body of water is called *Isaakaaqliq.* And, as the name CLEARLY implies, it is a staging area for molting and

Margaret Wesley of Noatak proudly displays part of her catch from ice fishing. Lael Morgan, staff

flightless waterfowl. Our plans for a floatplane access point, without regard to season, went back to the drawing board. Plans now reflect both the original name and the important resource related to the erstwhile Caribou Lake. And the Kobuk is a better park because of the change.

Accurate maps are no small concern to Park Service managers. Old place names can offer a deeper understanding of a region's history, and sometimes may act to avert hardship or danger. Like the short-lived Caribou Lake, the Ambler River had a name long before it became the namesake for a member of an early survey party. The original place name is *Natmaaqtuak,* or route for backpacking. This warns a traveler that the river's headwaters are steep enough to warrant carrying the sled load over the pass, since it is too hard a pull for dog team. Cultural landscapes of northwest Alaska are alive with rich and meaningful place names that can easily be lost with the passing of a generation in disuse. One of the longterm goals of the Park Service is to restore old place names, and thereby develop maps that are culturally credible as well as topographically accurate.

As a new member of the Northwest community, this agency also seeks to involve itself with appropriate research projects of common benefit to local people and other resource managing agencies. One such example is the ongoing project for monitoring the western arctic caribou herds. This important food source depends on substantial habitats that lie within boundaries of parks and preserves. Well coordinated management with the Alaska Department of Fish and Game and other land managing agencies — plus continuing input from local people — would help assure a well managed herd and an ample harvest. The same holds true for fire management. Park Service has already begun working with the Bureau of Land Management in developing fire management plans.

Subsistence is also an important concern. "Our past experience with Native American cultures will serve well in communities of the Kotzebue Sound region," notes Mack Shaver, the Park Service's newly assigned superintendent for Noatak, Kobuk Valley and Cape Krusenstern. Since 1916, the Kalapana Native people of Hawaii have continued their traditional harvest of shellfish at Hawaii Volcanoes National Park. And Arizona's Papago Indians still harvest cactus fruit in Organ Pipe Cactus National Monument since its establishment in 1937.

The best comparison with northwest Alaska occurs at Big Cypress National Preserve in Florida. Here the Seminole and Micosukee Indians carry out traditional subsistence hunting, gathering and fishing and retain full use of all ceremonial sites important to their culture. "The Park Service's longstanding mission to protect landscapes and maintain natural wildlife populations," Mack Shaver points out, "lends strong assurance that critical subsistence needs will be met, both now and in the future."

The most immediate challenge in the northwest Alaska communities is to clearly explain the Park Service's role to local people, and how our mission is distinctly different from other land managing agencies. Thus far the process has been steady but slow. The controversial nature of the d-2 lands issue has given rise to much speculation and surmise related to the Park Service's mission. But parks are made to last a very long time, and there already have been encouraging signs.

During a field trip along the Kobuk River in the early stages of park planning, several of us visited the fish camp of Jacob Johnson at *Siqlioruq,* just downstream of Ambler. By the time we stepped ashore, Dora Johnson had a kettle on the fire, and so we looked forward to a pleasant chat with two elders of the Kobuk River community. Over dried fish and steaming mugs of tea, the conversation inevitably

Bob Uhl points out safe dogteam trails to National Park Service anthropologists Ray Bane (in fur hat) and Dr. Zorro A. Bradley while they are enjoying the warm hospitality of the Uhl's winter camp near Cape Krusenstern National Monument. Robert Belous, National Park Service

BELOW — *The serene beauty of Kobuk Valley National Park, an elegant addition to the national park system, is captured in this photo of a Kobuk dawn.* George Wuerthner

RIGHT — *Entranced by the appearance of a rainbow across the river, rafters enjoy the warmth of a fire along the Ambler River.* Kit Marrs

got around to what the Park Service was doing in the area, and why.

Something called a park was quite new to Jacob. He thought a long time about such things as protecting the land. Why do it? Nothing really bad seemed to be happening to it right now. And why all the concern over where the caribou cross the river, and about park boundaries being here on the map or there? The fuss and sense of urgency was puzzling. It must all have seemed oddly irrelevant to a man who had seen more than 60 winters come and go along the river. But he weighed the ideas very carefully, and saved his best advice for last.

As we walked toward our boat to leave, Jacob pointed with his walking stick to the Jade Mountains and the hills of the Hunt River where caribou appear in fall time. "This land has been good for a long time," he said. "It gives us food and what we need." With a patient smile he said, "Maybe we should just leave it like it is."

The basic mission of the National Park System has never been stated more clearly. Certain places — like Jacob's Kobuk valley, Noatak, Cape Krusenstern — are already at their best the way they are. But they can be spoiled, degraded, by incompatible uses, as other lands have been spoiled and lost. The three parklands of northwest Alaska are set aside to be used and enjoyed in such a way that they remain unchanged, unspoiled, so that others who follow may use and enjoy and learn from them. The idea is really not new to the people of the region. Jacob Johnson would have felt very much at home back at Yellowstone in 1872. □

The Magic of the Caribou and the Shifting Sands

Ole Wik

The Waring Mountains are steep on the north side, but on the south they slope gently toward the Selawik Lowlands. Several bald, parallel ridges lead southward from the summits toward the marshes. Along the coast of each ridge, as neat and dark as a pencil line, runs a game trail worn by the hooves of thousands upon thousands of caribou. During April and May the animals cross the range in passing from their wintering grounds in Selawik country to calving areas on the north slope. These long, gentle ridges allow caribou to cross the Warings without venturing into extensive spruce woodlands that cover the rest of the southern exposures.

Descent on the north side of the mountains is steep, but the animals traverse the slopes with ease, leaving a tracery of lines and dots in the rotting snow. At the foot of the mountains the caribou step out onto a broad expanse of wind-rippled sand. Two or three miles farther north they ease through a thin strip of forest and come at last to good feed on high tundra between the sands and the Kobuk River.

The migratory urge is irresistible, but for now the animals drift without pattern, plodding eastward one day and westward the next. They wander a landscape of quiet, sub-arctic beauty with birch knolls and spruce-

A researcher from the National Park Service hikes along the southern perimeter of the Great Kobuk Sand Dunes where dune crests rise 100 feet above underlying peat bogs.
Pete Sanchez, National Park Service

lined sloughs sprinkled among stretches of featureless tundra and quiet, frozen lakes.

Day by day the sun climbs higher, and life on the tundra quickens. Finally cow and year-ling caribou set off toward the north, leaving the velvet-antlered bulls to follow later. Splashing through blue-gray slush on the ice of a thawing lake, their hundreds of hooves make a sound like a mountain stream bounding over smooth stones.

Moving as if with purpose now, the caribou head for places along the banks of the Kobuk where the forest strip is narrowest. They move quickly through the woods, cross the snow dune that covers the riverbank willows, and pass onto the river itself. More and more animals come, band after band, until they have carved ruts in the snow deep enough to

throw a dogsled. Bearing to the west of the Jade Mountains, they follow the Hunt River drainage to Noatak country and beyond to complete their spring migration.

Caribou have different migration routes, and they may suddenly abandon one route for another that has been long unused. The route just described has been fairly active for at least the last 20 years, and has taken on added human significance in that the route passes through the heart of newly created, 1.7-million-acre Kobuk Valley National Park.

The park, which sweeps from the Warings to the Jades and from Onion Portage well toward Kiana, embraces the most scenic lands in the central Kobuk valley, including the Great Kobuk Sand Dunes.

This undulating sheet of sand, an improbably tawny blanket tucked against the lower slopes of the Waring Mountains, seems totally out of place in a land of tundra and perpetually frozen ground. And yet the 25 square miles of active sands represent but a small fraction of the total dune field: at least 300 square miles of surrounding lowlands are wrinkled with stabilized sand dunes which now support open stands of aspen, birch, and spruce.

Like so many present-day land forms, the dunes date back to Pleistocene times when mountain glaciers were active in the Brooks Range. Broad, braided rivers carried abundant outwash material, and strong winds swept the sands and silts away to form the great dune fields. Disappearance of the glaciers eliminated the source of new material for the dunes, and the ridges of sand were gradually overgrown by vegetation, and became stable.

What is fascinating about the Great Kobuk

Sand Dunes, and a smaller group a few miles to the east, is that they alone have resisted revegetation through the centuries. How do they differ from the much larger tracts of dead dunes nearby?

The answer lies in a particular combination of winds and topography. The east wind, clearly, is responsible for the main motion of the dunes. Steep, spectacular slopes face Kavet Creek along the western margin of the field, and at least one old stream bed shows

Scientists prepare to attach a radio collar to a caribou. Usually Fish and Game personnel lasso two or three caribou in a group and pull them, one at a time, to the boat's gunwale, hold them by the antlers, and attach a radio collar and identification band. Once the collar is secure, the caribou is released to rejoin the migration.　　　　David Fritts

that the creek has been overwhelmed by sand and forced westward: the abandoned watercourse, its flow choked off, emerges full-grown from a steep wall of dry sand.

But if the east wind moves the sands, the north wind maintains them. It is no accident that the dunes lie against the foot of the mountains, for if that wall of rock were not there, the north wind would have carried the sands off to the south centuries ago. Lobes of sand lap at the slopes, as if the wind had lifted the grains upward until it could carry them no higher. The same winds desiccate and sandblast any seedling that manages to take root on the porous, sun-baked surface of the deep, well-drained sands; under such conditions, revegetation is impossible.

So the landscape is alive and changing as the sands inch slowly westward, and overwhelm even mature spruce trees. But hardy pioneering plants relentlessly colonize the quieter margins of the dunes, and the streams carry away a bit more sediment every year. Without a source of new sand, these dunes too must eventually die, and remain an undistinguished, sparsely forested hillside until the climate changes once again.

Only the fall caribou migration on the north side of the Kobuk matches the natural spectacle of the sand dunes to the south. At this season bulls, cows, and calves band together much more than they do in spring, and it is sometimes possible to see impressive concentrations of animals.

In a year like 1980, when unusually early snows whiten the north slope and the high country of the Brooks Range, caribou might reach the Kobuk early in September. But when mild temperatures continue well into fall, as they did in 1969, caribou may not arrive until well into November.

Either way, the first bands appear as faint lines along the lower slopes of the Jade Mountains. They seem to be always in motion, and yet they come no nearer; it might be a week before they reach the river. But one morning they come, and suddenly the snow is trampled and stained, and the air carries a barnyard smell of hundreds of animals.

———————

Gone are the faded, tufted, shedding, old coats of May; now the animals wear prime, sleek coats of brown, black, and purest white. The bulls have long, white beards below their massive necks, and carry antlers that have matured into great arching racks. These they scrape and polish against the trunks of the few small, lone spruces that dot the tundra, breaking off most of the trees' branches below five feet. Such sparring trees — all stem except for a turban of greenery at the very top — stand all year as witness that this tundra, for a few weeks every fall, still belongs to the caribou.

The herd is charged, now, with the energy of the rut. The animals have to stay together, and yet the bulls must have a certain space for their harems, a space from which rival males are excluded. This tension is audible in the intermittent clack and clatter of antler upon antler, as the great bulls square off, engage their challengers, and attempt to drive them away.

But such scenes are ephemeral, for the herds usually cross the Kobuk before the peak of the rut, and continue their southward drift toward wintering grounds. Within a few weeks the bulls' magnificent antlers, built up slowly for the better part of a year, drop uselessly to the ground, and become gnawing posts for mice and porcupines.　□

THE VILLAGES

Before the coming of outsiders, Eskimos of NANA region did not have villages as we think of them today, but moved seasonally, following the game. Although they spoke the same language, Inupiat, there were dialectical differences for they were divided into eight local groups or bands with slightly varying life styles governed by the diversified territories they held. Those who depended on the seasonal migration of caribou were forced to travel often, but others who had lands of richer bounty could afford to spend the majority of their time at home bases which ultimately became permanent settlements.

Kikitagamute, later known as Kotzebue, is one such site. Located near the mouths of three major interior rivers, in the heart of Kotzebue Sound just off the Chukchi Sea, it was a natural central meeting point for the earliest Eskimo traders from throughout the area as well as from Wales, Shishmaref, Point Hope, Saint Lawrence, Diomede and even Siberia.

A number settled in the area year-round and old-timers remember *Kikitagamute* as a place "where they took in people, even people who were chased away from other villages."

LEFT — *Kotzebue, largest town in northwest Alaska with 2,526 residents, clusters around the tip of Baldwin Peninsula. It serves as a supply point for 11 villages in the area and is headquarters for NANA Regional Corporation.*
John and Margaret Ibbotson

The original village site, where the FAA facility is headquartered today, was apparently abandoned when a tragic accident took the lives of most of the children and people of child-bearing age. According to the best recollection, villagers had gathered on the ice of a nearby lake for a game of football, and the ice broke beneath them, because of a taboo broken by a pubescent girl who was one of the players, causing all to perish. Newcomers settled in with survivors at the current Kotzebue location and about 200 were located in the area at the coming of the whites.

Buckland people lived for a time at Elephant Point, a long established beluga hunting site. Capt. Kotzebue, first on the scene in 1816, reported at least 100 people in this vicinity,

Visitors enjoy swimming in the hot springs at Buckland. Hot springs are a favorite vacation site in winter and older residents will travel a hundred miles to visit a springs. Some springs are shared by Indians and Eskimos, and in earlier times this was the only way they could meet one another except in war and trading.
Barb Askey

and Capt. Beechey counted 101 conical skin tents with about 150 occupants encamped there ten years later. Today Buckland claims 172 residents.

There was also a smaller settlement at the mouth of the Kiwalik River not far from the village of Candle and another farther west called *Inmachukmiut,* inhabited by Deering

TOP — *A modern school dominates this scene of Buckland, population 172, on the Buckland River in southern Kotzebue Basin.*
John and Margaret Ibbotson

ABOVE — *Inez Koenig had a phone installed in 1979 and no one explained the billing system to her until she ran up about $1,000 worth of charges phoning her son in New Mexico. Now Inez is making baskets the traditional way to earn money to pay off the phone bill.*
Lael Morgan, staff

people who spoke the same dialect. They impressed outsiders early with their militant hostility and apparently had a good track record of local warfare, but they were equally well known and admired for their fine pottery.

The Kobuk River area was also rich enough in game and fish to support settlement pretty much on a year-round basis. Some lived in scattered villages on the delta. Oksik, located a short distance below the Squirrel River near the place where the Kobuk divides into northern and middle channels, was reported to be the largest settlement on the lower river but its residents apparently moved to Noorvik about 1914.

Also well established was Kalla about seven miles above the present village of Kobuk, where most of the salmon fishing for the upper river was done. A smaller settlement between Oksik and Kalla was later named Coal Mine.

The majority of Kobuk people, however, lived near the mouth of the Pah River near where explorer Stoney built his winter camp by the Cosmos Hills. The settlement was called

Riley Camp, after a sternwheeler which supplied miners here, but was abandoned except for a couple of families by 1913.

Selawik Eskimos lived in tiny communities of 10 or 20 closely related people occupying two or three sod houses, throughout their plain area, fishing from myriad lakes, rivers, and ponds. A school was started with a wooden structure in 1909, but many residents continued to live outside the village, coming in only for the Christmas holidays, until well into the 1950s.

Upper and lower Noatak people also lived in small, scattered groups, but moved pretty much in a body to the coast to hunt seals and beluga whales every spring. A school was built at the present village site in 1911, but a sizeable number of holdouts continue to live upriver most of the year. In 1981 Noatak has 261 people.

Kivalina (population 208), also known as Corwin Lagoon, was a stopping place for travelers — mainly Kotzebue Sound people going to and from Point Hope — and a spring

CLOCKWISE FROM ABOVE —
►*Orderly rows of painted houses characterize the new village of Noatak, population 261. Many Noatak villagers still live upriver for much of the year.* John and Margaret Ibbotson

►*About 44 miles northeast of Elephant Point on the Selawik River lies the community of Selawik, population 580, second largest community in the Kotzebue Basin.*
►*Residents repair the pierced steel planking which serves as the runway for Kivalina, population 208, located on a barrier reef between the Chukchi Sea and Kivalina Lagoon 47 miles northwest of Cape Krusenstern.*
►*Young Alex Hawley of Kivalina wears a traditional Eskimo hunting parka with the fur on the inside. If the wearer falls through the ice, the hollow hairs of the caribou skin will add buoyancy.* All by Lael Morgan, staff

CLOCKWISE FROM LEFT —

▶ *Once an active gold-mining community, today Candle's permanent population numbers 5, but jumps to 12 if reindeer herders working nearby are counted.*
John and Margaret Ibbotson

▶*Neatly arranged houses of Noorvik, population 527, branch out from the shores of Nazuruk Channel of the Kobuk River.*
Lael Morgan, staff

▶*The new village of Shungnak, population 182, is built on a hill overlooking the old village which was subject to flooding.*
George Wuerthner

▶*Kobuk, population 60, originally called Long Beach, had its beginnings in 1899 as a supply point for mining activities in the Cosmos Hills.*
John and Margaret Ibbotson

About 340 residents look to modern Kiana on the Kobuk River as home. John and Margaret Ibbotson

shore base for Eskimos who lived inland on the Kivalina and Wulik rivers. The building of a government school there in 1905, and the location of a reindeer herd in the area soon attracted permanent residents.

Kobuk (population 60), originally called Long Beach, had its beginnings in 1899 as a supply point for mining activities in the Cosmos Hills. However a nearby settlement called Kalla had long been occupied by Eskimos.

Shore erosion from ice breakup flooding and a shift in mining activities caused the majority of Kobuk residents to move a few

miles southwest in the 1920s and to establish modern Shungnak (population 182). Residents renamed their town after the river on which it was established.

Deering (population 100) was built by miners at *Inmachukmiut* in 1901. A school, built there in 1906, lured residents away from the Eskimo village of Kuugruk on eastern hills.

Candle (population 12) went on the map in 1907 as a placer mining discovery, and later served as a supply point for reindeer herders as well as miners. Kiana also had its beginnings as a mining town in 1909, eventually taking the recording office and jail from Shungnak.

Noorvik was settled in 1915 by a contingent of Deering Eskimos led by missionary-teacher Charles Replogle who managed to

secure a 225-square-mile reservation through President Woodrow Wilson. The reason for moving, according to Replogle's report, was depletion of the fish supply at *Inmachukmiut* due to the hydraulic operations of miners and to the atmosphere of the mining town with its "drink and all night dances." Natives recall no problem with fishing, but there was a scarcity of firewood at the old site.

Noorvik, which means "a place that is moved to" was a well-forested, game-rich area where the village of Oksik had once prospered, and it immediately attracted 400 people and continued to grow, relinquishing its reservation status in 1971 to participate in the Alaska Native Land Claims Settlement.

Newest village in the region is Ambler, established by Shungnak people in 1958 at an

One of the fastest growing communities in Kotzebue Basin is Ambler, population 217, fourth largest community in the region.
Lael Morgan, staff

old summer camp called *Saisaapaat*. The move was made to the timbered area after bitter debate on the merits of declaring Shungnak a reservation. The no vote was 51 to 25, and many felt more comfortable moving on.

After the coming of the whites, the majority of the villages continued to grow. Exceptions were Deering which depopulated as mining slowed, and Candle which was devastated by fire in 1966 and has never made a strong comeback despite the fact that gold mining is still profitable in that area.

At this writing, excluding Kotzebue, Noorvik (population 527) and Selawik (population 580) are the largest communities, and ultra-modern Kiana (population 340) is running a close third with Ambler (population 217) fourth.

Kotzebue, which now ranks as one of the largest second-class cities in the state, doubled its population from 1950 to 1960, moving from 623 to 1,290 and recently doubled it again to

Deering, population 100, lines the shore where the Inmachuk River flows into Kotzebue Sound. The village was established at the turn of the century to supply mining camps on the Seward Peninsula, and was probably named for the schooner Abbie Deering *which cruised in nearby waters at the time of the community's founding.*
John and Margaret Ibbotson

2,526. The population for the region, established at roughly 3,000 to 4,000 at the coming of outsiders, now numbers about 5,000, of which about 85% are Inupiat Eskimos.

Under the Alaska Native Land Claims Settlement Act of 1971, Natives of the region united under NANA Regional Corporation, established to administer moneys and lands gained from the act, and all villages in the area, with the exception of Kotzebue, soon merged with their regional corporation, a precedent that several other corporations in the state are considering. □

CLOCKWISE FROM UPPER LEFT —

►*Enoch Howarth sprints for the finish line during field day events in spring 1980 in Kotzebue.* Debbie Myers

►*David Wright (left) and Nereus Wilson work a chemistry experiment with teacher Craig Eldred at Kotzebue School.*

►*From an old-time trading family, Frank Ferguson of Kotzebue serves in the state legislature and is president of the Alaska Federation of Natives.*

►*A resident of Kotzebue since 1932, George Francis is a longtime magistrate and still notary public. He married a local woman and lives in one of Kotzebue's oldest houses.*

►*While they do not yet have a McDonald's, the Dairy Queen has arrived in Kotzebue.*

All by Lael Morgan, staff

51

ANCIENT PEOPLES OF THE KOTZEBUE BASIN

— Douglas D. Anderson

Douglas D. Anderson first came to the Kotzebue area as a field assistant with an archaeological party from Brown University to investigate Cape Krusenstern in 1960 and returned in 1961 as a principal investigator for an archaeological survey of the Noatak River. With the late J. Louis Giddings, he was among the first to unearth the secrets of the Onion Portage and continued to work in this region through the late 1970s. Currently he serves as a full professor of anthropology at Brown University.

Ten thousand years ago the forerunners of the northwest Alaska's Inupiat Eskimos were already at home in the region of Kotzebue Sound. Actually, Kotzebue Sound did not exist then except, perhaps, as a narrow, 20-mile-long inlet extending southeastward from just north of Cape Espenberg. The rest of Kotzebue Sound was a great sandy plain, draining the combined deltas of the Noatak, Kobuk, and Selawik rivers, that was exposed when sea level was lower than now. Sea level was lower because the earth's waters were still locked up in great continental glaciers of the last ice age. At the height of this ice age between about 25,000 and 14,000 years ago, the lower sea level exposed a large land mass, called Beringia or the Bering Land Bridge, that connected north Asia with Alaska. Beringia, which reached its maximum extent when the sea was about 450 feet lower than now, began to flood about 18,000 years ago as the glaciers began to melt. The seas broke through Bering Strait about 14,000 years ago, but did not reach their present height until about 4,500 years ago. At

10,000 years ago, the age of our earliest archaeological finds in the Kotzebue Sound region, the still-rising sea level was probably about 50 feet lower than present. We cannot determine precisely where the coastline of incipient Kotzebue Sound was then, but it must have stretched northwesterly from near Cape Espenberg to Point Hope in an arc about 8 miles into the sea from the present shoreline. (Please see map, page 56.)

The early inhabitants of Kotzebue Sound and its environs, already separated by then from their north Asian neighbors with whom they had coexisted on Beringia, lived by hunting big game on land. Although no longer in overland contact with north Asia, these early north Alaskans continued to meet with Asians by boat or maybe across the ice and to share discoveries of new ways to survive in the north. We can surmise the existence of this early intercontinental communication network from the decidedly similar stone tools that evolved simultaneously in Arctic America and in northeast Asia as far west as the Aldan River, and as far southwest as northern Japan.

Also, the material culture of these early Kotzebue Sound residents, known in archaeological circles as the American Paleo Arctic cultural tradition, is similar to the material culture of groups in many other parts of Alaska, and this suggests that even at this early time most Alaskans were in continuous contact with each other.

We know little about the lifeways of the early peoples of northwest Alaska except that they hunted with antler-and-stone-tipped spears and cut up their game with large heavy stone knives and cleavers. Their tools, uncovered at the Onion Portage archaeological site mid-way up the Kobuk River, show them to have had a sophisticated stone-chipping technology which they used to make durable cutting edges for weapons and tools. Surface finds attributable to these people have also been reported from exposed hilltops in the tundra farther north. It is difficult to understand how they survived, however, for scientists tell us that their region was devoid of trees, except for some cottonwood, perhaps. Without access to wood, how could the people have made poles, shafts, and handles for spears, ice picks, and the hundred of other implements we consider necessary for survival in the north? Even the modern Inupiat of treeless northern Canada and Greenland have had access to trees, in the form of driftwood. The Kotzebue Sound region at that time was covered with a shrub tundra not unlike that in the Barrow region today. Although bleak, their habitat was not barren, for the tundra was sufficiently rich in grasses and other grass-like plants to support even more game animals than are present in the region nowadays.

Although many archaeologists believe that the early cultural remains found in the Kotzebue Sound area derive from the ancestors of Eskimos (the people who now live across the top of North America who speak the Eskimo language), others believe that they derive from the ancestors of Indians (all of the other people living in North America) who preceded the Eskimos into the New World during land-bridge times. Both arguments seem to me plausible, for if we could trace the entire genealogy of the early people who left the American Paleo Arctic artifacts, I think we would find that they were at least partly ancestral to both the Eskimo and the northern Indian populations of Alaska.

We do not know for how long or exactly where the immediate descendants of the Paleo Arctic people continued to live in northwest Alaska, but beginning around 6,500 years ago people with a different cultural tradition were in the region. Their tradition, known as the Northern Archaic, was a northern extension of a tradition derived from interior Alaska, southwest Yukon, and perhaps even farther away. Northern Archaic is characterized by side- and corner-notched projectile points and knives — very different from the slender antler spear points of the Paleo Arctic peoples; by the extensive use of stone skin scrapers, often of obsidian; and by large, oval knife blades. As with the earlier remains, Northern

ABOVE — *The author, a professor at Brown University, approaches one of the springs flowing from beneath the sand dunes along the Kobuk. Westward movement of the dune field has overtaken this spring, and buried its source. Numerous archaeological sites border the dunes.* Robert Belous, National Park Service

RIGHT — *The cache where archaeologist J. Louis Giddings kept his tools towers over Onion Portage archaeological site, a major clue to the life of early man in the Kotzebue Basin. In the foreground is the smoke hole of an Eskimo house.* Anore Jones

Archaic implements have been found along the Kobuk and Noatak rivers and also in exposed sites on the north slope.

It is easier to visualize the life of these people than it is to imagine the life of their predecessors, for the Northern Archaic people had access to trees. Although they hunted beyond the forest limits, they were never

Alaska Mural Artist: Jay H. Matternes, Smithsonian Institution Photo No. 72-5994

ABOVE — *When continental glaciers covered large areas of North America and Eurasia, much of interior Alaska became a refuge for many kinds of animals. Surrounding mountains received most of the precipitation, preventing build-up of permanent snow and ice in the central lowland. Alaska and Siberia were joined by the Bering Land Bridge, and many animals that were widely distributed across northern Asia crossed to Alaska. Other animals, ground sloths and camels for example, entered Alaska from farther south in the hemisphere.*

Fossil records show that the majority of these prehistoric animals were grazers, mainly bison, horses, and mammoths. The remaining animals were browsers and predators. The prevalence of grazers and fossil pollen evidence indicate a grassland environment in Late Pleistocene Alaska. The area is now forest and tundra, with browsers such as moose and caribou predominant.

Explorer Otto Von Kotzebue stumbled on to a remarkable deposit of mammoth and mastodon bones when he discovered Kotzebue Sound and Capt. Frederick Beechey investi-gated his discovery 10 years later, shipping fossils home to Dr. William Buckland, professor of Geology and Mineralogy at the University of Oxford and naming the river from whence they came in Buckland's honor.

Information for this remarkable recreation of the late Pleistocene epoch came from Russell Dale Guthrie, Department of Biological Sciences, University of Alaska, who is a leading expert in this field.

more than a few days' walk from the wood needed for their manufactures. As their predecessors did, they hunted caribou; because large animals like horse and bison had become extinct in the region (and moose had not yet arrived), they were largely dependent on this one source of meat. Perhaps because of this, they began to develop ways to catch fish in the rivers and streams. They appear to have had fish nets — or at least they made and discarded notched stones that resemble the sinkers used to weight the bottoms of fish nets in more recent times.

Because of the similarity between the Northern Archaic archaeological remains around Kotzebue Sound (and the north slope) and the archaeological remains of Indians in the deep interior of Alaska and beyond, the people of northwest Alaska who made the Northern Archaic tools obviously borrowed much from their interior Indian neighbors. They may, indeed, have been Indians who, during the unusually mild climates that reigned in the northern hemisphere between 6,500 and 4,200 years ago, spread beyond their present boundaries into arctic Alaska.

Other cultural remains that seem to date to this period have also been found in isolated scatters on tops of beach terraces just north of Kotzebue Sound and elsewhere in northwest

Alaska. These remains appear to derive culturally from the earlier American Paleo Arctic tradition, which suggests to us that between 6,000 and 4,000 years ago, tundra hunters continuing the American Paleo Arctic tradition may have coexisted in northwest Alaska with Indians of the Northern Archaic tradition.

Around 4,200 years ago arctic cultures again began to expand southward. This was the time of the Denbigh people, so-named after the site at Cape Denbigh in Norton Sound, where their tools were first found. Not only did they appear along the Kobuk River and other parts of northwest Alaska, but they also spread along the coast southward as far as Bristol Bay, and eastward as far as Greenland. The eastward extension of the culture was carried by migrants moving into the previously unoccupied eastern Arctic. This dynamic cultural tradition, of which Denbigh is the earliest period, is referred to as the Arctic Small Tool tradition, so named because of the diminutive size of the chipped stone blades the people made to edge their weapons and tools. This tradition may well be Paleo Eskimo — a term given to the hypothesized ancestral culture of both the Inupiat (northern Alaskan, Canadian and Greenland Eskimos) and the Yuit (southern Alaskan and Siberian Eskimos). The craftsmanship in shaping stone tools by flaking was so fine that many specialists today consider these Paleo Eskimos to have been the world's supreme stone workers of all time.

During Denbigh times Paleo Eskimos developed a subsistence that allowed them to harvest both caribou in the interior and seals at the coast. Perhaps more than any other single factor, this subsistence strategy, by which both land creatures and sea mammals were hunted during the times of their greatest seasonal abundance, allowed the people to inhabit most of the American Arctic and sub-Arctic. Their technology was so successful that the same tool kit was suitable for many dif-

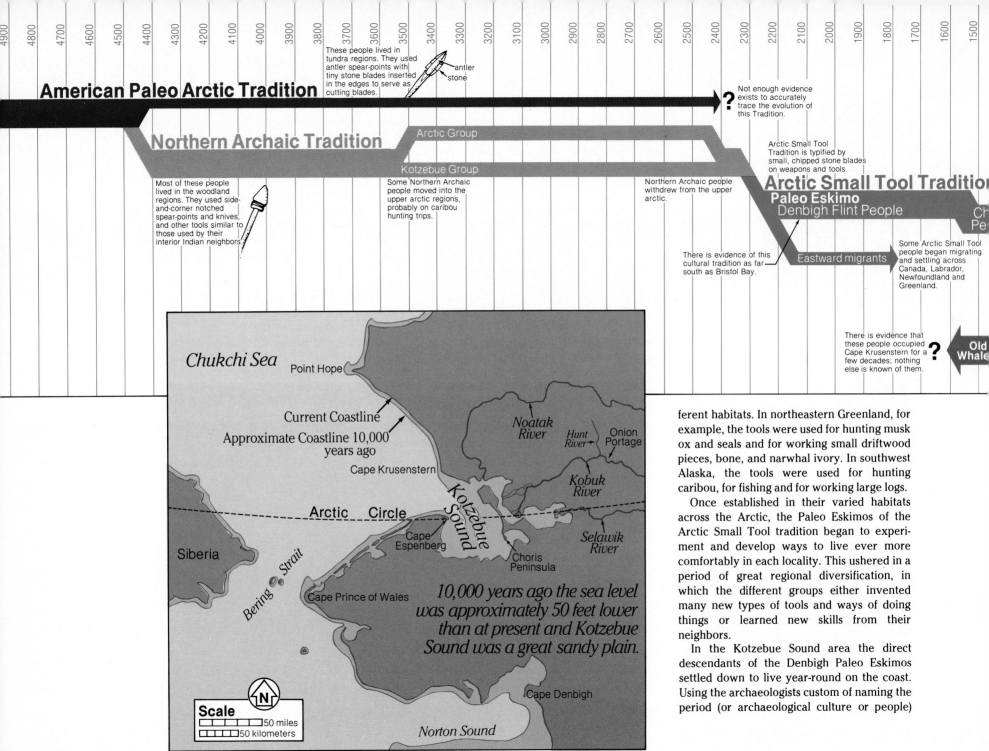

4900 4800 4700 4600 4500 4400 4300 4200 4100 4000 3900 3800 3700 3600 3500 3400 3300 3200 3100 3000 2900 2800 2700 2600 2500 2400 2300 2200 2100 2000 1900 1800 1700 1600 1500

American Paleo Arctic Tradition

These people lived in tundra regions. They used antler spear-points with tiny stone blades inserted in the edges to serve as cutting blades.

antler
stone

? Not enough evidence exists to accurately trace the evolution of this Tradition.

Northern Archaic Tradition

Arctic Group

Kotzebue Group

Most of these people lived in the woodland regions. They used side-and-corner notched spear-points and knives, and other tools similar to those used by their interior Indian neighbors.

Some Northern Archaic people moved into the upper arctic regions, probably on caribou hunting trips.

Northern Archaic people withdrew from the upper arctic.

Arctic Small Tool Tradition is typified by small, chipped stone blades on weapons and tools.

Arctic Small Tool Tradition

Paleo Eskimo
Denbigh Flint People

Ch
Pe

There is evidence of this cultural tradition as far south as Bristol Bay.

Eastward migrants

Some Arctic Small Tool people began migrating and settling across Canada, Labrador, Newfoundland and Greenland.

There is evidence that these people occupied Cape Krusenstern for a few decades; nothing else is known of them. ?

Old
Whale

Chukchi Sea

Point Hope

Current Coastline

Approximate Coastline 10,000 years ago

Cape Krusenstern

Noatak River *Hunt River* Onion Portage

Kobuk River

Arctic Circle

Siberia

Cape Espenberg

Kotzebue Sound

Choris Peninsula

Selawik River

Bering Strait

Cape Prince of Wales

10,000 years ago the sea level was approximately 50 feet lower than at present and Kotzebue Sound was a great sandy plain.

Cape Denbigh

Scale
50 miles
50 kilometers

N

Norton Sound

ferent habitats. In northeastern Greenland, for example, the tools were used for hunting musk ox and seals and for working small driftwood pieces, bone, and narwhal ivory. In southwest Alaska, the tools were used for hunting caribou, for fishing and for working large logs.

Once established in their varied habitats across the Arctic, the Paleo Eskimos of the Arctic Small Tool tradition began to experiment and develop ways to live ever more comfortably in each locality. This ushered in a period of great regional diversification, in which the different groups either invented many new types of tools and ways of doing things or learned new skills from their neighbors.

In the Kotzebue Sound area the direct descendants of the Denbigh Paleo Eskimos settled down to live year-round on the coast. Using the archaeologists custom of naming the period (or archaeological culture or people)

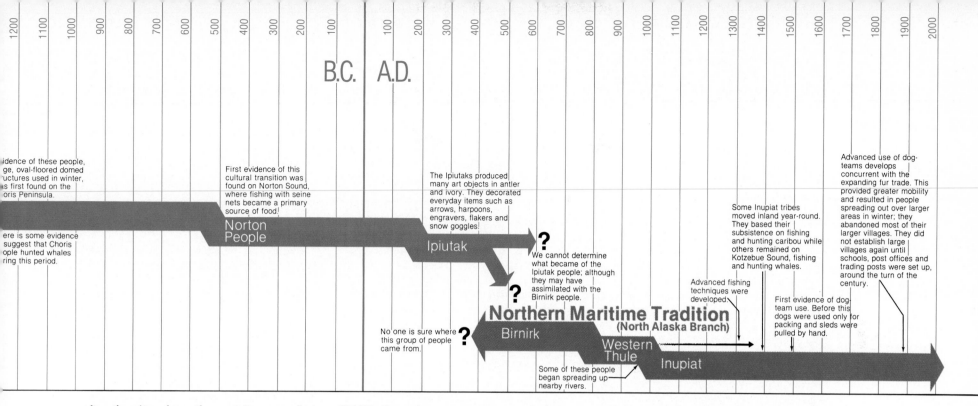

Timeline labels (B.C. left to right): 1200 1100 1000 900 800 700 600 500 400 300 200 100 | 100 200 300 400 500 600 700 800 900 1000 1100 1200 1300 1400 1500 1600 1700 1800 1900 2000 (A.D.)

...idence of these people, ...ge, oval-floored domed ...uctures used in winter, ...s first found on the ...oris Peninsula.

...ere is some evidence ...suggest that Choris ...ople hunted whales ...ring this period.

First evidence of this cultural transition was found on Norton Sound, where fishing with seine nets became a primary source of food!

Norton People

The Ipiutaks produced many art objects in antler and ivory. They decorated everyday items such as arrows, harpoons, engravers, flakers and snow goggles!

Ipiutak

?

We cannot determine what became of the Ipiutak people; although they may have assimilated with the Birnirk people.

?

No one is sure where this group of people came from. **?**

Northern Maritime Tradition
(North Alaska Branch)

Birnirk

Western Thule

Inupiat

Some of these people began spreading up nearby rivers.

Some Inupiat tribes moved inland year-round. They based their subsistence on fishing and hunting caribou while others remained on Kotzebue Sound, fishing and hunting whales.

Advanced fishing techniques were developed.

First evidence of dog-team use. Before this dogs were used only for packing and sleds were pulled by hand.

Advanced use of dog-teams develops concurrent with the expanding fur trade. This provided greater mobility and resulted in people spreading out over larger areas in winter; they abandoned most of their larger villages. They did not establish large villages again until schools, post offices and trading posts were set up, around the turn of the century.

---

after the site where the remains were first located, we call these the Choris people. Their winter homes, first located on the coast at Choris Peninsula, were large oval-floored domed structures that each must have housed many families.

The Choris Paleo Eskimos were not, however, the first people to winter along the coast around Kotzebue Sound. About 1,500 B.C. just before the Choris people settled on the coast, a sizeable group of people belonging to some entirely different cultural traditions occupied Cape Krusenstern for a few decades. Just who these people were remains a mystery to this day. We call them the Old Whalers and although their tools were made in very different styles from those that characterized the Arctic Small Tool tradition, some of their implements are reminiscent of much later Eskimo tools found in the large village sites of Point Hope and Barrow. Could it be that the

Old Whaling culture represents an early form of a long-evolving maritime arctic culture around Bering Strait that coexisted with the Arctic Small Tool tradition? In any event, the Old Whalers appear to have actively hunted whales, and may well have been the world's first whalers. So far, we know of their existence only from the one settlement at Cape Krusenstern.

In the meantime, while the Choris people of Kotzebue Sound developed a maritime living capability based on a local evolution of the Arctic Small Tool tradition, their relatives living along the Kobuk River were expanding their technology to fully utilize a riverine woodland habitat. Still other relatives, whom we also call Choris, were experimenting with making new types of tools and weapons to live more securely in the tundra farther north.

The Choris Paleo Eskimos — a term we now use to describe all of the Arctic Small Tool

tradition peoples residing in north Alaska between 3,600 and 2,500 years ago — were quite cosmopolitan. Those from the Kotzebue Sound area had contacts with coastal northeast Asians, and from them they learned the art of pottery making. Choris people also learned, presumably through contacts with southwest Alaska coastal relatives, how to grind slate into tools, a technique developed two millennia earlier along the North American Pacific coast. Choris Eskimos from the Kobuk River had contacts with Indians from farther in the interior of Alaska, obtaining from them exotic stones like obsidian for tool making.

We cannot yet say whether the Choris people of Kotzebue Sound hunted whales, but an unusually large number of whalebones were found on Cape Krusenstern beaches that they occupied between 2,500 and 3,500 years ago.

Beginning around 500 B.C., Norton people of Kotzebue Sound, the cultural descendants of the Choris people, refined many of the Choris techniques for making tools and weapons. Curiously, the Norton people — who got their name from their first archaeological site located in Norton Sound — did not winter along the shores of Kotzebue Sound as did their Choris ancestors — at least we have never found one of their winter houses there. Instead they preferred Point Hope (where they could hunt seals and, in the spring, whales) and the coast just northeast of Cape Prince of Wales. But in neither of these two areas did they congregate in large settlements. In contrast, their relatives at Norton Sound, the region from which the Norton people received their name, did establish large coastal communities, based primarily on fishing. Using long seine nets, they caught great quantities of salmon as the fish entered the rivers each summer. With such a predictable resource, the Norton people were able to maintain large, stable communities, supported during lean seasons or years by supplies of stored food.

What the Norton people of Kotzebue Sound and farther north lacked in numbers, they made up for in artistic talent. With tiny, stone-tipped engraving tools, they incised bold designs on antler in a style that is reminiscent of the spurred designs of the better-known early ivory carvers on Saint Lawrence Island. But it was the Norton people's descendants, the Ipiutak Paleo Eskimos, who, during the first few centuries after the birth of Christ, attained the pinnacle in artistic achievement in northern Alaska. Ipiutak artists carved human faces and fantastic animal figures in ivory and they incised intricate designs on both antler and ivory. They not only decorated such things as their arrows, harpoons, engravers, flakers, and snow goggles, but they also created a variety of art objects, mostly of ivory, that appear to have had no everyday use. These carvings included pretzel-like open-work pieces, chains, and shafts with ridges that look something like screw threads.

The first artifacts of the Ipiutak culture were found at Point Hope in 1939. Two decades later the Ipiutak culture was also found along the shores of Kotzebue Sound. There the Ipiutak people lived in settlements of tight clusters of small single-family houses around a single large house that perhaps served as a *karagi* (meeting house), an arrangement that characterized the Inupiat of the 19th century. They buried their dead in shallow graves, often clustered into small cemeteries. Most of the Ipiutak artwork found its way into the graves, but whether art was reserved for decorating burial objects, or whether decorated objects were so highly prized that they were customarily buried with the owners, we cannot say. The Ipiutak people represented the last Paleo Eskimo culture of the Arctic Small Tool tradition.

Co-existing with Ipiutak culture in northwest Alaska during the 5th to 8th centuries A.D. was a culture known as Birnirk. Birnirk, and its descendant Western Thule, are the earliest of what we can definitely identify as Inupiat culture, or, as it is named archaeologically, the North Alaskan branch of the Northern Maritime tradition. Just where Birnirk came from we cannot say. Some archaeologists believe it developed on the Northeast coast of Asia and the islands around Bering Strait; others believe it developed from the later periods of the Arctic Small Tool (Paleo Eskimo) tradition. We also cannot say what happened to the Ipiutak people, although they may have assimilated with the Birnirk people. Birnirk emerged first at Point Hope, Barrow, and Cape Prince of Wales, and then began to show up along the shores of Kotzebue Sound around 800 A.D., just before the Birnirk culture as a whole evolved into the Western Thule culture. Within 200 years, that is by around 1,000 A.D., the Western Thule people had spread up the Kobuk and other nearby rivers. The relation of the people of the Northern Maritime tradition to the earlier Paleo Eskimos or to the people of the Arctic Small Tool tradition is still something of a mystery. Both the Northern Maritime and the Arctic Small Tool traditions appear to be Eskimo, but they had different developmental histories: the earlier Arctic Small Tool tradition evolved on mainland Arctic North America, including the interior tundra regions, and the later Northern Maritime tradition evolved along the shores of the islands of the Bering and Chukchi seas.

One Birnirk settlement has been found at Cape Krusenstern, but, so far, nowhere else around or near Kotzebue Sound. Nor has Birnirk been found along the rivers draining into Kotzebue Sound. In fact, between about 700 and 900 A.D., the river drainages, and also the north slope, seem to have been pretty much abandoned, perhaps because caribou were too few during those centuries. Where the people went, we cannot say, but they may have moved to the coast.

Inupiat populations around Kotzebue Sound began to grow again during the Western Thule cultural phase around 1,000 A.D. The beginning of the second millennium A.D. seems to have been a time of plenty for the Kotzebue Sound Inupiat: not only were seals and caribou numerous, but baleen whales swam by close enough to northern shores of the sound to make whaling practical from Cape Krusenstern. This is the period when the Inupiat again moved to the rivers. At first they remained along the rivers only for the winters, preferring to be on the coast for the spring and summer seal and beluga hunts and for trade. Their main settlement along the Kobuk River between 1,000 and 1,300 A.D. was at Ahteut, just below the mouth of the Hunt River (an area that is now protected as part of the Kobuk Valley National Park), but they also lived at Onion Portage and undoubtedly at many other spots along the rivers.

By 1,400 A.D. the Inupiat along the Kobuk River had developed a fishing technology that allowed many of them to live all year in the interior. Presumably a few of their more itinerant members supplied them with sea-mammal products through coastal trading excursions. The Kobuk River Inupiat also intensified their trade with Indians at this time, and they began to adopt some of the Indian ways of doing things. For example, they began to make birch-bark baskets in the same forms that the Indians of interior Alaska made theirs.

Between the 11th and 15th centuries A.D. Inupiat fished primarily by spear and net along the Kobuk River, but by 1,400 A.D. they also began to fish by hook and line. For this they made and used beautifully carved ivory "fish lure" hooks, fashioned in the form of small fish. These same hooks were until recently made by residents of most of the villages and today are prized as heirlooms.

On the coast in 1,400 A.D., the Western Thule Inupiat lived year-round at Cape Krusenstern. Their primary occupation in the spring was whale hunting. They did not construct *karagit* in which to manufacture, repair, and store whaling gear, as their relatives in the modern whaling villages of Point Barrow did, but instead, the chief family of each settlement simply built an extra room on to its house for this purpose. Other Kotzebue Sound Inupiat lived in a village at the site of the present city of Kotzebue. They spent much of their time fishing.

Even with plenty of game in the region between the 11th and 15th centuries, the Inupiat people must have had a hard life. Traveling, for instance, must have been quite difficult, for, judging from the lack of harness parts in their archaeological leavings, they did not have dog teams until about the 16th century. Earlier Inupiat did have dogs and sleds, but the dogs seem to have been used for packing (and hunting) and the sleds, which were very small, were mainly hand-pulled and used to transport kayaks over sea ice. Even when dog traction first became popular in the 16th century the teams were very small. In fact, the large dog teams that we often associate with Eskimos only became practical after the development of the fur trade at the end of the 19th and beginning of the 20th centuries.

Another important innovation of the Inupiat that came into vogue during the Western Thule phase was the sinew-backed bow, introduced from Asia. This type of bow increased the Inupiats' ability to hunt caribou over long distances. Bows may also have been used for warfare. Slate armor looking something like Japanese *Samurai* armor appeared in the Western Thule period along the coast and interior areas of Alaska, but this may have been as much for show as for actual fighting or raiding, for we do not find evidence of increased violence in the village sites at any time.

Another custom often remarked upon by early explorers to northwest Alaska was the wearing of lip plugs for ornaments. It is interesting to speculate about the period when these decorations began to assume popularity in the Kotzebue Sound region. Lip plugs were made and worn back in Norton and Ipiutak times, and perhaps even in Birnirk times, but they were not worn during Western Thule times. They became popular again in the 16th century and remained in vogue right into the early part of the 20th century. Before they went out of fashion, some of the plugs were being made of bottle glass.

During the 19th century Inupiat of Kotzebue Sound and its environs seems to have abandoned most of their larger villages and spread themselves up and down the rivers and around the coast in isolated winter homesteads. There were several causes for this. One was the fur trade: as people began to engage in commercial trapping for furs they spread out more to maximize their chances of making a good harvest. Another cause was dog trac-

Labrets and other decorations adorned the faces of Kotzebue Sound Natives when explorer Otto von Kotzebue first saw these people in 1816. The likenesses were captured by his artist, M. Louis Choris.
Reprinted from *A Voyage of Discovery, into the South Sea and Beering's Strait . . . in the years 1815-1818*

tion, which had developed to the point where people were sufficiently mobile to permit both isolated living and frequent visiting. Other causes may have been diseases brought in from the outside that decimated the population, or food shortages such as those caused by the decline in the caribou populations. Whatever the reasons, the Inupiat again established villages in the region only after schools, post offices, and trading posts were set up.

Throughout the entire history of the Inupiat around Kotzebue Sound and the adjacent rivers, the people have shown a remarkable ability to accept and refine new techniques for living in their surroundings. Their past shows that they have managed resources and their lands well, and although they have suffered periods of food shortages, they have managed to adapt effectively to the ever-changing conditions. □

Eskimo Warfare

Anthropologists have made much of the idea that war did not occur among Eskimo people, and this may have been the case among Greenlanders, Canadians, and Alaska Yup'iks along the Kuskokwim. However the battles of ancient Inupiats are legendary, and much grisly evidence of them survives in the form of broken bones, crushed skulls, and bone and ivory armor.

One of the major deterrents to warfare in the Arctic was the fact that permanent settlement was seldom possible because of a scarceness of resources. To engage the enemy, one must first find him, and subsistence hunters were generally highly migratory. But the Eskimos of northwest Alaska were fairly rich in resources, and their seasonal migration patterns were well-established. Point Hope, just beyond the boundaries of the NANA region, ranks as the longest established permanent settlement in North America, and villages were also long entrenched around Kotzebue Sound.

Point Hope battles seem best remembered here, but the Kotzebue-Kobuk-Noatak-Buckland-Selawik warriers also quarreled among themselves and with Athabascan Indians whose territory to the south they progressively occupied over the ages.

Another formidable enemy was a people called the Arctics or *Inugutat (Innugutat)* who supposedly lived for centuries in the interior, and often plagued coastal neighbors. In older times the Arctics could have been Eskimos, but more recently these people seem to have been Indians. Archaeologists have had little success in documenting their existence, yet they are mentioned again and again in folk tales, and some believe in them yet.

The following recollection by James Tobuk is classic, not only because it deals with the Arctics, but because it tells of the all too common anguish of relatives caught on opposing sides of battle, and includes the Twins, oft-mentioned heroes of the past. James Tobuk has long been a resident of Anaktuvuk Pass but he and his family before him traveled widely throughout the Arctic, and he has meticulously preserved much history of the Kotzebue-Kobuk area.

Editor's note: A similar version of this story appeared in the Autumn 1980 issue of The ALASKA JOURNAL®, page 27. The dialect used by Mr. Tobuk is just one of many in the Inupiat language. Personnel at the National Bilingual Materials Development Center have provided translations (shown in parenthesis) for another dialect commonly spoken in the Kotzebue Basin.

Arcticers Attack Sickrik in Winter

James Tobuk

Ill. by J. O. Tobuk

Sickrik's family moved down to Sickriktook (Siksriktuuq). They named the village Edseakvick. [*Edseakvick (Iqsiugvik)* is translated by Kobuk people as "A place where the *innuqutat* or *iqsiut* are encountered."] Sickrik (Siksrik) build that village. Most of it underground tunnels to store enough supplies to last for months. Ice, wood and food; all can be reached through tunnels.

Sickrik (Siksrik) know he has bitter enemies, so he always well prepared to meet them. Build his igloo out of heavy timber covered with sod, sand and gravel; freeze them together so they don't have to go outside if attacked in cold winter.

One day he go out hunting ptarmigan up Kobuk River. Same time scouting around. See smoke far away where there was no village. He know they must be Arctics coming down again to get him. He feel almost certain they'll get him this time in cold weather and deep

continued

snow, so he hurry home to tell his neighbor and ask one of the reliable young men to go after the Twins who live about 30 miles up Sickriktook (Siksriktuuq), place called Mullghojark (Malgitchiak).

When Sickrik (Siksrik) get home to his young Arctic wives, he tell them that he saw smoke and he's very certain it's Arctic warriors coming again. Say that he send for Twins to help because he know he won't match so many men on soft snow, and because now he's aged, about 40 or 45 years old, and not so active as he used to be.

Messenger come in evening to Mullghojark (Malgitchiak). He tell the Twins Sickrik (Siksrik) very certain Arctic warriors coming down by the Kobuk. That they should be at Edseakvick (Iqsiugvik) by now. Twins don't hesitate a moment. Pick up their quivers full of arrows and little lunch. Leave immediately for the 30-mile run.

Arctic warriors camp close to Edseakvick (Iqsiugvik). They find out the village is underground. They know it will not be easy to get Sickrik (Siksrik) but they already come long ways. None of them willing to give up and return home without trying, so they dig out trenches in the snow and spray water on them so arrows won't penetrate.

Comic, an Arctic and cousin of one of Sickrik's (Siksrik's) wives, deliver package full of nice meat to Sickrik's (Siksrik's) igloo. When the girls go to the door to get it, one of them see her cousin. She whisper quietly, "Comic, you might as well go home before you get hurt." She tell him Sickrik (Siksrik) send for Twins, and they will soon be here.

Comic answer, "We are not after anything else but man."

She continue telling him to go home before Twins come every time she go out to give Arctics nicely cooked food, but Comic will not listen.

Sickrik (Siksrik) doesn't dare come out. They are too many for him.

At last Twins coming along. Daybreak soon, when they can see flying arrow. They know Arctics see them by now as they come out in open on a slough. No Arctics come out to meet them in open. They are afraid of Twins. They also know their heads would be big targets for well-trained Twins.

Arctics keep still in trenches. Twins can see the bows sticking out now. All at once lot of arrows swish over their heads. They slip their parka hoods on with two eagle feathers on each to see how many flint points will scrape them.

It's good daylight now. They can see the flying arrows. Dodging so many, it seems the air full of arrows. No chance to shoot back.

Comic get shot just above his heel. Most painful place. Cut his tendon cord, badly crippled. One of Arctic boys shout, "Comic got shot!" When girls hear that from inside they call out, "Comic, you better rush along home." Comic limping away in a hurry. Hitch up his dogs and leave for Arctic. Reach home safely.

Sickrik (Siksrik) shout inside igloo, asking Twins when to come out. Twins say "Not yet!" There are about 10 men around by the door waiting for him to come out.

The Twins seldom shoot. They are busy dodging so many arrows. They can't tell how many men they kill. Most of them fall into trenches. They guess about 15 by now. Sickrick (Siksrik) kill two or three that try to come inside through the top window.

Twins don't miss. They hit every shot. They very active and small, about five feet tall, and quick as a flash. If Arctics knew them, perhaps would never come to attack Sickrick (Siksrik) that winter.

Sickrik (Siksrik) getting restless. He know the Twins exhausted by now. They have been traveling all night on snowshoes, then fight all morning. Twins try to clear doorway but they getting short of arrows. They would have enough but some broken by Arctics' arrows.

One of the Twins get close to igloo. Shouted, "Come out now. We got no more arrows!"

Sickrik (Siksrik) come out like a flash and say, "Take a rest, boys. You didn't leave me enough Arctics to fight."

He kill all them that were after him. They defeated because they wouldn't surrender. Twins escape with few scratches and holes in their clothes. Sickrik's (Siksrik's) family and their neighbor evacuated Edseakvik (Iqsiugvik) because too many dead bodies in it. They move to other village. Sickrik (Siksrik) very tired of civil war with Arctics for many years now. He wish they would cease fighting but he couldn't do nothing. They just keep on sneaking attacks on peaceful Kobuks.

One of Sickrik's (Siksrik's) wives got killed while picking berries. She forgot to put on her Arctic dress and was mistaken for Kobuk girl. When Sickrik (Siksrik) went out to bury his wife, people said he must be very dangerous.

The Twins were chosen to guard the villages along the river. I never heard of them been killed, neither Sickrik (Siksrik). □

Trading on the Edge of Nowhere

Jimmy Huntington

Her name was Anna, and her father was a native trader. All year he traded among his own people. Then, with the first long days of March, he would make his way down the Hogatza to the head of the Dakili River, the divide between the Eskimo and the Indian lands, where he would meet Schilikuk, the Eskimo trader. This was permitted because each needed things that only the other had, and it was the only known peaceful contact between the two races.

As soon as Anna was old enough, she began to accompany her father on these trips, and so she learned the Eskimo language. They would load up the sled with their goods and set off toward the Dakili, a five-day trek for a good strong dog team, and make camp on the south slope of the boundary hills. This was as far as it was safe to go. On the other side, Schilikuk the Eskimo would be making his way south along the Selawik River, and the great trading ritual was about to begin. In all the years that Anna went with her father, it never changed.

First the old man would walk, alone and unarmed, to the top of the divide. He carried only a long pole. If he saw no signs of the Eskimo trader he would stick his pole straight up in the snow and return to camp. Every day that it was not storming he walked back up the long hill, looking to see if a second pole had been stuck in the snow alongside his. That was the sign that Schilikuk had arrived, and that trading would begin the next day.

Then my mother would help pull the sled up the hill — they could not use the dogs for the two teams would have fought to the death — and they would lay everything out on the snow. There were tanned hides, and wolverine fur for parka ruffs. There was a mound of soft red rock found only among the Koyukuk, which could be dipped in water and used to paint snowshoes a brilliant red. Meanwhile the Eskimo was laying out his stuff, too — salt from the Bering Sea and sealskins to make mukluks, a kind of boot worn in the spring and fall to keep out the wet.

Making believe they couldn't care less, the two traders would then inspect each other's goods. Say the Eskimo wanted a handful of red rock. He would pick it up, walk over to his own pile of things and toss a sealskin off to the side. That meant he was offering to pay that much for the rock. If my grandfather wasn't satisfied — and of course it was part of the ritual that he had to pretend to be insulted by the first offer — he would pull a second skin out of the Eskimo's pile. This was Schilikuk's signal to look hurt. He'd snatch back both skins and they'd have to start all over again.

All this took a long time and a lot of patience. There was always the danger of tempers really flaring, and day after day there was the hard work of hauling the sled back up to the top of the divide. Once Anna told her father: "You could trade everything on the first day if you didn't have to go through that business of acting so mad at each other."

My grandfather smiled: "Ah, but the Eskimo's sled is heavier than mine. Soon he will get tired of pulling it up the hill and then I will be able to buy his goods cheaply."

Years later Schilikuk the Eskimo would tell my mother that he had used exactly the same strategy. ☐

Editor's note: *Jimmy Huntington, descended from an Athabascan trader in the Galena area, carefully detailed barter between warring Indians and Eskimos in his delightful autobiography,* On the Edge of Nowhere, *Crown Publishers, Inc., New York (1966), and reprinted here by permission. Huntington's account was written (as told to Lawrence Elliott) from the recollections of his Athabascan grandmother.*

It should also be noted that in 1972 Huntington, with other Galena families, hosted an Eskimo baseball team from Kotzebue, marking the first official delegation of Eskimos to make a peaceful visit to the area. Old-timers were tense at their coming, but the games were much enjoyed; Eskimos winning one, Indians one, and the third ending in a diplomatic tie.

Among both teams were several Native leaders and when they negotiated border disputes for the land claims settlement a few weeks later, they did so far more amiably than was managed by Kotzebue and Eskimo cousins of the arctic slope region to the north.

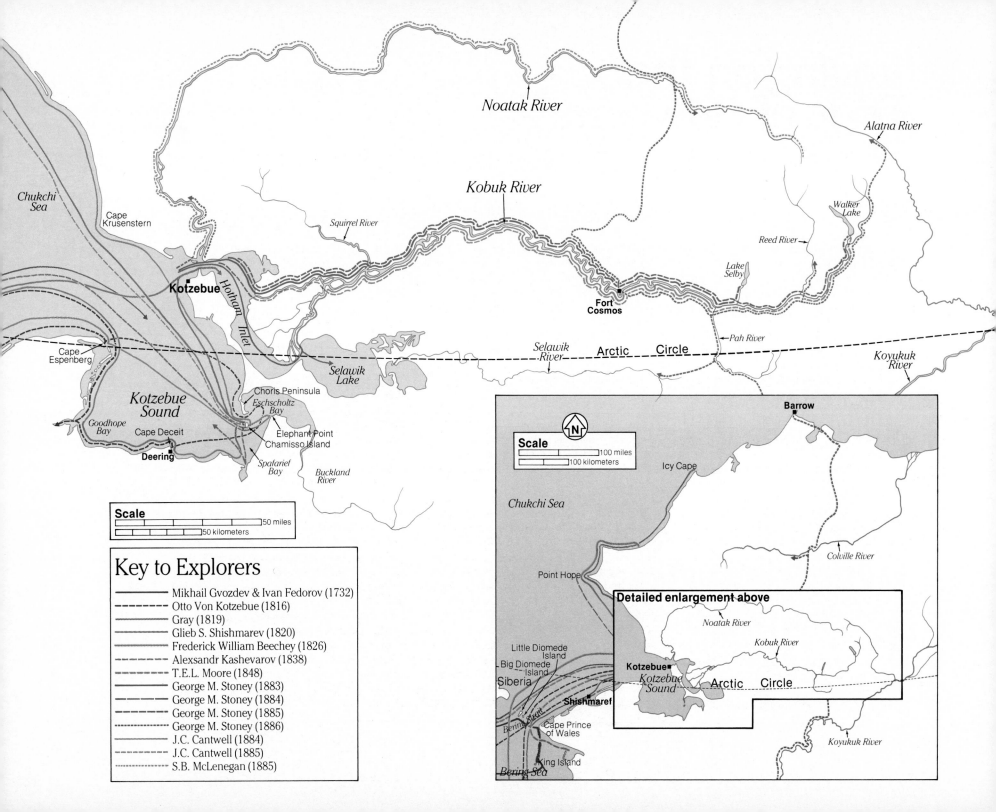

Noatak River

Alatna River

Chukchi Sea

Cape Krusenstern

Kobuk River

Walker Lake

Squirrel River

Reed River

Kotzebue

Hotham Inlet

Lake Selby

Cape Espenberg

Fort Cosmos

← *Pah River*

Selawik River

Arctic   Circle

Koyukuk River

Selawik Lake

Choris Peninsula
Eschscholtz Bay

Kotzebue Sound

Goodhope Bay

Cape Deceit

Elephant Point
Chamisso Island

Deering

Spafarief Bay

Buckland River

Scale
50 miles
50 kilometers

Key to Explorers

——————— Mikhail Gvozdev & Ivan Fedorov (1732)
– – – – – Otto Von Kotzebue (1816)
——————— Gray (1819)
——————— Glieb S. Shishmarev (1820)
——————— Frederick William Beechey (1826)
– – – – – Alexsandr Kashevarov (1838)
· · · · · · · · T.E.L. Moore (1848)
——————— George M. Stoney (1883)
– – – – – George M. Stoney (1884)
– ·· – ·· – George M. Stoney (1885)
· · · · · · · · George M. Stoney (1886)
——————— J.C. Cantwell (1884)
– – – – – J.C. Cantwell (1885)
· · · · · · · · S.B. McLenegan (1885)

Scale
100 miles
100 kilometers

Barrow

Icy Cape

Chukchi Sea

Colville River

Point Hope

Detailed enlargement above

Noatak River

Kobuk River

Little Diomede Island

Big Diomede Island

Kotzebue

Kotzebue Sound

Arctic   Circle

Siberia

Bering Strait

Shishmaref

Koyukuk River

Cape Prince of Wales

King Island

Bering Sea

EXPLORATION AND DEVELOPMENT

Because the Eskimos of northwest Alaska had traded for centuries with their Russian cousins, the Chukchi, their presence was known to the earliest explorers, yet white men came late to their region.

Well before Bering officially discovered Alaska, Dmitrii Pavlutskii, who had successfully warred against the Siberian Eskimos, sought to expand his conquests and ordered Mikhail Gvozdev, a surveyor, with seaman Ivan Fedorov to reconnoiter what was then known as the Large Country.

They sailed in the *Gabriel* in 1732, landed first at Big Diomede Island which had been discovered four years earlier by Bering, then went on to Little Diomede Island where they were refused permission to land. They also anchored about two and a half miles off mainland Alaska, apparently near Wales, and were attempting to approach the southern shore where they could see huts when they were forced back to sea by a rising wind. Sailing southward they came to King Island where again Alaskans would not allow landing. However here they encountered a man in a kayak who told them he was Eskimo and that Eskimos lived in the Large Country where there were forests, streams and animals.

There is reason to believe that Bering carried Gvozdev's and Fedorov's map on his voyage of discovery in 1741, but his landfalls were far south of their route and for some reason their account was long lost in history.

John Cochrane, an Englishman visiting Kamchatka, met two Alaska Eskimos at the Anyui trade fair in Siberia in 1821, and wrote that the Russians had known about Kotzebue Sound for "more than 100 years." Yet Cook missed Kotzebue Sound completely in his trip to the Arctic in 1776, and no Eskimos living in this area and northward have folk tales about the white man coming from Siberia during this period.

German Estonian Russian naval officer Otto Von Kotzebue found the Eskimos less than awe-struck, however, by his official discovery of Kotzebue in 1816. On rounding Cape Espenberg in the *Rurik* he was met by five skin boats containing 50 armed men ready to trade on their own terms.

Their first request was for tobacco, for which they apparently had a long-standing addiction, and the explorer noted trading beads and three types of iron knives among them.

The introduction of scissors did prove a novelty to the Eskimos, and they fell flat on the bottom of their boats when the explorer became annoyed with them and fired his cannon, although the reaction seems to have

While commanding the Rurik *in 1816 for the Russian Navy, Otto von Kotzebue officially discovered Kotzebue and gave the sound his name.*
Courtesy of Rotislav von Kotzebue

been one of prudence rather than surprise. On recovery the Eskimos invited Kotzebue and his men to come to the beach, "promising us women."

According to an account in *The Eskimos of Bering Strait 1650-1898* (1975), Kotzebue justified his gunfire by the "ambiguous attitude of the Kotzebue men ... they took willingly the objects we offered them, but wished to give nothing in return," but his hostility may also have been due to jangled nerves. At Shishmaref, his previous stop, well-armed Eskimos had threatened to seize his ship — "with piercing crys and hideous grimaces, they threatened us with their lances," and shortly after his Espenberg arrival, some 40 additional skin boats, each with a dozen to 20 men, paddled up to threaten him.

The expedition soon sailed east in pursuit of its assignment to find a northwest passage to the Atlantic, but a month later Kotzebue concluded there was no such route, and anchored 10 miles northeast of Deering. Here, again, he reported the Eskimos treated him with contempt. He sailed to a headland south of Cape Espenberg, naming it Cape Deceit because it wrongly appeared to be the entrance to a bay and because of treachery encountered there at the hands of locals.

He also named neighboring Goodhope Bay, "as I might really hope to make a very remarkable discovery here," and gave the larger sound his own name "in compliance with the general wish of my companions. . . . Inconsiderable as the discovery of this sound may be, it is an acquisition to geography and may serve the world as a proof of my zeal; for, in truth, even Cook has treated this coast rather negligently."

The following year the explorer attempted a return visit, but ice blocked his way through Bering Strait as late as July 10, and he gave up. His Russian sponsors were convinced his expedition was a failure, but it did put Kotzebue firmly on the map.

In 1819 an American trading captain named Gray (not Captain Robert Gray), sailing the *Sylph* for John Jacob Astor, sounded the area to check Kotzebue's chart for the governor of Kamchatka, and later returned with the *Forester* and the *Pedler*, also of Astor's trading fleet. Some believe they arrived on the scene even earlier, and hold them responsible for first selling the Eskimos guns, contraband goods by Russian law.

The Russian government bitterly contested America's right to trade in their waters, and quickly moved to increase their own knowledge of the regions. In 1820 G.S. Shishmarev, von Kotzebue's former lieutenant now in command of the *Good Intent*, surveyed the coast between Cape Krusenstern and Icy Cape with M.H. Vasiliev in command of the *Discovery*. Although the place was thought to be uninhabited, Shismarev discovered a settlement of 101 conical skin tents near Elephant Point and encountered about 150 occupants armed from head to foot with bows, arrows, spears, and "even long rifles."

Despite the hostile introduction, Eskimos enticed the Russians ashore to trade, and entertained them with song and dance. Shishmarev reciprocated by giving their chief a medal and inviting him to dine, but afterward the Natives became obstreperous because the Russians would not sell them powder and shot.

The crew took quick leave, only to be forced back to shore by rough weather. There followed an uneasy night during which Russians claimed the Eskimos pilfered their supplies, and when they decamped the Natives pursued them, firing arrows and shot. Finally Shishmarev ordered a cannon ball fired at the largest of the bidars, wounding one man and ending the attack.

The climate of hostility prevailed when Captain F.W. Beechey in command of HMS *Blossom* arrived in Kotzebue Sound in the spring of 1826 to rendezvous with Captain

William Parry who was attempting the northwest passage from the Atlantic with Sir John Franklin.

Beechey entered Kotzebue Sound in late July dispatching a barge to explore an inlet he named Hotham, and stopping to bury a cache of flour for Franklin at Chamisso Island before sailing north. On return Beechey discovered the ground strewn with iron hoops from his flour barrels, and was met by Eskimos who "put their fingers to their tongues and spit into the sea in disgust," thus betraying their knowledge of the cache.

Although locals later proved more hospitable, Beechey reported they would not permit writing in notebooks; refusing to talk when the notebooks were open. And when Beechey attempted to sketch a local girl, her father called for a clean piece of board and promptly sketched Beechey, aping his manner.

Beechey and party explored the sound between Spafarief Bay and Cape Espenberg discovering Pleistocene mammoth remains by the Buckland River.

After wintering in San Francisco, Beechey returned, and continued to explore farther north. Meanwhile, the ship's barge wrecked off Choris Peninsula in a sudden gale with the loss of three lives.

Beechey's lieutenant, Edward Belcher, "an able if disagreeable officer" according to one biographer, reported Eskimos on shore had refused to come to the rescue of the foundering barge and later robbed the wreckage.

By other accounts, Belcher had been hauling wood to build an observation tower when the storm came up, and when he tried to rescue his barge-bound men, his shore boat became badly damaged.

Eskimos nearby in a skin boat apparently saw the futility of trying to launch a boat in the gale, however Belcher forced them at pistol point to help. The Natives did give the shipwrecked men some fish but when Belcher tried to buy some fur trousers, he discovered the price had risen drastically.

By the time the *Blossom* arrived, Eskimos outnumbered the whites three to one and scavenging increased. When sailors tried to take wreckage from local salvage crews, Eskimos drew their knives but Beechey kept control at gunpoint, carrying off a hostage.

The explorers did not want to alienate the Eskimos with whom the missing Franklin party might one day have to deal, and soon released the man unharmed, but hostilities broke out again. Noting Natives were donning protective eider duck garments and uncovering bows and arrows, Beechey sent a company of marines ashore to protect men already there to gather water, and apparently provoked attack. Three marines were wounded in the melee and one Native shot; the first recorded killing of an Eskimo by a European in North America.

Although this incident blackened the record, the Beechey expedition proved remarkable in the quantity and quality of information it gathered. It was Beechey who first recognized the Natives as Eskimos, and who correctly delineated Norton Sound as the dialectical border dividing Inupiat speakers from Yup'ik. He compiled an Eskimo

LEFT — *Frederick W. Beechey (1796-1856) commanded the HMS* Blossom *on expeditions to Kotzebue Sound.*

Reprinted from *To The Pacific and Arctic With Beechey, The Journal of Lieutenant George Peard of HMS 'Blossom' 1825-1828;* ed. Barry M. Gough, Cambridge University Press, courtesy of the Historical Photograph Collection, Archives, University of Alaska, Fairbanks

BELOW — *Natives paddling baidars met Frederick W. Beechey and the* Blossom*'s crew as they entered Kotzebue Sound in 1826.*
Reprinted from *Narrative of a Voyage to the Pacific and Beering's Strait*

An artist on one of George Stoney's expeditions into the Kotzebue Basin sketched this scene of a summer fishing village along the Noatak River. U.S. Naval Institute Proceedings

vocabulary for the area, and through his observations many aspects of the early culture were preserved.

"During our stay we purchased almost everything there was in the village disposable, more for the sake of their gratification than our own," observed crewman James Wolfe whose detailed diary survives to this day.

Beechey's report may also have prompted convergence of whaling ships on this area. The *Plover* under the command of T.E.L. Moore arrived at Chamisso in 1848, "in consequence of the success of one of their vessel's last season" which returned home with 4,000 barrels of whale oil representing six weeks of whaling after reading Beechey's description of multitudes of whales in the Arctic.

Alexsandr Kashevarov, a Kodiak-born Native fathered by a Russian and educated in Europe, explored the sound by skin boat in 1838 but added little to general knowledge of the area. The next reconnaissance fell to searchers for the missing Franklin expedition. Although the British explorer had last been seen in Baffin Bay, his government thought he might have succeeded in sailing through to the Chukchi, and between 1848 and 1854 the British Navy dispatched eight ships and a yacht in an attempt to find him. Kotzebue Sound was the base of operation for some of these ships, and this time relations between local Eskimos and outsiders were amicable.

The whaling fleets and traders that came north in ever increasing numbers during this period headquartered at Point Hope or further north. Kotzebue people had less contact with them than those of most coastal villages, but the outsiders' introduction of store-bought goods; utensils, stoves, clothing, and new foods brought rapid changes in the Eskimo life style. Many Kotzebue area families hunted seasonally at Point Hope, and traders often ventured south in search of furs.

It was during this period that liquor was introduced, but while it did take a toll among residents of the sound, they were less adversely affected than those in direct contact with foreign fleets. The region's interior had yet to be penetrated, and white contact was still a rarity for large numbers of inlanders. Rumors of great wealth in this region persisted but were countered by the Eskimos' warlike reputation.

"Owing to the hostile character of the natives and for other reasons I never penetrated this region," explained naturalist E.W. Nelson in a letter to a fellow scientist in the early 1800s, "but met and interrogated numerous intelligent Indians who live in the district and from whom I bought various jade objects. . . ."

It was John Simpson, surgeon of the *Plover,* who first recorded the existence of the Kobuk River. In 1849-1850 he visited Hotham Inlet, measured the width of the Kobuk's main channel, tracked its course into the "pines," and learned of several villages upstream. But it was not until 1883 that any white man made real headway in this area.

First to arrive was Lieutenant George M. Stoney who, with one other white man and two Eskimos, explored the Kobuk as far as Squirrel River, and returned the following season under U.S. Navy sponsorship with a steam cutter, three petty officers and eight men. Some 275 miles upriver the party abandoned its power launch and proceeded in a skin boat, finally reaching a tributary flowing from Lake Selby.

En route they encountered a competitor, Lieutenant J.C. Cantwell of the Revenue Cutter Service who had beaten them upriver by a few days, made it nearly to the mouth of the Pah, and been forced to turn back for want of supplies.

Next year the two expeditions again competed. Cantwell arrived first, making it to the Selby tributary in a steamer, then going on in a skin boat to discover Walker Lake. Stoney's party wintered over, however, establishing Fort Cosmos at Cosmos Creek; exploring the Noatak, Selawik, Alatna, Colville, and Reed rivers and even traveling overland to Barrow.

News of these discoveries was delayed. Cantwell did not publish an account of his first venture until 1887, while that of his second expedition appeared 13 years after the fact. Stoney's report was not made public until 1902, a year after the first U.S. Geological Survey expedition had been sent to the area.

The earliest recorded exploration on the Noatak was made in 1885 by S.B. McLenegan of the Revenue Steamer *Corwin.* With a seaman named Nelson, he traveled upriver to the headwaters in a 27-foot skin boat. The Noatak Canyon was not detailed until C.E. Griffin came through for the U.S. Geological Survey in 1911.

The area was also slow to open to white settlement. While the Evangical Mission Union of Sweden established a post at neighboring Unalakleet in 1886, the Catholics moved into the Yukon area in 1888, and the Episcopals into Point Hope; Kotzebue saw no whites except for an occasional trader or prospector.

During this period Uyagaq, a Selawik Eskimo who had married at Unalakleet, brought home word of Christianity. The crusader, whose English name was Rock, was fluently bilingual and well-traveled. Rock had been sold on the advantages of religion, education, and medical care various missionaries were providing, and in vain he pleaded with church backers to expand into Kotzebue Sound.

In 1896 the Eskimos of Kotzebue held council, and decided to act on their own, dispatching two local men 250 miles south by skin boat to Cape Prince of Wales where they took a sail boat to southeastern Alaska, some 2,000 miles distant, in search of a missionary.

The call was answered by the Friends Church. In July 1897 Robert Samms, 32: Carrie, his 19-year-old bride; and Anna Hunnicutt, a lively spinster; arrived in Kotzebue with Uyagaq as their interpreter, and immediately started work on a mission.

The Kotzebue Women's Club meets around the turn of the century. With the arrival of Friends missionaries in 1897, the change from a culture influenced by shamans to one influenced by Christianity and 20th century organizations and activities began.

Courtesy of Mrs. Fletcher Gregg

Their first church meeting, held outdoors in a windscreen of umiaks, was attended by some 500 Eskimos and, although some later got drunk (on brew of fermented molasses and flour introduced by the whalers) and threatened the new arrivals, the Friends were ultimately allowed to live, teach, and doctor in peace.

By most accounts, the Samms and Miss Hunnicutt were remarkable people. They spent most of their lives in the Arctic and like many who followed, they were dedicated, living with little or no luxuries in a fashion closely akin to the Eskimos they had come to proselytize.

The Samms immediately began learning Inupiat, and adopted Eskimo food, and clothing. The women had brought their skates, introducing the sport, with reading and writing of English, and math.

Their coming coincided with a period of want among the Inupiat. Game was scarce and the missionaries provided meals for their school children and sometimes local families. With their teaching, their practice of medicine, and by personal example, the missionaries broke many cruel and seemingly senseless Native taboos and at the same time broke the power of the shamans. But in their zeal, the Christians broadly condemned the good with the bad.

Initially the Samms had been entertained by Native dancing and danced themselves until they witnessed an unusually primitive Wolf Dance which frightened them into banning all further performances. The use of Inupiat was soon forbidden in the school system and children were disciplined and sometimes beaten for infractions.

Mass marriages were performed to legitimize long standing Eskimo unions and, on at least two occasions, local residents were issued burlap bags, and sent to collect the bones of friends, relatives and ancient ancestors that had been left in the open

ABOVE — *Tom Berryman, one of the region's earliest traders, stands in front of the store in Kotzebue, now the site of Walker's Liquors. Berryman married a local woman and spent the rest of his life in the Arctic.*
Nichols Collection, Courtesy of Mark Ocker

RIGHT — *Visiting a fish camp at Deering in 1912, Boris Magids, a wealthy trader, watches Eskimos clean fish. Magids preferred a military-style uniform although apparently he did not serve in the military. A Russian, Magids immigrated to New York and came to Alaska to join his brother. During his days as a trader, he made a yearly buying trip to Seattle where dealers eagerly sought him out to get a piece of his large orders for goods.*
Courtesy of R.A. Dailey Collection, Alaska Historical Library

The Traders

The small group of whites in the Kotzebue area during the early 1900s constituted an interesting mix from numerous nations. Among the earliest were whalers who jumped ship and turned to prospecting, trading, and living off the land. Others, including a colony of Japanese, drifted in from the Klondike and Nome gold stampedes. And more than a few came north to avoid military service during World War I. Shungnak is sometimes referred to in old records as a "haven for draft dodgers," and one sourdough recalls the brothers of a prominent Kotzebue family arrived from the Lower 48 in their early 20s outfitted in knee pants as part of their cover to avoid the induction board.

While missionaries and government teachers were among the best educated of the new arrivals, they were certainly not the most cosmopolitan.

First in this field, perhaps, was beautiful Margaret "Gretchen" Echardt who had sung in the Vienna opera, but had been forced on hard times at the end of World War I. She once confided that she had come to America (Chicago) as a mail order bride, but she certainly

was very much her own woman as the wife of Hugo Echardt, a trader who arrived in Kotzebue just after the turn of the century.

Friends recall that when the couple ran a fox farm up the Noatak, she worked like a farm hand during the day, but boggled visitors in the evening by dressing for dinner and serving the meal in style, complete with candlelight. They also recall the thrill of hearing her clear voice for miles across the tundra when she decided to stage a concert for her own entertainment.

She was best known, though, for her quick wit. When the bottom fell out of the long-haired fur market in the mid-1930s, the Echardts moved back to Kotzebue, and Gretchen took on the job of running the business of a trader who was known for his dishonest dealings. By all accounts she made him a good profit, and at the end of the season he praised her highly but told her, alas, he had no money on hand to pay her.

"That's all right," she answered lightly. "I took 10% off the top every day, anyway."

Among the most successful of early businessmen were Sam and Boris Magids who immigrated to the east coast from Russia and were apparently sent to Alaska with Jewish backing. Their father was a banker in the Russian middle class, but those who have seen their correspondence say they considered themselves aristocrats.

"Boris Magids dominated trade," recalls John Cross, a pilot who flew for him when he was based out of Deering. "He'd go outside in the spring for a week or two and wholesalers would come to his hotel . . . he didn't have to go to them. He'd order thousands of cases of milk . . . more than came into Nome at that time.

"He was a banker at heart. His word was good for any amount of money unless the stakes were really high. It shocked me when he jumped a contract with the Seattle Fur Exchange."

Other traders in the area were Louis Rotman whom Magids initially backed in the Selawik area but who went on to become a serious competitor; Tom Berryman who came to Kotzebue as a very young man, expanded his enterprise to Kivalina, and stayed a lifetime; Harry Brown of Kobuk who, Cross recalls, had previously served as a bouncer in a Nome bar; Walter Blankenship of Kiana and Warren and Archie Ferguson who started at Shungnak and traded

throughout the region. Warren drowned when a truck he was driving plunged through black ice on the lagoon behind Kotzebue, and Archie raised his three youngsters; Frank, now a powerful legislator and head of the Alaska Federation of Natives; Raymond, who runs NANA's reindeer operation; and Don, a pilot. Archie expanded their business after Magids' death to the point that Fergusons dominated trade.

Life during this early period was hard, even for those of the relatively well-heeled white community. Mail from home came spasmodically at best in summer, and isolation was complete after freezeup. Yet photos of the era show the pioneers dressed fashionably, dining at well-appointed tables in homes of reasonable elegance.

The jail at Kiana boasted a piano. Well-outfitted young people are shown playing tennis on the beach in front of the Quaker mission about 1914. Deering had a dance band. And many, who had simply come to the area to get rich quick and go home, lingered for a lifetime. Many of their last names are still listed in local phone books today, and their heirs and descendants make up the majority of today's Eskimo leadership. □

Warren Ferguson (sitting on the railing with one foot on the snow and one foot on a dog sled) and his brother Archie were leaders in bringing commercial enterprises to the Kotzebue Sound region. Here Warren has gathered with his friends at Shungnak in the early 1930s. He died when his truck went through the ice at Kotzebue Sound.
Courtesy of Lona Wood Collection

71

because of taboos against touching the dead. These remains were interred in a mass grave with formal Christian ceremony beside the Friends Church, and thereafter it was made clear Inupiat were to be properly buried.

A clean break with the past, acculturation, was the goal not only of the missionaries and government teachers who followed, but also of some Native people. These Natives were convinced that their children should get into the white system with its checks and balances against the vagaries of nature which often plagued subsistence hunters and fishermen, its store-bought conveniences, and its ministry of love.

New values were reinforced by a flood of miners who moved into the interior, at least 800 on the Kobuk alone the winter of 1898-1899 and another thousand or so in the years to follow. With the miners came resident traders and fur buyers who established a source of store-bought goods, and the means to acquire them. There were jobs for a limited number in the mining camps, and the government promoted the reindeer industry as another alternative to subsistence living.

A small number of Eskimos made the transition with seeming ease. Joe Sakanik, a Kivalina man crippled from youth by a skating accident, gleened enough education from two years of schooling to serve as a government teacher, from 1918 to 1922, and went on to open a store, and become an accountant.

Eskimo View of the Gold Rush

Editor's note: *The National Bilingual Materials Development Center, Anchorage, graciously supplied this translation of oral communications presented at the Elders Conference, 1977.*

Charlie Sheldon recalled the Kobuk gold rush from stories his mother told him, and in 1977 shortly before his death, he chose that subject to speak on at an Elders Conference.

"It is said that the white people came in 1898 and they say it was then there were many *mainnats* (miners)," Sheldon began. "They heard about gold in Alaska and came here from Nome, eager to find gold. All lusting and dying for gold.

"In that year my parents, Iyagun and Nataagnaq, were young and had twin sons. We lived up the Kobuk River. We were *Itqiliagruk* (Eskimo word for part-Indian) and (my people) lived from above the Paa (Pah) all the way above the Aqusriugvik or even up to the Reed River.

"One of the miners who went upriver was named Sam Pepper. Mother called him commissioner. My father was hired to work and Bob Snyder and Jack Little or Jack Pecker were also working for Sam Pepper.

"When winter came the white people settled on an island. Two brothers took care of people who lived in the jail. The first fireplace that was built on the Kobuk River was in that big house. My mother would encourage me to go see this fireplace which the Inupiat had built. . . . Recently my wife and I went to look for it and did find it. There is a tree that grows in the middle of it and (the tree) is naturally bent, perfect for a sled.

"In 1898, from Ugii to Kigutiligauraq, it was filled with white people. There were also Japanese. They were not so big men who lived in cavelike structures, digging their way in the ground and putting on a door. They lived away from the white people. The *Pusrkhiurat* (Portuguese) also lived by themselves and also the Russians.

"Sam Pepper and his wife were very young when they came to our area. Sam Pepper built a house, somewhere maybe near Beaver Creek on a large hill, and my parents lived in that house.

"1899: this was the year when the trouble began with the white people. It was said that Sam Pepper controlled the killing along the Kobuk River and thus did not have any records of killings at that time. However, there were murders along the Noatak and the Selawik rivers whenever the Natives could not understand the white people or vice versa. Along the Kobuk, whenever a Native got in a disagreement with a white, he would run away from that area.

"1899 was the year when the white people suffered. Sam Pepper told them to go home. When they had gone down to the mouth of the river they made small dories and started to cross the large lakes. Although the Eskimos told them not to try to cross the river, they did not listen and ended up drowning when it became windy.

"There were so many drifted like that, it is said that even the lesser scaup ducks were eating them when they rotted. Gordon Mitchell recalled that once when they were traveling down the Noatak River he noticed something which was covered with white

Samuel Anaruk, a Buckland man who attended Carlisle Indian School and roomed with Jim Thorpe, returned to Alaska to teach 38 years for the Bureau of Indian Affairs. His Eskimo wife and his daughter, now Sophie Lieb, also taught for the government. Tony Joule, a well-known whaler and athlete from Point Hope, attended Mt. Herman School in Massachusetts to become fully accredited and taught for the BIA in his home region for 44 years.

Other Eskimos trained as ministers. By the end of 1928 Eskimo pastors included Lester and Lulu Young of Selawik, Frank and Kitty Wells of Deering-Noorvik, John and Mary Wright of Kotzebue, Harry and Flora Cleveland of Selawik, John and Lillie Savok of south Kotzebue Sound, Whittier and Edna Williams of the coast, and Ruth Egaq of Buckland as field evangelists.

A small number of Eskimo reindeer herders eventually became affluent. Several became airplane pilots, and a Candle man gained the distinction of becoming the first Eskimo movie star.

Ray Wise, later known in Hollywood as Mala or Agnaachiaq, ran away from the Friends School in Kotzebue at the age of 12, picking up work as a cook or mate on Arctic expeditions including that of Knud Rasmussen, then finding work as a cameraman at Universal studios. Chosen to play the lead in Ewing Scott's *Igloo*, he proved an actor of con-

canvas. He asked his father what it was and his father said it was some dead white men. Some of their boots were sticking out from underneath the canvas. It must have been there were so many that were dying that the others did not even have the time to bury them.

"There were also many who froze to death because they tried to walk such distances in the bitter cold.

"Sam Pepper had a steamboat. He told my parents that if they followed him to Nome he would give them all his things, but they did not go because of their twins. Later Aqpiksraq (a brother) went to school at Chemawa, Oregon, and was in Seattle. He looked up the Peppers and they welcomed him, asking him if he was one of the twins, but no, he was one of the younger sons. Still, they welcomed him and asked about everyone. They had opened a candy store."

One of the few Eskimos to make a profit from the rush was "Yukon" Charlie Coffin, according to Sheldon's recollections.

"He was a big miner and had Inupiat and white people working for him numbering more than 30. However, Qupatquq (Coffin's Eskimo name) did not act as if he was a big shot. He would give his workers gold dust and then, with the rest, he would send for food that would last him two years. This Eskimo man, although he had not had formal education, when his brain is good and his actions are good, wise, and smart, he can be like an educated man.

"However as Qupatquq lived, things got bad for him. His wife left him and he worried about it so much that he began to play cards and soon he had only four dogs and carried only mittens. However later he became a Christian and died a happy man."

Another successful Eskimo prospector was Sivaaya, according to Paul Green whose father was traveling with Sivaaya at the time of the find.

"They had been walking by Auliniq (up the Noatak River) and separated there. After being separated a while, they met again and went to Mayuumaruq and caught a Dall sheep there. The next day they noticed something nearby and it looked as though it was a thermal area where the snow melts continuously. Sivaaya went there and came back with something in the front of his parka. He gave my father one of them and told him that these little things were heavy. He put the rest in his pack. . . . He said if anyone wanted to pack much of that stuff, there was enough for anyone to pack all they wanted."

The next year when Green's father went to earn a bit of money working on the docks, he was surprised to discover Sivaaya had purchased two boatloads of supplies with the little rocks he had found at Mayuumaruq and Auliniq.

"The following summer there were many white people . . . tents all over," Green recounts. "They all spoke of Sivaaya but after what happened Sivaaya died.

"Many (of the prospectors) tried to go toward the Noatak River with small boats and many of them drowned. They asked everyone where Sivaaya found the money. My father never told them. . . ."

Green's father died shortly thereafter leaving a map with his friend, Putumii, pledging him to include Green and his sister when he staked his claims. But Putumii, who was Green's cousin, said he lost the map and although he staked many claims (none for Green and his sister), Putumii does not seem to have gotten famously rich. So the legend of Sivaaya's gold lingers on to tempt yet another generation of prospectors. The last grandchild of Sivaaya died in 1979, but Eskimo legend predicts something from the ground of value to a newcomer will yet be found. ☐

Dreams of wealth and a comfortable life brought miners to the Cosmos Hills in the Kobuk valley. These miners gathered at old Shungnak in 1909. Courtesy of Esther Norton

male to become a doctor, and returned to Anchorage.

Early on, Kotzebue area schools had been segregated with Natives attending one large facility, and white children attending a smaller one with youngsters of mixed blood. In 1938 the system was integrated, and class consciousness began a slow wane. For the majority, transition was a tough assignment. Whites controlled the government, schools, reindeer industry, transportation, and trade.

Nor, initially, was there a choice of religion or even escape from it, for Friends missionaries ran not only the churches but the schools, and filled numerous important government positions.

The extent of their influence became evident in 1928 when George Morelander replaced Quaker missionary-teacher Sylvester Chance as superintendent of the Northwest District of the Bureau of Education, and charged Eskimos were being misled by mission teachings to the detriment of their progress.

Adding to the controversy was a division among fundamentalist Quakers, then in control, and those like Robert and Carrie Samms who emphasized the disciplined life but were less hard-nosed regarding observance of the Sabbath and tithing.

During this period the Catholic Church moved into the area, scandalizing Quaker elders with its "moral laxity" which included sponsoring free dinners, card playing, dancing, and movies in an attempt to establish a Kotzebue church.

Fervently and publicly, distraught Friends prayed that the interlopers be deterred until two visiting priests were killed in a plane crash that also took the life of pioneering bush pilot Ralph Wien in 1930. The tragedy helped dampen the battle, and today 11 different faiths are established in Kotzebue, although the Friends still have by far the largest membership.

siderable depth, and later dazzled moviegoers in Metro-Goldwyn-Mayer's classic, *Eskimo.*

Ultimately Wise settled in Hollywood, introduced the fad of kayaking to swimming pool owners, became a squash champion of the Beverly Hills Athletic Club, and spoke eloquently against inequities suffered by his minority.

At his death his will stipulated that his son, Ted, then seven, remain in California where he could get a better education than was available to Natives in Alaska. The wisdom of this decision was borne out in 1976 when young Mala became the first Alaska Native

RIGHT — *Tony Joule with his arm on his wife Anne poses with Lucy Mills (right) and an unidentified woman. Joule, a whaler and athlete, became the first fully accredited Eskimo teacher hired by the Bureau of Indian Affairs and served the area for 44 years.*
Courtesy of Reggie Joule

BELOW — *Worshippers leave the church at Noorvik shortly after the town's founding in 1915. Noorvik was the only village that had a clock. A missionary installed the timepiece to teach Eskimos to become more punctual, but the lesson was lost when a Selawik man hit the clock with a stick, forever putting the clock out of commission.*
Courtesy of R.A. Dailey Collection, Alaska Historical Library

BELOW — *According to her own account, Mrs. Louise Nichols of the Kotzebue Friends Mission gives a "lesson in cleanliness" to her young charges in 1914.*
Nichols Collection, Courtesy of Mark Ocker

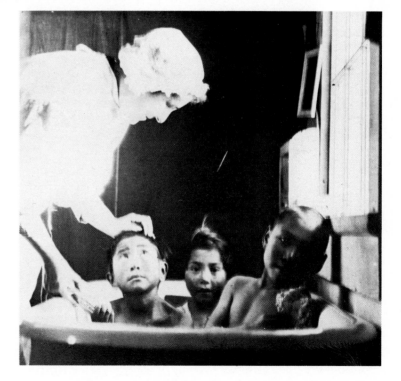

Throughout this period health standards continued to improve. A government hospital was established at Kotzebue, and Indian Health Service doctors and nurses routinely began to travel the territory.

Delbert Replogle, son of a Noorvik missionary family, built the first radio set in the region. When word came of the flu epidemic of 1918, Replogle dispatched progress reports via dog team, enabling local villages to quarantine potential carriers, and sparing the area sickness that wiped out five-sevenths of the population of neighboring Wales and other Inupiat settlements along the coast. By contrast the population of Kotzebue Sound began to expand.

It was service in World War II, however, that helped reestablish the Inupiat. Short of manpower, the U.S. government left the Arctic unprotected, and Major Marvin "Muktuk" Marston enlisted Eskimos to fill the gap, forming the Territorial National Guard under the Alaska Command.

The men of this region served well, bringing them statewide and national attention and their backer, Marston, became an outspoken champion of the Eskimo way, doing much to enhance the Natives' opinion of their own worth.

Partly through Marston's efforts, at war's end the Alaska Territorial Legislature passed the first anti-discrimination law in the nation, providing equal treatment for Natives and whites in business establishments and public

UPPER LEFT — *The Deering Band, complete with an imaginative variety of broom and can instruments, performs for the July 4th celebration in Deering in 1908.*
Courtesy of R.A. Dailey Collection, Alaska Historical Library

LEFT — *These Eskimos, photographed by missionary-teachers in 1914 in Kotzebue, make use of both traditional and modern items in their daily living.*
Nichols Collection, Courtesy of Mark Ocker

Dr. Herbert N.T. Nichols took this photo of Kotzebue's school children gathered outdoors while he and his wife were living in Kotzebue from 1913 to 1916.

Nichols Collection, Courtesy of Mark Ocker

RIGHT — *Crippled by a skating accident in his youth, Joe Sakanik taught at the government school at Kivalina from 1918 to 1922 even though he only had two years of formal schooling. Joe received so little schooling because he could only attend when someone could carry him. After his stint at teaching, Joe successfully operated a store and worked as an accountant.* Courtesy of Mrs. Edith Kennedy

ABOVE — *Races in traditional skin boats were serious but fun business. These paddlers push their boats through Kotzebue Sound near Sealing Point in 1914.*
Nichols Collection, Courtesy of Mark Ocker

RIGHT — *At a cabin banked with sod just in back of the Kotzebue schoolhouse, missionary Nichols captured the smiling images of Joseph Jessup, Clara Perish, and Jerry Cooper about 1914.* Nichols Collection, Courtesy of Mark Ocker

places, but the battle was far from won. Eskimos still had no real representation in government, no say on how their children were educated and no title to the land on which they had lived for centuries.

In 1951 the Bureau of Land Management auctioned off most of downtown Kotzebue, almost entirely to whites. Few Natives understood the auction process and those who did, did not have ready cash for purchases. But the economic climate was changing. Also in 1951, John Bullock and Louis Rotman joined forces to form B&R Tug and Barge company. Until this time there had been no way to cash a check in Kotzebue and B&R's main competitor, like other traders in the area, issued his own money (bingles), or paid off workmen with store credit. Now Bullock and Rotman offered a large cash payroll, freeing recipients from the barter system that had long indebted them to certain traders. The opening of a bank in Kotzebue in 1960 further encouraged the use of cash.

Although short-lived, local attempts to produce jade and asbestos proved lucrative for a few. Building of a small Air Force site at

Kotzebue stimulated jobs, and the aborted development of Bornite Copper Mine by Kennecott caused a flurry of activity.

In addition, Kotzebue Eskimos played a key roll in pioneering tourism in the Arctic. In 1954 Wien pilot Frank Whaley enlisted Chester Seveck as a tour guide, and recruited other Eskimos to dance, and help run a modest airline hotel to accommodate visitors.

Seveck, who "gave up reindeer herding for herding tourists," and worked at the job until his death in 1981, recalled the early days with amusement. At one point the company's

ABOVE — *Even though life was hard, people usually had time for games including this women's snowshoe race held at Shungnak in the 1920s or 1930s. The six contestants closest to the camera are: (from left) Hannah Jackson, Susie Gray, Hadley Ferguson, Dora Johnson, unidentified, and Annie Skin.*
Courtesy of Lona Wood Collection

LEFT — *After many years as a reindeer herder, Chester Seveck joined the ranks of tour guides and helped organize a tourism program for Kotzebue. Here he shows tourists a whale bone.* Frank Whaley

big-wheeled, open-air transport vehicle got mired in the mud on the airstrip, and all the tourists had to get out and push.

That first year he escorted 1,454 visitors, and the neat figures in his meticulously kept diary show a slow but steady increase; 1,661 by 1964, almost 9,000 annually a decade later, and more than 10,000 in 1980.

In 1966 Willie Hensley was elected to the Alaska Legislature and with Eskimo and Indian leaders from other areas he helped form a voting block which for the first time brought real legislative power to bush residents.

Hensley, part Native, part white, had been raised nomadic by his Eskimo grandparents, had entered late into the Kotzebue school system, but showed so much promise that a Baptist family that befriended him sent him outside the state for better schooling. Later, at the University of Alaska, Hensley chose to examine the murky legal question of Native land ownership, and during his second legislative session got through a bill saying the state would give Natives a royalty on minerals found on state land if the federal government recognized Alaska Native lands claims.

During this period Hensley also helped organize the Northwest Alaska Native Association (NANA) with local leaders like Robert Newland and John Schaeffer, and a statewide coalition of Natives, the Alaska Federation of Natives, of which he ultimately served as president.

Laura Bergt, daughter of a Kotzebue bush pilot and one of the few Native women active in the claims fight, helped the cause along by renewing an old acquaintanceship with then vice president Spiro Agnew in 1971. Later that year Congress awarded 40 million acres of land and nearly a billion dollars to claimants.

Locally, too, Eskimo pride came to the fore when Natives overcame stout opposition of the Friends Church and many of their own brethren to allow continuation of an Inupiat dance class in the Kotzebue School System.

"A lot of kids are getting up and coming to school at 8 A.M. — before classes officially start — to take Eskimo dancing," defended Nellie Ward, then president of the student body. "Some of them like it so much they're even getting interested in the Eskimo language. It's beautiful."

The next year the state legislature passed a law requiring that when 15 students or more in any school spoke a language other than English, bilingual education must be added to the curriculum. Youngsters who had been punished for speaking Inupiat soon found themselves enrolled in formal Inupiat language classes.

Under the Native claims settlement the state was divided into 12 regions, and Natives of each were directed to form a profit making

Native leader Willie Hensley of Kotzebue presented the keynote address at the 1980 annual convention of the Alaska Federation of Natives. Lael Morgan, staff, reprinted from *ALASKA*®magazine

corporation which was endowed with money and land. Northwest Alaska Natives incorporated NANA for this purpose, and were awarded $42 million and 2 million acres of land.

NANA ranks as one of the most successful regional corporations in the state, providing a considerable increase in local jobs as well as dividends to stockholders. In 1980 NANA became the first Alaska firm to build an oil rig (in joint venture with two Arctic Slope Region village corporations and VECO, Inc. of Anchorage) and has done well on numerous other ventures.

Maneuluk was also incorporated by Eskimo stockholders as a nonprofit arm of NANA, and now administers health and social service programs with councils set up under the Indian Reorganization Act.

With state decentralization of education in 1976, the Inupiat at long last gained control of their school system, instituting a curriculum carefully tailored to the area's needs with heavy emphasis on Eskimo values.

A measure of local autonomy also came from the Friends Church which recently deeded about 40 acres of church land back to the Eskimo congregation, and has set aside 60 more acres for this purpose.

Kotzebue has also become headquarters for National Guard units in the area. The state program, an extension of the old Territorial Guard, has expanded to a point where it has equipped the Kotzebue unit with a modest air force with which to fly search and rescue missions.

The sudden emergence of Eskimo power and affluence came as a shock to minority groups that had long controlled the region, and in 1972 verbal hostilities between Natives and whites briefly made headlines. Both factions quickly denied there was a problem, however, and since that time have shown remarkable teamwork in planning the firm foundation for an exciting future. ☐

SUBSISTENCE LIVING ON KOTZEBUE'S COAST

A Personal Sketch
Bob Uhl

In the past 130 years of northwest Alaska history there have been at least two kinds of settlers coming into the region. The first and most obvious were empire builders and developers. Whalers, traders, missionaries, doctors, miners, biologists, and educators represent this group. To a very great extent these people brought their worlds with them, seeking to reestablish the living standards and living patterns from which they came.

Some though not all of the second group of settlers have come since the 1950s, and differ from the first group in that they want to join the life style already here. My wife Carrie, a Kotzebue Sound Eskimo, and I, a transplanted California caucasian, have since our marriage in 1948 been a team in the second group seeking a satisfying life in the things of both cultures that seem good to us.

Our first 20 years together were taken up with the struggles of parenthood, dominated overall oddly enough by complete dependence on an 8- to 12-member dog team. We are now, in 1980, more than halfway through our

A musher and dog teams head across the sea ice looking for seals near Cape Krusenstern.
Ken Ross

ABOVE — *Some families move seasonally from the interior to the coast to harvest a variety of marine and land mammals. Anore (left) and Keith Jones and their two daughters Willow and Arunya reside in Ambler in the winter and Sisualik in the summer.* Lael Morgan, staff

OPPOSITE — *Wind whips the snow around these sled dogs at a whaling camp in the Chukchi Sea ice.* Ken Ross

second 20 years together dominated by mechanical, economical, and spiritual considerations.

From 1948 to 1968 nearly every family unit in the Kotzebue region depended on a string of dogs for fuel, food, and long distance regional travel.

Resources needed to exist in the Kotzebue Basin at that time required some method of transport. We had to reach out to the resource, and haul it back home. In some cases distances might be short. In others we might have to travel 100 or more miles to secure marine mammal or caribou meat.

Several hundred pounds of load to be moved these distances required some help. A dog in harness with some training can exert several pounds of continuous pulling force for many hours. A team of dogs with a leader, working together, can move a thousand-pound load in a 14-foot basket sled with good runners 50 miles in a day.

We had to haul huge quantities of fuel to maintain the fire in our home 18 hours a day through 9 months of freezing temperatures. Daily water for home use came from melted lake ice hauled in by sled. Nets might be set under the ice 15 miles from home. Caribou might be 50 miles up a local river. Running an extended trapline to supply the necessary furs to earn hard cash required a dog team. We might make as many as four seasonal moves to different living-harvesting locations to take full advantage of changing seasonal abundance of different species. Our whole household, people and things, had to be loaded on a 12- or 14-foot sled and with several round trips moved 20 to 50 miles to the new location. Even our dwellings in some seasons had to go along.

Under the discipline of the times these were not things that could either be done or not depending on whims, they were things that had to be done to survive as a viable family unit. Therefore the care and well-being of our dog team held priority over all else. In times of food scarcity the dogs must be kept alive at all cost because the mobility they provide is all important to survival. In tight times then it was not easy to see family members go to bed hungry because the last meat or fish must be distributed among the dogs.

Dogs, of course, have the advantage over things mechanical in that they eat fish and meat — renewable resources that are found on the land and in the rivers and seas. We could not depend on any sure cash income, and though living was tough, it was possible with what the land provided.

Subsistence living provides us with a wonderful feeling of independence. But we do not become independent of people. Most persons taking on a rural subsistence life style (except real hermits) find that people in small doses become one of their most highly valued necessities. No matter how refined and expert our hunting, fishing, and gathering skills become; chance, health, and complex

LEFT — *Arunya Jones visits with Carrie Uhl at Sisualik. The canopy over the bed is a local invention that keeps out mosquitoes in summer, keeps in heat in winter, and protects privacy in a crowded cabin.* Lael Morgan, staff

BELOW — *At Sisualik Bob Uhl boils beluga* muktuk *to store in oil. The remains of the beluga lie on the shore while the last of summer's sea ice floats just offshore in this July photo.* Anore Jones

resource dynamics work together to *make* us good neighbors and to appreciate those neighbors we have.

Our living from and with the land occurs in the midcoastal portion of the NANA region centered now in Cape Krusenstern National Monument. Marine mammals (bearded seal, common ringed seal, spotted seal, beluga whale, and an occasional walrus) supply our most basic food, trade, and handicraft raw material needs. Fish of different species in season are equally important, especially since a commercial salmon fishery has provided a cash base from which other subsistence activities can be followed with more efficient technology. Land animals, birds, and plants have their important place.

Beginning with the Marine Mammal Protection Act of 1972 there has been a slow but steady federal and state regulatory pressure that makes it more and more difficult, and in

ABOVE — *Don't you have days like this and ain't it fun at the top?*   Anore Jones

UPPER RIGHT — *Subsistence living requires using available natural resources such as this arctic hare from the Kotzebue area coast and snowshoe hare from the interior.*   Manya Wik

ABOVE — *A musk ox enjoys the lush grass at Cape Krusenstern.*   Peter Connors

some instances impossible, to continue a viable life style that the freedom of the times made possible for us. Some of this pressure was and is necessary. A good deal of it is not.

If the world of nature is viewed as a system with man as steward given use privileges as well as species-maintaining responsibilities, then it seems wrong and a waste not to utilize those natural resources that can sustain harvests.

Much of the pressure in northwest Alaska generated in recent years that seems to make subsistence living more difficult has come from national interest groups that do not see living natural resources as a crop to be harvested and maintained, but as separate life forms to be preserved or worshipped. We believe there is unbalance in this last, and though we appreciate aesthetic values to the highest degree and wish to preserve species, we find that we still have stomachs to feed and bodies to clothe.

Our spring and summer camp is located in Carrie's native allotment land parcel on Sisualik peninsula in the northeast corner of Kotzebue Sound a few miles west of the Noatak River delta. Fresh-water delta channels and sandbars meet Chukchi Sea waters here, and just as spring ice moves out, great numbers of beluga, small, toothed whales, enter shallow water here. Hunters captured them historically in kayaks and skin boats, now the hunters use outboard-powered boats or nets. Two layers of skin plus a thin layer of blubber lightly dried, cooked, and put down in rendered oil make the staple delicacy *muktuk.*

From ice out in early June till freezeup in late November a more or less constant parade of some kind of edible fish, marine mammal, bird, or shellfish passes our beachfront on Sisualik Spit. With proper-sized nets, marine-mammal harvesting equipment, and sufficiently fierce storms to deposit shellfish on the beach, the Sisualik dweller has a diverse diet.

In November after ice and snow cover have become thick enough, we move back six or seven miles from the beach to our winter camp in one of the small white spruce patches that make up the extreme north and west boreal forests of North America. Caribou, moose, ptarmigan, snowshoe hare, and a few furbearers provide material sustenance as well as aesthetic pleasures and pains for the six winter months until May when we return to the coast to welcome migratory birds back from southern climates.

Marine Mammals
Lifeblood of Coastal Subsistence

The sea provides a bountiful harvest of flesh, skin and oil to sustain Kotzebue Basin's coastal residents. Marine mammals, particularly several species of seals, and beluga whales constitute chief ingredients of this bounty. Prized above all is the bearded seal *(oogruk)*, largest of Alaska's earless seals which can weigh more than 500 pounds. Seal skin covers skin boats, and forms raw material for clothing and storage containers. Seal meat is eaten and rendered into seal oil. Seal organs, as well as those of belugas, become garments and other useful items.

ABOVE — *A Native near Kotzebue prepares seal gut to be made into waterproof clothing about 1914. The gut is blown up and dried, then worked with a scraper and teeth to make it supple.* Nichols Collection, Courtesy of Mark Ocker

RIGHT — *Carrie Uhl inflates a seal poke for drying at Sealing Point in 1967. Fourteen years later the Uhls still visit the point and Carrie still inflates the pokes.* Ken Ross

ABOVE — *With an ulu, Carrie Uhl flenses blubber from the hide of an* oogruk, *or bearded seal, at Cape Krusenstern.*

RIGHT — *Bob Uhl stores seal blubber in a poke for self-rendering into seal oil, or* uksruk. Both by Robert Belous, National Park Service

Perhaps no other season so well demonstrates the poignant joy and pain of subsistence living. Surely spring is the season which is most difficult for extreme conservationists and folks living from the land to find common ground.

Marine mammal harvest is also primarily a spring activity as the ocean side of Sisualik Spit reflects. Meat drying racks, wooden barrels, semi-underground store houses, and hard working, *ulu*-wielding women characterize late May and June here. A whole winter's supply of oil, dried meat, and clothing skins can be had with good fortune and hard work.

June progresses and marine-mammal-bearing ocean ice moves farther west and north until it is finally out of reach. Great ground swells then signal the arrival of ice-free months. Salmon return to waters they left four years earlier. Kotzebue Sound commercial salmon fishermen gather their gear, and by mid-July are actively involved in their month-and-a-half of cash earning for the year. Many salmon fishermen have other forms of income, but for some the cash made fishing will constitute most of their yearly income. In these

Commercial fishermen check a set net curved into an S shape by the changing tide of Kotzebue Sound. In the foreground grows ryegrass, typical of beach vegetation in this area. Anore Jones

days of tighter and more stringent regulations, perhaps it would be useful to have limited entry for subsistence commercial fisheries in western Alaska since the money earned by the majority of local fishermen is as indispensable as the meat, fish, furs, wood, and berries that make their life style viable.

September brings an end to commercial salmon activity. Berry picking (blue, salmon, black and cran) continues to full swing, and fall land animal harvest gets under way. Because of widespread mechanical freezer ownership in recent years, this September harvest of caribou, moose, sheep, bear, and waterfowl is possible a few weeks earlier than previously. This presents some game management problems since some people are yet dependent on the natural outdoor freezer that in the Kotzebue Sound area is not safely used until October.

In years past, especially if we go back far enough, we find the people of this region inexorably tied to seasonal migration patterns of wildlife. Different species also go through long range cycles of abundance and scarcity. In earlier times it is very easy to see how awe, fear, and reverence might develop toward those forces that influence resource abundance or scarcity. High value was placed on animals, birds, fish, and plants. The worst possible sin for these pure subsistence people would be to not have made use of an opportunity to harvest in time of plenty, and then face starvation later in the year. This attitude is ingrained in the subsistence personality. When great migrations of caribou, whitefish, char, and other species move through the country each fall, much effort, time, and skill are expended to take enough of the resource.

In the mid-1800s many changes began with the coming of other peoples. These changes continue today; some good and some not. One thing lost by the people of the country to some degree was the awe, reverence, and respect for the surrounding environment and the living species of it. The exploiter with his lust for money and fame showed little respect for other forms of life in the north. Missionary-teachers of the era also tended to draw Eskimos from nature worship and may have contributed to the problem. At any rate the old reverence for things of the natural world was shaken.

By 1960 through the 1970s, when much environmental awareness and concern for natural resources of the world began to make headlines outside and land ownership and management became important in northwest Alaska, the scene was set for misunderstanding and frustration. The good from these sometimes painful upheavals was a learning and sharing between cultures, a reassessment of important values, and a chance for all individuals who were willing to broaden their scope of being. This process, of course, continues into the 1980s.

Freezeup in October makes possible large harvest operations of those species that at this time pass within reach of our camp. Each year varies but whitefish, caribou, seals, ptarmigan, and an occasional walrus, or bear can be expected each fall as waterfowl leave the scene with freezing temperatures that make their habitat unusable.

By early November, especially if there has been sufficient snow, we move inland to our winter quarters where taking a moose or two and readying trapping equipment for the upcoming season become the primary concerns. How wonderful to be again in the fragrant spruce woods with shelter from drifting snow and an unlimited fuel supply.

Bob Uhl, a transplanted Californian and long-time resident of Kotzebue Basin, prepares to build a fire at his camp at Sisualik while dog Snoopy keeps an eye on things. Lael Morgan, staff

with its limited sky, bordered by ragged spruce spires; she rejoices for the unlimited horizons of spring camp.

We are often asked how we think it will be to live within the newly created national monument areas administered by the National Park Service. "Won't the necessarily more stringent regulations make it impossible to continue a living from the land life style?"

Well at this point it is difficult to say what the future will bring. All of the bills that have come before congress have extensive subsistence sections that seem to provide at least the promise of continuence for those families and their descendants now living by subsistence. Interim and present regulations drawn up by the National Park Service seem reasonable, and no change has yet been felt in our area of activity since the act was made law. Much of our hopes for the future are based on what is written into subsistence considerations of the Antiquities Act, or pending congressional action. Much of the working out of these provisions remains at the discretion of the incumbent Secretary of the Interior. Just how subsistence considerations will be worked out on the grass roots level will depend much on how the written rules are interpreted. The National Park Service has gone to greater pains than any other state or federal agency to at least gather base information on people, creatures, and general environmental information of the areas involved. At best to us, the national monument does not seem to be the lock-up complained of by many in the state and at least one possible way to have some control over the two factors sure to bring a halt to present life styles: *overpopulation* and *uncontrolled* use of natural resources. ☐

December and January are months of very short daylight hours and often either extreme cold or stormy, milder weather with no visibility. Four or five hours of rather dull daylight is typical of these months here and though trapping, hunting, and fishing continue, it is a time of long evenings, holidays, and thinking.

With the longer days and higher, warmer sun of February and March preparation for a new harvest year gets under way. Fur taking continues, and ice fishing for various species begins. Firewood, and spruce poles for meat and fish racks must be cut and hauled the ten miles to Sisualik while ice and snow provide a good haul road. When weather conditions make open leads in the ocean ice available, common ringed seals can be taken, and on land small game, hares and ptarmigan, provide variety in the soup pot.

Late April thaws signal the time for moving again to the ocean beach, and the beautiful unlimited horizon the arctic coast provides. Carrie tends to feel cooped up after a few months in our spruce-patch winter quarters

LIVING OFF THE LAND IN THE KOBUK VALLEY

Ole Wik

Every so often we read that primitive man waged a constant struggle for survival. We visualize a ragged band of nomads camping in one area until they had cleaned out all the game, and then moving hungrily on to another — always wandering, always wanting.

Perhaps there were areas in North America where life really was like that — but northwest Alaska was not one of them. Even today, there are far more big game animals in the region than there are people. The springtime skies ring with the calls of waterfowl, the pure rivers teem with fish, and even in deep winter the willow flats can be counted on to yield a meal of rabbit or ptarmigan.

It is true that the hunting life would have been a constant struggle if these creatures were evenly spread in space and in time, but they are not: many of the important fish and game species are themselves nomadic. In the course of their various migrations they pass certain choke points in remarkable numbers, so that for a few days or weeks, in certain choice locations, nature's generosity is enormously magnified. Soon enough the creatures

A musher heads his dog team cross-country during spring thaw in the Kobuk valley near the Jade Mountains.
Anore Jones

disperse and perhaps all but disappear, but before long something else is on the move, and it is harvest time again.

A more accurate image of northwest Alaska, in other words, is of a land rich in food resources *which wax and wane with the seasons.* It is undoubtedly true that the primitive Eskimo, like the Natives of less favored regions, sometimes suffered episodes of dire want, but these were interspersed with periods of *almost unimaginable abundance.* And though the ancient Eskimo often wandered, it was not in desperation: he was moving either to position himself for the next great wave of life that would bring him something to eat, or else to build a comfortable camp in which to enjoy the previous harvest.

The Kobuk people capture the essence of the old way of life in a single word: *niqimaliqaat,* meaning "they followed the meat." The Old Time People moved from camp to camp in response to the life cycles of the various creatures that supported them, skimming a living from a whole series of temporary abundances that were nicely spaced throughout the year. Well-developed food preservation techniques (drying, immersion in seal oil, natural freezing) closed the cycle of the seasons, enabling the Eskimos to face lean times with a remarkable variety of wholesome foods laid away.

Nowadays the people spend less time in camp, and more in permanent villages. The establishment of schools brought the people in to town, and the responsibilities of jobs often keep them there. But beneath the increasing bustle of modern occupations, life still throbs to the rhythms of the many wildlife migrations that punctuate the year.

Following the hunting, fishing, and gathering activities of the people in Ambler, in the central part of the Kobuk valley, gives a good idea of the yearly harvest cycle of the inland area of northwest Alaska.

In early summer, even before the river has completely cleared of ice following breakup, villagers set gill nets in the side sloughs. In this time of gentle weather the land seems to be at rest, but a great deal of movement is taking place beneath the placid surface of the swollen river. Northern pike, mud sucker, and small whitefish known as *qalgiq* are all moving. Conditions are just right for drying their flesh: breezy, not too hot, few flies. This is also the time for gathering *masru* (Eskimo potato), and

RIGHT — *Bernice Custer cleans and guts a tubful of chum salmon. The fish resource is key to successful subsistence living in the upper Kobuk.* John and Margaret Ibbotson

BELOW — *Caribou are extremely important to subsistence living in northwest Alaska. Though both male and female caribou have antlers, large branching racks characterize bulls such as this one from the western arctic herd.* George Wuerthner

Birch Bark Basketry
Necessity Becomes an Art

Making baskets from birch bark, once done out of necessity, has now become an art, passed down through families over the years. Originally used for cooking, a well-made basket is watertight, fashioned with elegant simplicity from a single sheet of bark. Uses for the baskets are unlimited, from carrying water to holding the day's berry harvest.

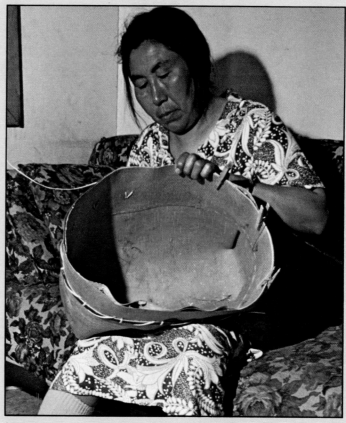

Ambler resident Clara Lee, one of the Kobuk valley's best basket makers, harvests a sheet of birch bark (above); she ties the roll of freshly cut bark with a willow bough (center); and splits spruce root for use in the outer binding of the baskets (right).

Minnie Gray of Ambler fashions the traditional birch bark basket used for berry picking known as an aimmaq.

All photos by Robert Belous, National Park Service

93

BELOW — *In earlier times a person's life could depend on the kind of rope he had. The rope hanging on the right side of the branch is made of* oogruk, *or bearded seal skin, and will be ready to use after the hair is cut off.*   Anore Jones

RIGHT — *Maude Cleveland removes the hair and quills from a porcupine in this 1966 photo by Ken Ross. Porcupines are good eating and their quills are used for decoration.*

ABOVE — *Lorry Schuerch of Kiana makes his living from trapping. Here his son Brent sits in his chair in the kitchen with some of Lorry's catch of red fox and lynx.*   Lorry Schuerch

RIGHT — *Seal skin and sinew are two essential elements of traditional subsistence living. The sinew from caribou, most often taken from along the back, was the choice for sewing parkas and all lightweight skins.*   Anore Jones

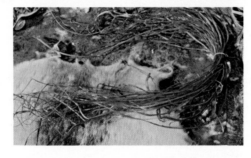

the first summer greens — bluebell and willow leaves, louseworts, and fireweed tips. A little later women collect sacks of wild rhubarb along the cutbanks.

Toward the end of June, fishing gradually tapers off. Warm air and the midnight sun give a sense of well-being, but in fact this is one of the hungry times, a time between migrations. No fish are moving, and as the remaining resident fish are cleaned out of the eddies, the nets yield less and less.

At this time, more than ever, residents sense the crucial importance of the river. One tends to think of Eskimos primarily as hunters,

forgetting that they are also skilled fishermen who rely heavily on the produce of their healthytaters. It is likely that a serious disturbance of the Kobuk's fisheries would have more impact on the local people than a crash of the caribou herd.

The lean time of midsummer ends with the appearance of the first salmon and the prized shee. By mid-July their delicious flesh is appearing on tables throughout Ambler, perhaps garnished with wild chives, and by August the racks along the beach are heavy with orderly rows of fish, cleanly split for drying.

In late summer the women, seized by berry fever, spend as much time as they can in the woods and on the tundras. Though the delicate cloudberry (salmonberry) is usually scarce, the women can usually gather "any much" blueberries, which they put up by the gallon. The bland crowberry is welcomed for mixing with blueberries, and for adding to sourdock to make a fermented dish called *qaugaq*. All of these berries require special care to hold them over into the colder months, but the lingonberry, which ripens later, is virtually indestructible and will keep perfectly well in an ordinary cardboard box.

River Life Style

Molly McCammon

CLOCKWISE FROM LEFT —
►*Neighbor Jim Kowalsky ministers wedding rites to Wilbur Mills and Molly McCammon at their cabin in a remote river valley in Kotzebue Basin in 1977.*
Courtesy of Molly McCammon
►*Wilbur Mills hauls his mother Helen Mills of Seattle in a canoe up a tributary of the Kobuk.* Molly McCammon
►*Molly McCammon peels white spruce logs for a new cache.* Wilbur Mills

A small log cabin nestled among spruce trees in a valley about halfway between the Kobuk and Noatak rivers is home for my husband and me most of the year. Sitting at our table sipping tea, we look outside the large picture window that frames the rugged mountains that dominate this valley.

Migrating caribou have worn a trail 50 yards from the window, and we watch them pass by in the fall. Often moose will follow our paths, curious about these strange forest creatures called humans. Occasionally we see a black or brown/grizzly bear foraging for roots on a mountain slope.

Our valley is settled by a group of young people who staked public land opened by the Bureau of Land Management in 1973 and 1974. Most of us are products of the 1960s and still a rather transient bunch. But even if we travel to Fairbanks for an occasional stint of work, or visit family Outside, this valley is still home.

As for most people living a bush life style in this area, life patterns depend on cycles of food gathering. Fall is the busiest time. Days are spent combing the woods for bright red cranberries, vitamin-rich rose hips, and the last of the juicy blueberries. Mushrooms are eagerly sought as a welcome addition to the winter stew pot. Late September sees us hunting caribou and moose, enough to last through spring. Rabbits and ptarmigan provide a nice change of diet. Whitefish, grayling, and arctic char are netted at fish camp 18 miles away, where our neighbors fish heavily for dog food.

Winters are spent on quiet, indoor projects interspersed with lots of visiting, and an occasional trip to town. This is also the time for any trips outside — a brief respite from cold and dark. Spring finds us all on the move — by dog sled or skis. This is the time for intensive traveling — exploring the beautiful country that surrounds us. In summer we undertake our various income-producing occupations.

As a photographer, my husband Wilbur Mills, has spent the last ten years documenting the beauty and wildlife of the Brooks Range. We both do a little guiding in the summer, taking hikers and boaters out to experience the arctic wilderness.

For us the beauty of living up here is in getting to know a wild area intimately. We are both travelers and explorers; our psyches need an adventure fix on a regular basis. Discovering a bubbling spring surrounded by exquisite mosses and ferns, climbing a peak that has probably never been climbed before, seeing two wolverines in one day, watching streams of caribou flow down the river valleys — these experiences are what makes everything worthwhile. □

Cora Cleveland of Ambler holds a net which has spread out under the ice to capture passing fish.
                                    Manya Wik

In September the glorious yellowing of aspen signals the onset of the greatest harvest period of the Kobuk year. Washtubfuls of *qalgiq* (whitefish) and of the even smaller *qallusraq* are taken in seines; increasing numbers of egg-laden char appear in the nets; and the shee again pass the village, this time on the return trip downriver.

On land, black and brown/grizzly bears roam the tundra, fattening sweetly on berries. Moose also begin to wander, impelled by the mating drive that powers all deer in the fall.

And in due course come the caribou, trailing single file through mountain passes, across the tundra, and down to the river.

If freezeup is late and the water is ice-free, the Kobuk presents little barrier to the animals' southward march. Led by a cow, a band will slip into the river and paddle lightly across, single file, the antlers of the bulls forming a kind of fence across the water.

But if freezeup is early and the river is running ice, the leader may turn the herd back to the tundra. The river temporarily becomes a choke point, even as band after band of new arrivals join the animals already congregated on the north side of the river. This is the time to sense just how rich the tundra can be.

Once the river ice becomes thick enough to support them, the caribou continue southward to their wintering grounds. But by then the hunters are busy setting nets under the ice for the all-important *qausrilyuq*. Ambler people harvest tons of these large whitefish, heavy with eggs, in two or three weeks of intensive fishing.

Clouds of grayling gather around the nets, snapping up the eggs that constantly dribble from the struggling whitefish. Fishermen in turn jig for the grayling, adding hundreds of them to their growing hoards of frozen fish.

Just after sunset the fishermen may switch to larger lures in order to hook for burbot, which are also on the move as the river

freezes over. These unlovely mudsharks are prized not only for their delicate flesh but also for their sweet livers. Not too many years ago the more ambitious fishermen used to catch mudsharks by the dozens in woven willow traps set beneath the ice.

The mudshark run tapers off by late November, and then another lean time begins — the long one of deep winter. Now the taste of fresh meat can only be met with small game — rabbits and ptarmigan, mostly. Young boys also like to test their skill and their .22s on the easy spruce grouse that live in the forest, and that mean so much to the old people.

But what is winter for, after all, if not to feast on food that was put away in more generous times? Even a family without modern refrigeration can spread the table with half a dozen species of dried fish, and as many kinds served frozen. There will also be moose and caribou jerky — with as much as you want of the indispensable seal oil, bought or bartered from the coast — and perhaps a meat soup as well. To finish, there will be a bowl of berries, a bread or cracker of some kind, and of course tea.

Oddly enough, it is the forbidding northern climate, so easily regarded as a burden, that makes much of this abundance possible. The great natural deep-freeze not only keeps fresh meat in edible condition for half a year, but slows the deterioration of important supplies of dried meat and fish that hang in the cache for use as needed.

So passes the winter. Then, one day in late April, a hunter brings back word that he has heard the first wild geese, heralding the onset of the miraculous rebirth that accompanies breakup. Within a few weeks dozens of kinds of birds return to breed, the velvet-antlered caribou drift toward calving grounds on the north slope, and bears come out of hibernation, hungry and cranky but still fat and tender. Children's lips glisten with beaver fat and goose grease. Once the ice rushes out, the nets go down again, and people savor a treat as old as human occupation of Alaska; the first fresh fish of a new summer. □

Dan Denslow, Working the Wind

Ole Wik

Dan and Joyce Denslow came to the Kobuk valley in late summer 1963, as schoolteachers, and immediately liked the country, the people, and the way of life. In those days there was open land, and by the following spring they had decided to take a year off and build a sod igloo in the forest. Little did they dream that their year in the woods would become a life style, or that their place would become a model of self-reliant Alaska living.

The early years were taken up by the problems that face all settlers, of whatever race, in whatever place or time: building a home, and securing a living. Dan was dedicated to serving others, and he was a pilot —so it was only natural that he established Ambler Air Service. Charter flying provided an income, and work on the home continued as time permitted.

The Denslows were deeply impressed by the Eskimos' use of the resources of the land, and wished to base their life style on a gentle harvest of those resources: meat, fish, berries, building materials. But Dan also saw the value of certain carefully selected tools and technologies from industrial culture, and used his engineering background to adapt them to rural Alaska conditions.

The results, after more than a decade of effort, were a snug home insulated with poured-in-place urethane foam, a large and

Dan Denslow climbs the tower of his wind mill in Ambler with his daughter and neighbor children.   Lael Morgan, staff

productive organic garden, a fine shop, and — centerpiece of it all — a wind-electric system based on a reconditioned 2.5 kw Jacobs mill and a large battery bank.

The wind blew more than anyone had noticed, and the wind generator produced more power than Dan, Joyce and their daughter Corie required for their simple needs. So, typically, Dan strung wires to the two nearest neighbors so that they might also enjoy the simple luxury of electric lights.

By this time — the late 1970s — Dan had

sold the air service, and was flying only part time, as a replacement. His shop, equipped with a variety of wind-powered tools, was on the way to becoming an income-producer through woodworking, welding, repair, or whatever. Dan had also been awarded a grant from the Department of Energy to construct a wind-powered, walk-in freezer which would have multiplied the possibilities for living off the land. Both shop and freezer would have been demonstrations of the power of individuals to provide for their own needs in rural Alaska.

Once he stopped flying full time, Dan had more time to devote to his research. His hands-on experience in homestead-scale wind power quickly propelled him to the forefront of the budding Alaska alternate energy movement. He was invited to speak at various conferences where his knowledge of life in the bush, his grasp of the technical details of wind power, and his witty, charming delivery were great assets.

His work was interrupted early in 1980 when he temporarily took on flying duties once again. On the intensely cold morning of January 14 he was called out to fly a charter to the neighboring village of Shungnak. On final approach to the fog-shrouded runway the engine failed, and the plane crashed on the tundra. The accident claimed six passengers, along with their dedicated pilot.

The winds of sudden change blow over the Denslow homesite. Joyce and Corie have left the valley, for now, and we shall not have the joy of knowing how their Kobuk life style would have evolved.

But the big wind machine, still facing into the north wind, continues to spin our power for Dan's neighbors. He would have liked that.   ☐

SEASONS OF THE NOATAK

Molly McCammon

We had been walking for hours, and the pass was still not in sight. Every twist and bend in the river gave the illusion of the pass being directly ahead, but instead, only another rock wall, another talus plateau to climb. No wonder it is called Blind Pass.

Two days of hiking had brought us this morning to the end of spruce forests and the beginning of a limestone canyon cut by a torrential creek. At lunch next to the river, a young grizzly paused on a piece of shelf ice still left after breakup. One look at our small group, and the bear fled. It was hopeless to try following the creek through that canyon filled from wall to wall with swirling, rushing whitewater. Our only alternative was to crawl through the thick alder forest overhanging the canyon walls, and reach the bare tundra above. An hour of sweaty climbing brought us into the open. From here the valley gradually turned to the east, toward what appeared to be an impregnable barrier of sheer rock.

Tundra soon gave way to rock. Our path followed the course of the creek, exiting the canyon; the water was flat, then cascaded

A tributary of the Noatak pushes through a narrow, limestone-walled canyon in Gates of the Arctic National Park and Preserve. Wilbur Mills

down to deep aquamarine pools. We climbed toward a wedge of ground below the rock wall, scoured flat, the melting snow now exposing thick mud. The fluted and spired mountains surrounded us, snow clinging in each gully not reached by sun. *Croak, croak!* A rock ptarmigan, still in its winter white, called out a warning. That, and the drip drip of melting waters were the only sounds in this vast amphitheater lost in space and time.

Sheer willpower picked up our feet, and moved us toward the notch in the rock walls. Snow still covered much of the ground, and every third step we would sink to our thighs in the heavy, wet stuff. Hiding from the wind behind a rock, we wolfed down a few dried apples. One last push, and we were there.

The view was awesome and somewhat frightening. The Arctic in springtime, late May and early June, is a land just beginning to awaken from the long winter. Directly below us snow continued downward for another mile before reluctantly giving way to rock. Ice still covered the creek bed as it dropped rapidly to join the main river below. Mountains crowded the sky, lit with pink alpenglow; minutes later these same mountains showed black and white — black rock alternating in bands with white snow, sloping down into a dreary, dead-looking valley floor. Here the land was brown,

save for large snow patches and pools of water, and seemingly void of life. A river cut swiftly around limestone walls and faded toward a large valley in the distance — the valley of the Noatak.

That was my first view of the Noatak, and as if under a spell, the river has lured me back time and again. Its sweeping vastness and the intricate struggle for life that takes place there reminds me of the desert where I lived as a child. At about 425 miles in length, the Noatak drains one of Alaska's largest river basins, and is considered by many to be one of the most wild and pristine in the United States. Archaeological evidence indicates that the basin was occupied by man as long ago as 12,000 years, although the valley remained unexplored by white men until late in the last century. Inupiat Eskimos successfully adapted to the harsh arctic environment over the years, and even today continue to rely on the basin's resources for their survival.

One meaning for the word *Noatak* is "deep inside," and truly the river's very headwaters lie deep inside the central Brooks Range. Straight from glaciers still clinging to the sides of 8,510-foot Mount Igikpak, the Noatak begins its course across more than a third of arctic Alaska before emptying into the sea near Kotzebue.

From its source, the Noatak flows for about 50 miles through a steep glacial valley surrounded by rugged mountains before crossing a major moraine belt marked by glacial land forms and occasional rapids. There the river enters the Aniuk Lowlands, a vast glacial till plain characterized by immense sweeps of tundra dotted with ponds and marshes and fringed by mountains, hazy blue in the distance. At the Anglungak Hills the valley narrows again into a canyon 65 miles long called the Grand Canyon of the Noatak with surrounding mountains of 2,000 and 3,000 feet. The canyon's lower seven miles form a true gorge with vertical walls some 200 to 300 feet high.

Below the canyon the river descends through a valley that gradually widens, the current slacking off and the river dividing into numerous channels. One final cut through the Igichuk Hills, and then the Noatak flows into its delta.

BELOW — *Calm waters of the Noatak River reflect images of Mount Igikpak (8,510 feet) and other peaks of the central Brooks Range.*
John and Margaret Ibbotson

RIGHT — *Near where the Kugrak River joins the Noatak 41 miles southwest of Survey Pass, the view to the northwest shows the Noatak meandering through a valley in Gates of the Arctic National Park and Preserve.* Wilbur Mills

Springtime in the Arctic is that brief, ephemeral time between breakup and the deepening of summer, the first mad burst of activity. Unlike the south slope of the Brooks Range, the Noatak gets little snow, usually no more than a foot or two. The long, sunny days of late May and early June quickly bare the tundra, leaving pools of water and newly formed streamlets everywhere, wending their way down to the numerous creeks and streams that form the tributaries of the main river.

Melting snow waters flow downward, carving channels through the ice in creeks and riverbeds. Sometimes these small channels keep eating away right through the winter's thickness of ice, opening up the main river gradually. Other times, pressure builds up, and the rotting ice starts to move with grinding motions. Soon a mighty force sweeps the ice all away toward the sea, leaving only the shelf ice and huge fields of what is called *aufeis* or overflow. These ice fields are usually formed in braided stretches of the river where the water freezes to the bottom. Since the water that is still flowing in the river has nowhere else to go, it pops out of a crack or hole in the ice, and spreads out before freezing. This continual process of overflowing, and then freezing creates huge thicknesses of ice, some of which never melt completely during the brief arctic summer. These fields of ice make vast highways for traveling in springtime, and provide freedom from insects for many large mammals later in the summer.

Rivers run high and muddy now, carrying large amounts of sediment washed down from the saturated tundra, cutting away at side banks, creating new channels at random. The ground is wet and spongy. Here and there a

The author enjoys a turn on cross-country skis through spring snow near her home in a valley between the Noatak and Kobuk rivers. Wilbur Mills

Erosion eats away the banks of the Noatak, exposing cones of permafrost. John Clayton

tiny green shoot pops up from under last year's rubble of grasses and sedges. Tiny buds on willows and dwarf birch open tentatively. In a cloven rock outcropping next to the river, a flash of color reveals the purple mountain saxifrage. At the edge of a melting snow bank, a northern anemone follows the sun in an arc across the sky, exposing its bluish undersides in the gentle breeze. The young, tender shoots of dwarf fireweed and willows are gathered along the now-exposed gravel bars, and greedily devoured in exotic-looking spring salads. The earth vibrates with activity.

There could be no spring without return of the birds. With leads along the ponds and lakes growing larger each day and with the rivers now flowing, ducks and geese return, some to stay, most to continue on north to their nesting grounds on the arctic plain. A northern phalarope spins on the water of a small pond like a wind-up toy, stirring up insects from the bottom. An arctic tern, having just flown in from Antarctica, takes up residence on a large willow overhanging the river's edge. A walk

through the willows scares up a group of ptarmigans, the males still in their winter plumage, giving an outraged croak before settling down to feed again in another batch of willows. Lapland longspurs add to the general commotion with songs tinkling like Japanese wind chimes. The plaintive whistle of the American golden plover matches well the lonely vastness of the tundra. The air is filled with the sounds and bustle of mating and breeding activity.

A group of caribou, bulls and yearlings, look up curiously from feeding on horsetails. Their coats are ratty-looking, eaten by warble fly larvae which burrow into the animals' skin to overwinter. Now they enjoy the peaceful spring days, still free of mosquitoes. Cows are already on calving grounds to the north where most of their young are born during the first week of June.

Mount Igikpak dominates the entire upper Noatak area of the Brooks Range. The peak's granite walls rise over 5,000 feet from the valley floor, support several glaciers up to two miles in length, and sport a massive double turret topping a swirl of knife-edged ridges.

One summer I led a group of hikers on a 70-mile trek, circumnavigating the entire granite massif. A day hike to its base started up a small alpine valley filled with flowers at their summer height: pink woolly louseworts, covered with fine hairs to trap warmth, an aid in the short, cool growing season; yellow poppies nodding at any breath of wind; fields of dryas whose leaves form a ground-hugging mat common to alpine tundra. Snow still lingers in patches shadowed from the sun with early spring plants just emerging at the meltline. Enough fireweed and willow shoots, as well as the delightfully tart mountain sorrel, are found for a luncheon salad.

Grassy slopes give way to rocky moraines left by the retreating glacier. A cold wind blows down over the ice, and ominous black clouds swirl around the mountain's summit, which refuses to reveal itself. The glacier is dirty, strewn with rubble flung from the rocky heights and wisps of tundra blown from nearby meadows. A ridge leading up toward the next valley over tempts us and up we climb, clambering over slippery, lichen-covered rocks, the water-logged soil sliding under our feet. Brilliant red and yellow lichens, clinging in intricate patterns to rocks, capture our attention. Strange plants are these: part alga, part fungus, together working in symbiosis. The fungus absorbs and stores large amounts of water, but lacking chlorophyll, cannot make food. The single-celled

Hikers rest and scan the far slope with their binoculars during a journey through the Brooks Range near the Noatak's headwaters.
Steve Warble

106

algae provide that necessary ingredient, and make organic compounds by photosynthesis.

Fields of dryas cover the ridgetop. Clouds part and we lay on the warm tundra, basking in the sun's warmth. In the distance stand the craggy spires and minarets of Arrigetch Peaks. To the south lies a tributary of the Kobuk River, the dark green along the river indicating dense alder thickets which soon give way to spruce trees. The remainder of the Noatak lies hidden behind the dominating presence of Igikpak.

From the base of Igikpak the ten miles to Lucky Six Creek are covered quickly. Summer

is now at its peak, yet a hint of fall is already in the air. Bear scat is abundant and we clap hands loudly while beating through the willow thickets found in small draws. A cow and calf moose jump out of one such thicket, mama twitching her ears at us. How casually they run across the tussocks, those tufts of grass and sedge that are the bane of all hikers in the far North.

Up ahead a sow brown/grizzly and three cubs chase each other playfully across the tundra. Mama stops suddenly, rearing straight up on her hind legs and sniffing the air, her cubs following suit one by one. Catching our scent, she turns in one fluid motion and runs toward a boulder-strewn creek bed, family in tow. The sun glistens on the blonde hairs of her coat, and we can see the powerful muscles ripple rhythmically as she runs.

LEFT — *John Clayton tows his kayak across sand bars at the mouth of the Noatak.*
Courtesy of John Clayton

BELOW — *A hiker moves through cotton grass on a tundra meadow high above the Noatak River bottom near the village of Noatak.*
Janelle Eklund

Another beast we encounter frequently is the famed arctic mosquito. When they are out en masse, many prayers are offered in hopes of a strong wind or a sudden cold snap, 40° appearing to be about the insect's critical activity temperature. Mosquitoes can literally drive large animals quite mad. I have seen caribou with glazed eyes running frantically in all directions, attempting to escape the hordes. Usually the gravel bars or a dry, windswept ridge are the best places to be during a bad stretch.

As we hike along, I think of Samuel McLenegan and a lone companion, both from the revenue cutter *Corwin*, dragging their canoe up this river in July 1885 as part of a government survey in Alaska. His account details the miseries endured during the month-long ascent, yet the explorer was also struck by the beauty of the country.

I think about Philip Smith of the U.S. Geological Survey, who worked his way in the summer of 1911 up the Alatna River with huge freight canoes, portaging them over Portage Creek Pass and down to the Noatak, floating on to Kotzebue. How easy we have it today with airplanes and light-weight equipment. Yet the spirit of adventure is still the same, the love of wildness and open space that calls.

Setting up camp next to Lucky Six Creek, we discover that we do not have the valley to ourselves after all. Orange surveyors tape marks a landing field across the tundra, and a pile of gear lies nearby under an old tarp. Following the creek up, we come upon a large mosquito-net tent hidden behind a boulder the size of a house. We are almost at the tent by the time the man inside hears us, jumps up and reaches for his gun. "I thought you were that bear that's been hanging around," he explains with obvious relief.

The man's name is Ralph, about 26, from Fairbanks, and a modern-day gold prospector. He and his partner had been searching for gold up the creek using a small, portable

LEFT — *Dall sheep cross tundra-covered slopes in the Brooks Range above the Noatak. Portions of the river valley under National Park Service administration have preserve rather than park status to allow for continued hunting of Dall sheep.* John Clayton

RIGHT — *Changing temperatures bring a blaze of color to tundra vegetation in this early September photo of the middle Noatak valley.* Wilbur Mills

suction dredge. Just the other day his partner had cracked up his Cessna 180 while flying in some gear, and was now in Fairbanks getting it patched up. "So far we've found about $600 worth of gold," Ralph laughed, "about enough to pay for our airplane repairs."

The man was definitely quite bushy, talking as if he had not seen a soul for months. Just out of curiosity, I asked him if he realized he was mining in a national monunent. "Oh hell, we just took the maps out and saw this creek on it. With a name like Lucky Six, there just had to be gold here. We didn't look to see who owned the land. What's a national monument anyway?"

We left him at the creek picking over that morning's batch of creek bottom he had sucked up with his dredge, singing "Oh my darling, Clementine" at the top of his lungs.

It has been another rainy summer, and several days later we are waiting for our pilot, now two days overdue, to come in and pick us up. Out of food we are down to true subsistence — feeding ourselves from what we can obtain from the land. We come up with a true feast: fresh grayling, potfuls of steamed puffballs, sauteed *masru* or Eskimo potato (the root of *Hedysarum alpinum*) and succulent blueberries.

Fall is a special time in Alaska, and there is nowhere better to spend it than on the Noatak. The days are still long and warm. Nights are cool and dark enough for stars and the aurora borealis, those shimmering curtains of colored lights that dance across the northern sky. The tundra is ablaze with color. One of the Noatak's side valleys is completely red with dwarf birch and bearberry leaves that have changed color. Another, dominated by willows and dryas, is completely gold.

These small, alpine side valleys, their marble and limestone rock carved by ancient glaciers, provide some of the most striking alpine scenery in the Brooks Range, especially at this time of year. Although most of the peaks are below 6,000 feet, they are very steep and rugged. Valleys average about 15 to 20 miles long, and often originate in deep cirques or glacier-scoured passes. Here fall colors are more overpowering because of the intimacy created by the valleys' smallness. For me the charm of the Noatak lies not so much in the vast river valley itself, but in these small miniatures of the whole.

Scattered groups of bull caribou dot the landscape, fat and sleek after a summer of good eating, thick coats ready for winter. We stalk them in pairs, the front person lifting arms straight up like imitation antlers, the back person sticking a leg out to the side in the classic alarm pose, and then grunt like female caribou. On calving grounds I have had calves and cows grunt joyously in return, and run straight for me. These bulls are unimpressed. They look up curiously; start running; stop for a second look, not quite believing; then really head out.

We scan the hillsides with binoculars, looking for sheep. Two rough-legged hawks circle above us. A small band of ewes and lambs is spotted above a gray band of limestone rock. The rams remain elusive, grazing high up in the most inaccessible meadows, far away from any threat.

It is a cold night. The next morning the ground is covered with a light dusting of snow, and ice rims the water bucket. Longjohns feel good. It is time to get home and gather firewood and cranberries, and hunt for our winter meat. Most of the birds have already left for their winter homes in the south, the frantic mating and breeding season over for another year. Flocks of geese call above us, this time heading south. Some of the moose are also heading south, across the passes into spruce country. We take heed and head for the shelter of the boreal forest.

In late September temperatures drop and a thin sheet of ice covers the ponds, thickening rapidly. Slush ice flows down the river until it jams and becomes solid. A storm moves in from the Bering Sea, and drops snow instead of rain. Winter has arrived, and will remain until the ground is once again snow-free in May. The overwhelming sound is the silence. All the noises of water are stilled: no bubbling creeks, no rushing rivers, no wind blowing through the cottonwood and willow leaves along the banks. The cries of only an occasional gray jay or raven pierce the cold air. The quiet is deafening.

We visited the Noatak one winter in March, skiing from its headwaters back to our home south of the arctic divide, and experienced some of the magic of winter on the Noatak.

Newly arrived ptarmigans were everywhere, scratching up grit from gravel bars beneath the snow. White gyrfalcons patrolled willow thickets regularly, looking for a meal, and occasionally meeting with success. An eagle soared up high.

We went first class this trip with a wall tent, wood stove, and enough food for a month, all to be pulled in small sleds by our group of four.

Skiing was good on the river with about five to six inches of snow on top of overflow ice. But we paid whenever we tried to cut the long, meandering bends of the river. The tundra had little snow and was rough and hummocky with exposed rocks, causing too much drag for our sleds. We were forced to follow each bend, some days skiing 10 or 12 miles but making only 4 down the valley.

On some sections of the river, snow had literally been blown out of the country. Both river and tundra were bare, and skis were abandoned in favor of foot power. Other days, a stretch of fresh overflow, bank to bank, blocked our passage, the water steaming in the cold air and spreading fast. We were forced to thrash across the tundra around it. Pingos along the route gave us good vantage points for looking for wildlife. These mounds are formed in the centers of drained tundra lakes as permafrost freezes in from the sides. When the center finally freezes, the ice can only expand upward, creating a low hill.

Lois (front) and Ward Irwin skiing the Noatak in March. Ward is pulling a sled full of supplies for the trip. Courtesy of Ward Irwin

Just above such a pingo, a group of Dall sheep observed us from a windblown slope. They seemed unafraid, sensing that we were not wolves after them. A small red fox perched on the riverbank, watching us intently. Caribou were here too, small groups that have spent the winter in this valley, pawing beneath the snow for remnant horsetails.

Sled tracks surprised us one day. We had not seen another person in a month, nor heard an airplane. We later found out the tracks belonged to a trapper from Anaktuvuk Pass, camped farther down the river. When Lieutenant George M. Stoney of the U.S. Navy explored the upper Noatak by dog sled in December 1885, several small villages of Eskimos existed in the area, subsisting almost totally on caribou. Older residents of Kobuk villages still remember traveling with their parents over the mountain passes to the upper Noatak in the summer to hunt, dry meat, and obtain summer caribou skins for clothing. Now the upper river is seldom visited in winter, save for a few Eskimos traveling by snow machine between the Kobuk River villages and Anaktuvuk Pass, and a few men from Anaktuvuk who trap in the valley extensively for several months at a time.

In the last few years the Noatak has received enormous amounts of publicity from the debate over putting some of Alaska's federal lands into national parks, refuges, and forests. The numbers visiting this river in the summer have increased drastically, making it now one of the most popular float trips in the state. Changes are coming. No longer is the basin as isolated and seldom-visited as it once was. I can only hope that somehow, the qualities of wildness and solitude, of immense space and timelessness, will always remain unchanged, throughout all the seasons of the Noatak. □

THE SALMON RIVER

John McPhee

Editor's note: *This material appeared in* Coming Into The Country *(Farrar, Straus & Giroux)* ©*1977 by John McPhee, and originally appeared in* The New Yorker. *Reprinted here by permission.*

Acloud, all black and silver, crosses the sun. I put on a wool shirt. In Alaska, where waters flow in many places without the questionable benefit of names, there are nineteen streams called Salmon — thirteen Salmon Creeks, six Salmon Rivers — of which this one, the Salmon River of the Brooks Range, is the most northern, its watershed wholly above the Arctic Circle. Rising in treeless alpine tundra, it falls south into the fringes of the boreal forest, the taiga, the upper limit of the Great North Woods. Tree lines tend to be digital here, fingering into protected valleys. Plants and animals are living on margin, in cycles that are always vulnerable to change. It is five o'clock in the afternoon. The cloud, moving on, reveals the sun again, and I take off the wool shirt. The sun has been up fourteen hours, and has hours to go before it sets. It seems to be rolling slowly down a slightly inclined plane. A tributary, the Kitlik, comes in from the north-

Jack Hession (left), John McPhee, and Pat Pourchot look over parts of their kayaks on a Salmon River shore. John Kauffmann, National Park Service

The Salmon River flows south from its source in the Baird Mountains 60 miles to the Kobuk River several miles northeast of Kiana.
Heritage Conservation & Recreation Service

west. It has formed with the Salmon River a raised, flat sand-and-gravel mesopotamia — a good enough campsite, and, as a glance can tell, a fishing site to exaggerate the requirements of dinner.

There are five of us, four of whom are a state-federal study team. The subject of the study is the river. We pitch the tents side by side, two Alpine Draw-Tite tents, and gather and saw firewood: balsam poplar (more often called cottonwood); sticks of willow and alder; a whole young spruce, tip to root, dry now, torn free upriver by the ice of the breakup in spring. Tracks are numerous, coming, going, multidirectional, tracks wherever there is sand, and in gravel if it is fine enough to have taken an impression. Wolf tracks. The pointed pods of moose tracks. Tracks of the barren-ground grizzly. Some of the moose tracks are punctuated with dew-claws. The grizzlies' big toes are on the outside.

The Kitlik, narrow, and clear as the Salmon, rushes in white to the larger river, and at the confluence is a pool that could be measured in fathoms. Two, anyway. With that depth, the water is apple green, and no less transparent. Salmon and grayling, distinct and dark, move into, out of, around the pool. Many grayling rest at the bottom. There is a pair of intimate salmon, the male circling her, circling, an endless attention of rings. Leaning over, watching, we nearly fall in. The gravel is loose at the river's edge. In it is a large and recently gouged excavation, a fresh pit, close by the water. It was apparently made in a thrashing hurry. I imagine that a bear was watching the fish and got stirred up by the thought of grabbing one, but the water was too deep. Excited, lunging, the bear fell into the pool,

and it flailed back at the soft gravel, gouging the pit while trying to get enough of a purchase to haul itself out. Who can say? Whatever the story may be, the pit is the sign that is trying to tell it.

It is our turn now to fish in the deep pool. We are having grayling for dinner — Arctic grayling of firm delicious flesh. On their skins are black flecks against a field of silvery iridescence. Their dorsal fins fan up to such height that grayling are scale-model sailfish. In the cycles of the years, and the millennia, not many people have fished this river. Forest Eskimos have long seined at its mouth, but only to the third bend upstream. Eskimo hunters and woodcutters, traversing the Salmon valley, feed themselves, in part, with grayling. In all, perhaps a dozen outsiders, so far as is known, have travelled, as we have, in boats down the length of the river. Hence the grayling here have hardly been, in the vernacular of angling, fished out. Over the centuries, they have scarcely been fished. The fire is high now and is rapidly making coals. Nineteen inches is about as long as a grayling will grow in north Alaska, so we agree to return to the river anything much smaller than that. As we do routinely, we take a count of the number needed — see who will share and who can manage on his own the two or three pounds of an entire fish. Dinner from our supplies will come in hot plastic water bags and be some form of desiccated mail-order stew — Mountain House Freeze Dried Caribou Cud — followed by Mountain House Freeze Dried fruit. Everyone wants a whole fish.

Five, then. Three of us pick up rods and address the river — Bob Fedeler, Stell Newman, and I. Pat Pourchot, of the federal Bureau of Outdoor Recreation, has not yet cast a line during the trip. As he puts it, he is phasing himself out of fishing. In his work, he makes many river trips. There will always be people along who want to fish, he reasons, and by removing himself he reduces the number.

He has wearied of take-and-put fishing, of molesting the fish, of shocking the ones that, for one reason or another, go back. He says he wonders what kind of day a fish will have after spending some time on a hook. John Kauffmann has largely ignored the fishing, too. A National Park Service planner who has been working for five years in Arctic Alaska, he is a New England mastertouch dry-fly fisherman, and up here his bamboo ballet is regarded as effete. Others taunt him. He will not rise. But neither will the grayling to his Black Gnats, his Dark Cahills, his Quill Gordons. So — tall, angular — he sits and observes, and his short gray beard conceals his disgust. He does agree to time the event. He looks at his watch. Invisible lines, glittering lures go spinning to the river, sink in the pool. The rods bend. Grayling do not sulk, like the salmon. They hit and go. In nine minutes, we have our five. They are seventeen, eighteen inches long. We clean them in the Kitlik, with care that all the waste is taken by the stream. We have a grill with us, and our method with grayling is simply to set them, unscaled, fins intact, over the fire and broil them like steaks. In minutes, they are ready, and beneath their skins is a brown-streaked white flesh that is in no way inferior to the meat of trout. The sail, the dorsal fin, is an age-old remedy for toothache. Chew the fin and the pain subsides. No one has a toothache. The fins go into the fire.

When a lure falls into the water, it can become arrested at the bottom, and you tug and haul at the line and walk in an arc, whipping the rod, four-lettering the apparent snag that has spoiled the cast and is stealing your equipment. Tug some more. Possibly a small boulder or a sunken log has stopped the lure. Possibly not, too. You may have a pensive salmon. He contemplates. He is not yet ready to present his response. Not long before this river trip, I was fishing in lake-and-stream country northwest of Anchorage and

John McPhee lines his boat about seven miles below Sheep Creek on the Salmon River.
Heritage Conservation & Recreation Service

the line became snagged in a way that to me suggested big things below. When I tugged, there was a slight movement at the other end, a gesture in my direction, the signal — obviously — of an irritated salmon getting ready to explode. I strained the line. It moved a bit more in my direction. A couple of minutes later, I landed a Safeway Stores Cragmont orange-soda can, full of silt and sand.

Over the fire now, I tell that story, and Bob Fedeler responds that that country near Anchorage, where many people have summer cottages, has long since been virtually fished out and is now supplied with stocked rainbows from a state hatchery. "That is the myth of Alaska," he says. "The myth is that in Alaska there's a fish on every cast, a moose behind every tree. But the fish and the moose aren't there. People go out with high expectations, and they're disappointed. To get to the headwaters of a river like this one takes a lot of money. The state needs to look to the budgets and desires of people who cannot afford to come to a place like this."

John Kauffmann, sitting on the ground and leaning against his duffel, shifts his weight uncomfortably. "You can charter a lot of aircraft time for the cost of summer cabins and Winnebagos," he says, and he bangs his pipe on a rock.

Fedeler shrugs. He scratches his cheek, which is under a mat of russet beard. He is compact, sturdy, not particularly tall, with a wide forehead and intelligent brown eyes. He would resemble Sigmund Freud, if Sigmund Freud had been a prospector. Fedeler says that he and his wife, Lyn, almost left Alaska during their first year, because they saw so little, and could afford so little, of the outdoors, of the wild — let alone of wildlife. In 1972, he took an advanced degree from South Dakota State and straightway headed for Alaska. To support themselves, he and Lyn found jobs in Anchorage. He worked at McMahan's Furniture. He is a wildlife biologist. The state work he sought was given preferentially to people who had been resident in Alaska for at least a year. Meanwhile, in Anchorage — a city sealed away by water and mountains, a city that would be right at home at the west end of the George Washington Bridge — he had to go to the movies to see anything wild. He did not have the hundred dollars an hour needed for air charter. He did not have a hundred dollars. He knew the wilderness was out there — several hundred million acres of it — but he lacked the means to get to it, and his soul began to stale. Fortunately, he stuck out the wait, went on shoving McMahan's furniture around. At last, he got the work he wanted, his present job as a wildlife biologist with the Alaska Department of Fish and Game, based in Fairbanks.

Pat Pourchot, of Anchorage, puts in that he finds plenty to do near home. He climbs cliffs. He kayaks on fast white rivers.

Stories emerge about others like Fedeler —for example, a young man I know from Arkansas, who came to Alaska a year and half ago specifically to fish and hunt. He drove a cab in Anchorage until he couldn't stand it anymore. Taking a two-month vacation, he went home to Mountain Home. Then he came back to Alaska and his taxi. "It was the prettiest spring I've ever seen," he reported. "The dogwoods and redbuds blossomed and

Grayling cook over an open fire at one of the camps along the river.
Heritage Conservation & Recreation Service

they just stayed and stayed. I got all the fishing I wanted, in Arkansas. You need the bucks for the good hunting and fishing up here. Fishing is supposed to be, you know, so out of sight here. It really *is* out of sight for me. I haven't made the bucks."

People from outside write and say to friends in Alaska that they want to come stay with them and fish. "Fine," says the return letter, "but you'll have to charter. Air charter." "No," says the next letter. "We just want to stay at your place and fish from there." Urban Alaskans shake their heads at such foolishness and say, typically, "These people in the Lower Forty-eight, they don't understand."

Something in the general drift now has John Kauffmann on his feet and off to the river. He assembles his trout rod, threads its eyes. Six feet three, spare, he walks, in his determination, tilted forward, ten degrees from vertical, jaws clamped. He seems to be seeking reassur-

ance from the river. He seems not so much to want to catch what may become the last grayling in Arctic Alaska as to certify that it is there. With his bamboo rod, his lofted line, he now describes long drape folds in the air above the river. His shirt is old and red. There are holes in his felt hat and strips of spare rawhide around its crown. He agitates the settled fly. Nothing. Again he waves the line. He drops its passenger on the edge of fast water at the far side of the pool. There is a vacuum-implosive sound, a touch of violence at the surface of the river. We cheer. For two minutes, we wait it out while Kauffmann plays his fish. Adroitly, gingerly, he brings it in. With care, he picks it up. He then looks at us as if he is about to throw his tin star in the dust at our feet. Shame — for our triple-hooked lures, our nylon hawsers, our consequent stories of fished-out streams. He looks at his grayling. It is a twenty-five ounce midget, but it will grow. He seems to feel reassured. He removes the fly, which has scarcely nicked the fish's lips. He slips the grayling back to the stream.

Grayling are particularly fast swimmers. In Arctic Alaska, where small rivers like this one for the most part freeze solid, grayling can move big distances rapidly to seek out safe deep holes for winter. They are veterans of runs for life. They are indices, too, of the qualities of a stream. They seek out fast, cold, clear water. So do trout, of course, but grayling have higher standards. Trout will settle for subperfect waters in which grayling will refuse to live.

The sun, which two hours ago was behind the apex of a spruce across the Kitlik, is now far to the right of that and somewhat closer to the ground. All day, while the sun describes a horseshoe around the margins of the sky, the light is of the rich kind that in more southern places comes at evening, heightening walls and shadowing eaves, bringing out of things the beauty of relief. It is ten-thirty, and about time for bed. □

PLANTS AND TREES

Anore Jones

Trees

Traveling west through this region the great blanket of forest covering much of interior Alaska begins to shrink and to disperse into isolated patches and bands along the rivers and mountain bases. Approaching the coast, tundra predominates although several small forests stretch down to brackish-water inlets. Just north of Kotzebue a few stunted spruce grow on the edge of Kotzebue Sound.

White spruce *(Picea glauca)* predominates with some trees reaching 20 inches in diameter along the upper Kobuk River, although the average large tree is smaller. Black spruce *(Picea mariana)* grows smaller and more stunted throughout the same general area. In days past, spruce provided logs for fuel, rafts, and houses, and milled lumber for boats and houses. Today, with imported-lumber houses and fuel oil in fashion, the forest is mostly being saved for future generations to enjoy. However each

The headwaters of the Kobuk River flow out through forested slopes of Gates of the Arctic National Park and Preserve where black spruce grow in bogs and low-lying areas and higher, better-drained slopes support white spruce. The lighter-colored trees are birch that grow in many places along the Kobuk's winding course to the sea. Wilbur Mills

year finds more people restoring wood stoves to their homes and enjoying the healthy exercise and low expense of getting their own sweet smelling wood. Recent forest surveys have shown a rich resource of wood that is adequate on a sustained yield to supply all the needs of people on the upper Kobuk with a small surplus to market on the coast.

Large spruce roots are excellent material for carving into bowls, spoons, net floats, etc. Pencil and smaller-sized roots are split, peeled, and used to wrap willows that bind the edge of birch bark baskets.

Such a lovely tree is the birch with graceful dark branches, and white bark peeling off in layers of pastel abalone hues. Waterproof, flexible, and very durable, birch bark has always been an ideal basket material, and is still today being made into many kinds of baskets from watertight traditional berry- and food-storage baskets to those made for tourists. In fact this home basket industry has left most straight and proper-sized birch within easy walking distance without its protective bark. Stripped trees live but tend to develop rot more quickly. Studies of old stripped trees seem to indicate that some old-timers were extra skillful in removing the bark so the underlying cambium was undisturbed and could grow new bark.

But bark is not the only useful part of birch. Its tender, young leaves are good for salad and

tea, and the trunk can be tapped for sap in early spring for a refreshing beverage, birch syrup, and even candy if boiled long and carefully enough. As the primary native hardwood, birch is used to build lightweight sleds, kayaks, bowls, and other useful items. Birch and alder are very hot, long-lasting firewoods, good to put on a fire at night so plenty of coals will remain for morning. Alaska paper birch *(Betula papuryfera)* is often intermixed with cottonwood, aspen, and willows in spruce forests, but birch also grows alone.

Paper birch hybridizes with Dwarf birch *(Betula nana)* which is a dwarf to shrubby plant widespread throughout the area in both tundra and forest. These blends can create trees with copper- and wine-colored bark or shrubs with white bark.

Sixteen different species of willows grow in northwest Alaska, ranging from the dwarf coastal and mountaintop species only 1 inch high to the 15-foot-high trees along the upper Kobuk River. These large willow patches, often in the bend of a river, provide food and shelter for moose and thousands of rabbits and ptarmigans.

Old-timers also had many uses for willows. Some were used to build kayaks because the wood was lightweight and strong. Old-timers strung fish on hoops of the branches, built tent frames with the wood, burnt it for fuel (especially far north and west of the spruce

LEFT — *Ideal as basket-making material, birch bark is peeled from trees and worked into a variety of shapes. Stripping the bark does not kill the trees, but does make them more susceptible to rot. Old-timers apparently knew how to remove the bark without disturbing the cambium layer so the bark could grow back as it is doing here.*

BELOW — *Sap drips from a tapped birch tree. Sap, collected in early spring, makes a refreshing beverage, syrup, or a delicious candy if boiled long and carefully enough.*

RIGHT — *It may not look attractive, but spruce gum is not all that bad. Of the three types shown here, the yellow is softer and longer lasting.*

All by Anore Jones

found throughout the region. Knowledge of the location of the few balsam poplar groves along the windy coast used to be important for the traveler in search of fuel and shelter. Poplar is also used for lightweight sleds and carving. In lieu of blueberries in quantity, balsam poplar bark cambium provides a good laxative used with caution.

Quaking aspen *(Populus tremuloides)* grows mixed with balsam poplar, birch, or alone through the eastern half of the Kobuk valley. Like poplar, aspen burns well when dry, but with much ash. In the fall half-rotted aspen bark has a powerful perfume.

Shrubs

Two shrubs are locally used as medicine. Common juniper *(Juniperus communis)* as a tea is a good tonic. Its berry can be chewed to ward off cold. Artemisixa, or sage, is very effective as a poultice to draw out infection.

Tundra

There are many types of tundra, each determined by the location and wetness of the ground and the plants that cover it. After absorbing the vastness of the tundra, the next most memorable impression is the overpowering aroma from the crushed leaves of Eskimo tea, also known as Labrador tea *Ledum palustre).* The leaves can be dried for year-round use alone or with other teas. The leaves contain a poison, Iodol, and must be used in small amounts. The lovely white flower has its own delicious perfume.

Other characteristic plants of the tundra are cotton grass sedges and grasses.

Alone or mixed with other plants, cotton grasses form most of the sod and tussocks covering the tundra for which the North is famous. Caribou, and birds such as cranes and ptarmigan find cotton grass flowers their first fresh food in the spring.

forests), wove baskets from the roots, and made fish nets and strings from carefully prepared inner bark.

No willow is poisonous, and two are especially good to eat. River willow *(Salix alaxensis)* has a sweet inner bark and young shoots which taste refreshingly like watermelon and cucumber. Young leaves of Diamondleaf willow *(Salix planifolia* ssp. *pulchra)* at first taste acrid and unpleasant. After one or two minutes of chewing the taste becomes sweet and leaves the mouth feeling fresh. This willow is also high in Vitamin C.

Red-dyed leather on Eskimo yo-yos or mukluk ties was probably dyed with alder bark which gives a deep red-rust color to woods and leathers that are tanned with the bark. Alders *(Alnus crispus)* rival birch as a hot, long-lasting fuel, and as a good wood for carving. Alder leaves are good fertilizer.

Alder roots have nitrogen-fixing bacteria that enrich the nearby soil and fallen leaves are rich with nitrogen. The best ground for a garden is where willows and alders have been growing.

Balsam poplar *(Populus balsamifera),* locally known as cottonwood, is another tree

Campers brew Labrador tea during a May outing near Selawik.　　　　Barb Askey

119

Wild iris is just one of the many species of flowers that brighten the tundra landscape. While people of the region eat many wild plants, many other species, including wild iris, are reported to be poisonous to some degree.

Anore Jones

Children play in the 4½-foot-tall grass growing in the Kobuk valley. The grass is cut to make beds for dogs.
                                                    Anore Jones

In fact the showy cotton flowers, which make lasting bouquets if picked when they first appear, are not flowers at all, but rather the tiny seeds which are covered with cottony strands so they will blow in the wind much the same as real cotton. Cotton grass abundance indicates how good the salmonberry crop may be since both plants thrive under the same weather conditions.

The lower three or four inches of stem of cotton grass are sweet and good to eat. In the ground grows a one- to two-inch section of root that mice trim of rootlets to store in underground caches. People gather these roots to eat with *masru* or Eskimo potato.

Hundreds of flowers grow throughout the region — some the same types as domestic garden varieties: iris, daisies, aster, lupine, dandelion. Others are special arctic versions of familiar garden flowers such as delphinium, rhododendron, geranium, rose, and violet. And some are unique to the far North or high mountains like moss campion, alpine, azalea, heathers, and andromeda.

No discussion of edible plants is complete without mentioning poisonous ones, and there are several in the region. Poison water hemlock *(Cicuta mackenziana)* may be the most dangerous, especially its roots, one of which has been known to have killed a child. Death camas *(Zygadenus elegans)* has a greenish-cream flower with a plant and root vaguely resembling wild chive. Chive, however, smells like onion and has a hollow

stem. The death camas stem in cross section angles in a v-shape. Other plants in the region that have been reported as poisonous *to some degree* include: delphinium, aconitum, iris, some daisies, andromeda, narcississ-flowered anemone *(Anemone narcissiflora),* wild sweet pea *(Hedysarum mackenzii),* lupine *(Lupinus nootkatensis),* astragalus, oxytropis, cowslip *(Caltha palustris),* Eskimo tea *(Ledum palustre),* pallas buttercup *(Ranunculus pallasii),* and wild chives *(Allium schoenoprasum).*

Wild sweet pea could be mistaken for *masru,* but may only make those ill who eat it without seal oil. Raw leaves of cowslip contain a poison — helleborin — which is destroyed in cooking. Pallas buttercup has anemenol which

Wild chive is good to eat, but a similar-appearing plant, death camas, is highly poisonous.
                                                    Anore Jones

is destroyed in cooking. Leaves of wild chives can cause an upset stomach when picked too old or stored too long. Lichens in the raw state are indigestible by humans, but partially digested lichens from inside a caribou stomach are good food because the caribou's stomach has the enzymes necessary to break down the lichens.

Greens

Wild greens come up earlier than gardens in spring, and are eagerly sought for salads. Fireweed shoots, when they first appear, are a favorite salad base. To be most tender and mild, fireweed shoots must be picked young while they are still purple and the leaves are still partially closed. Large shoots even smell like asparagus when lightly boiled for a hot green with butter and a dash of vinegar.

Other favorite salad greens include willow and both types of birch leaves, which, like fireweed shoots, can be eaten in quantity and to which garden vegetables and stronger-tasting greens can be added.

A timeless Eskimo way of preserving the good taste, bright color, and healthy vitamins of wild spring greens to enjoy through the winter months is by storing them in seal oil. Vegetable oils do not seem to work as well. Two favorite greens are the sura (leaf buds of Diamondleaf willow) and coastal Sea Lovage leaves *(Ligusticum scoticum),* known locally as *Tukkaayuk.* Seal oil not only preserves the leaves, they also keep the seal oil fresher longer. Many other leaves and vegetables taste good eaten with oil, but most will not

RIGHT — *Salt-water sourdock, one of the regions most important wild staples, is collected by the gunnysacksfull for fermenting in a sourdock barrel.*   Anore Jones

BELOW — *May Brown (left) and Pauline Gooden preserve sourdock, a wild edible, at Selawik in the early 1940s.*
Courtesy of Lona Wood Collection

keep well because seal oil can only preserve a limited amount of moisture.

Perhaps the largest quantity of wild greens picked in this region are rhubarb upriver and sourdock along the coast. These greens are harvested by the gunnysacksfull, brought home, cleaned, chopped, and boiled to be stored in barrels for the winter. Both are highly acidic, and tend to ferment in a delicious way when not kept very cold. Both are eaten with sugar and often seal oil for a dessert, and feel just right after the usual meat meal.

Sourdock fermented in a barrel is just the start of a processing sequence that produces increasingly delicious sourdock as the season progresses. A gallon or more of boiled blueberries is added to the barrel for flavor, color, and fermenting power. Then ripe blackberries (crowberries) are stored in the sourdock, as many as can be stirred in, making the sourdock sweet enough so it does not need any sugar. Sourdock is even acidic enough to pickle half-dried trout bellies.

Wild rhubarb *(Polygonum alaskanum),* known locally as *Qusrimmaq,* grows along inland rivers. Although in a different genera, wild rhubarb tastes much like the garden variety. The main difference is that the leaves as well as the stalks are eaten — domestic rhubarb has poisonous leaves. Wild rhubarb can be eaten raw with oil, boiled like sourdock, or cooked with dried fruits like apples and raisins. Wild rhubarb can also be substituted for domestic rhubarb in most any recipe, the main difference being wild rhubarb's greenish color.

Berries

Cranberries and blueberries are usually the most abundant berries upriver, while salmonberries or cloudberries and crowberries grow thicker, better fruit near the coast.

Of the 13 kinds of berries growing in this region, crowberries, salmonberries (cloudberries), cranberries and blueberries are most commonly picked. In a good berry year a family may harvest 50 to 100 gallons each of berries that are abundant in any particular year and perhaps 5 to 20 gallons each of the other berries. Given abundant berries, an experienced picker can pick 10 gallons a day, although 5 gallons may be more average.

First to ripen are salmonberries, known also as *akpiks (Rubus chamaemorus).* They are orange-apricot-colored with a faintly similar taste, and they certainly fill a similar niche in the diet. Like other berries, salmonberries are most often eaten for dessert with sugar and seal oil. Beyond their immediate table use, salmonberries are an important medium in which to store blackberries.

Crowberries, known locally as blackberries or *paungak (Empetrum nigrum),* are a good berry for eating, being not as strong as

blueberries or cranberries. They also have larger, nutlike seeds which make a more satisfying food when eaten in quantity with seal oil. It is wise to eat seal oil when consuming a large amount of these berries since the seeds can have a constipating effect.

Blackberries grow on low, ericaceous shrubs that often carpet the gravel and tundra. Since some berries ripen first, it is best to pick the extra large, sweet berries leaving the rest to ripen later. If the fall is long enough, all the berries will swell big and sweet.

These flat circles of miniature shrubs keep expanding year after year, somehow maintaining a core of life through the long, harsh winter — frozen solid, wind blasted, and occasionally flooded with ocean water. Yet each June new shoots grow from old branches,

Edible berries (shown here clockwise from top left are blueberries, lowbush cranberries, crowberries [blackberries], and tinnik *or* kinnikinnick) *constitute one of the cornerstones of subsistence living in the Kotzebue Basin. Some berries keep well; others do not keep at all. But all provide vitamins and other nutritious elements, and mix well with other subsistence foods.* Manya Wik

some with male and some with female flowers so tiny they can scarcely be seen. Only from the female branches do berries grow. And each August the land is again spread with a feast of sweet berries, more than enough for all.

Tingaulik is a favorite fall treat made with a

paste of trout or tomcod livers and blackberries. The first ripe berries of the season usually go into this, and seldom are there more than enough to satisfy everyone's *Tingaulik* appetite.

Everyone loves blueberries. People in this region enjoy cookbook recipes, but the traditional way — eating blueberries with seal oil and sugar or rich milk, or in *akutuq* (Eskimo ice cream) — still predominates.

Blueberries ferment much faster than any other berry, creating a storage problem. The colder the blueberries are stored, the better they will keep. One good way is to bury them in the ground near the frost zone. They must be dug out at freezeup though because then

Ripe tinnik, *also known as* kinnikinnick, *is best picked in September and October, and stored for several months in bear fat or seal oil to allow the berries to sweeten and the seeds to soften.*   Anore Jones

the ground gets warmer. Half-dried trout bellies are delicious pickled in blueberries. And blubber that is too strong to eat can be pickled in blueberries that are too fermented to enjoy. Together they both taste better.

Unlike blueberries in keeping ability, lowbush cranberries *(Vaccinium vitis-idaea),* also known as lingonberries, keep well even for two years. Cranberries are best known for their tartness which is usually offset with a lot of sugar, or before sugar was introduced, with fat. Cranberries are the perfect compliment to a meal with a lot of seal oil or fat meat.

Another favorite food is *Ittukpalak* — raw cranberries and raw fish eggs (any fish except salmon), in about equal proportions, mashed, and whipped together. *Ittukpalak* makes a foamy, pink dessert that must be eaten right away or quick frozen — it does not keep.

Tinniks (Arctostaphylos uva-ursi), also known as *kinnikinnick,* are an often misunderstood berry either dismissed as inedibly dry and mealy, or confused with the insipid alpine bearberry *(Arctostaphylos alpina).* In this region *Tinniks* are sought and stored in oil before being eaten because the longer they are stored in oil, the better they get. The dry, mealy pulp becomes sweeter and juicier, and the large, hard seeds get softer. Then they are ready to eat with oil or put into *akutuq.* Less important berries in this area include: highbush cranberries, nagoonberries, rose hips, red fruit bearberries, bog cranberries, American red raspberries, and northern red currants.

Roots

Masru or Eskimo potato *(Hedysarum alpinum),* is the main root harvested to eat. Although it grows throughout the region, *masru* is only worth harvesting where it grows lush and in sandy soil that is easy to dig. The cream-colored, sweet roots look something like a branched parsnip and can be 20 inches

long, tapering down from a 1 inch or smaller diameter. After being dug and washed, the roots are cut up and stored, either raw or cooked, in oil.

Mice often fill their underground caches with *masru,* and sometimes people of the region can find the caches and take out the best pieces. Mice also store hairy roots of cotton grass or the little black balls from horsetail roots. Both are sweet and good eating, but much too tedious for people to dig, so let the mice do the work.

The author found this giant puffball mushroom near Noorvik. While many mushrooms are edible, others are poisonous. Mushroom picking and eating demands knowledge and caution.   Anore Jones

Mushrooms

Of numerous delicious mushrooms, puffballs and boletes are widespread. Inland one can find morels, orange delicious, inky caps, pig's ears, and sulphur shelf mushrooms. Because mushrooms can be poisonous, gathering them requires knowledge and caution. The Eskimo word for mushrooms — *argaingnat* —means "that which causes hands to come off," a stern warning.   □

BIRDS

Bob Uhl

A variety of bird species add to the beauty of tundra and mountains surrounding Kotzebue Basin. Among common species which boost bird-watching along the coast are glaucous gulls, first of the water birds to return in late April; and three species of jaegers: pomarine, parasitic, and long-tailed. Cries of mew gulls create a constant din at nesting time. Among predators, short-eared owls, golden eagles, gyrfalcons, peregrine falcons, and northern shrikes line up for their share of smaller birds and small mammals.

Arctic and red-throated loons, and northern and red phalaropes take advantage of countless ponds which dot the tundra.

Coastal lowlands provide suitable habitat for various waterfowl: brant, snow geese, white-fronted geese, Canada geese, whistling swans, harlequins and pintails. Eiders and old-squaws clamor constantly from leads in the icepack in May and June. A loud, noisy call signals the arrival of sandhill cranes.

Numerous shorebird species, including western and semipalmated sandpipers, dunlin, long-billed dowitchers, common snipe, golden plovers, whimbrels, and bar-tailed godwits join the throngs on the tundra searching for sustenance and nesting sites.

Showing the gray nape and black throat that characterizes this species, an elegant arctic loon rests on a nest of grasses and mud near Cape Krusenstern.   James D. Young

The tinkle of calling lapland longspurs and savannah sparrows mingle with notes of other passerines: robins, ruby-crowned kinglets, tree swallows, bank swallows, and white-winged crossbills.

The bird scene changes in Kotzebue Sound not only seasonally but also apparently over the long term. With their ever-present cousins, arctic terns, aleutian terns now rest in the Sisualik-Krusenstern area where they were unknown by residents until 15 years ago. Black turnstone eggs have recently been found, and the numbers of Hudsonian godwits, apparently low for many years, seem to be increasing. Tree swallows now occupy nest boxes in nearly every coastal camp where 20 years ago there was not a box or a nest to be found.

Several species that regularly spend time in Alaska but return for the balance of the year to other continents can be seen at different locations near Kotzebue Sound. Wheatear, yellow wagtail, and bluethroat are among the most regular visitors; less common are white wagtails, ruff, dotterels, spoonbill sandpipers, and rufous-necked sandpipers. Great knots and whooper swans are rare, but may occur more often than records indicate since a discerning eye and ear are needed to differentiate these species from similar but more common ones.

At least one species, sharp-tailed sandpiper, a Siberian nester, visits regularly as an immature, but seldom as an adult.

Another species, Kittlitz's murrelet, spends its life at sea except for the time the bird flies 40 miles inland to the top of a bare mountain to lay an egg and rear a chick, and then returns to the ocean environment in which the species normally exists.

Very few eggs of Kittlitz's murrelets have been found. Near Cape Prince of Wales on the Seward Peninsula one egg was found in 1935 on bare rock on a mountainside; another was found in 1943 presumably in the same mountain environment. In 1978 a geologist involved in work on the Lik-Red Dog mineral discoveries at the Wulik River headwaters, 40

LEFT — *Thousands of shorebirds, primarily dunlins, long-billed dowitchers, western sandpipers, and sharp-tailed sandpipers, gather on tundra ponds near Sisualik in preparation for fall migration.* Peter G. Connors

ABOVE — *Alert to any unusual sound or movement, a semipalmated plover sits on its nest at Cape Krusenstern. Plovers, distinguished from sandpipers by their shorter bill and large eyes, are just one of the many shorebird families that mass on lowlands of northwest Alaska before beginning their southerly migration.* James D. Young

BELOW — *A hawk owl keeps a sharp eye on photographer Frank Bird from a spruce tree along the Noatak River.*

RIGHT — *An immature gyrfalcon migrates along the coast of northwest Alaska. Largest of the falcons, gryfalcons feed primarily on ptarmigan and seabirds.* Peter G. Connors

A female willow ptarmigan goes into a distraction display near her nest at Cape Krusenstern.
Peter G. Connors

miles inland from Kivalina, flushed a bird he described as looking like a "small football with wings" from a single egg on bare rock on a mountainside.

A few hardy species brighten the long winters of Kotzebue Basin. Ravens can show up anytime throughout the region. At the right snow-covered seal breathing hole may be found a winter-plumaged black guillemot. These birds, white in their winter coat, can be expected in any mid-winter open lead in the Chukchi Sea ice off Kotzebue Sound. Open areas of the coast may produce snow buntings, ptarmigans, gyrfalcons, and snowy owls. In timbered areas fly gray jays, chickadees, and northern three-toed woodpeckers. Spruce grouse sit in the shelter of a white spruce, ever alert to avoid the talons of hawk owls and goshawks. Years of snowshoe hare abundance may entice great horned owls to Kotzebue Basin's spruce forests.

Travelers searching for the oddest sight in a mid-winter cold spell (-30°F to -50°F) might well head for one of the open springs scattered throughout NANA-land to watch a gray, wren-like bird, bouncing with flashing eye, walk deliberately into a riffle, and on into deeper water. With toes grasping pebbles on the bottom, the dipper, or water ouzel, searches the bottom of the pool for a meal.

Some species of birds have been a source of food for indigenous people in seasons when other game or fish were not available. The very existence of some cultures may have depended on birds for the pot and for clothing. This need has not entirely been whisked away by welfare support, food stamps, general economic affluence, and nearly universal access to the village store. Several species continue to be harvested in considerable number each year. Pintails, American wigeon, Canada geese, white-fronted geese, brant, oldsquaws, and some eiders are the preferred species for human consumption. Cranes and whistling swans often find their way into the pot. Of species wintering in the area, willow ptarmigan and rock ptarmigan are by far the most sought. Only minor use is made of snowy owls and spruce grouse.

Eggs of several species are gathered in moderate numbers. Large, delicious eggs (two or three per nest and more a few days later) come from glaucous gull nests in late May and early June. Seabird colonies at Cape Thompson and Chamisso Island yield murre and puffin eggs to brave cliff-climbers. Smaller numbers of arctic tern, Aleutian tern, and miscellaneous waterfowl eggs are taken at every opportunity.

Residents of northwest Alaska are both bird watchers and bird hunters. They are also aware of the dangers of overuse for they have

A western sandpiper hovers near its chick which is camouflaged to blend with summer tundra near Cape Krusenstern.
Peter G. Connors

their counterpart to the passenger pigeon. E.W. Nelson, in 1887, reported the Eskimo curlew around Kotzebue Sound. A few years later Joseph Grinnell reported seeing none in the area, and today the Eskimo curlew is believed to be extinct. Though the major factors contributing to this species' extirpation apparently occurred farther south, on its migration flyway, this lack is still a shock to bird watchers who know that a species their grandparents may have snared and netted near Kotzebue Sound will never again return to that area. □

Birds of the Upper Kobuk Valley

Editor's note: Many bird species found along the coast range farther inland; others come only to interior river valleys and hills. Ole Wik, of Ambler, offers these observations of birds along the upper Kobuk River.

The most striking thing about the birds of the upper Kobuk valley is that they differ so little from those found elsewhere in interior Alaska. A birder from Fairbanks would feel right at home in Kobuk country.

There are only a few species of birds that remain in the valley all winter. Boreal chickadees seem impossibly delicate for the climate, but their pleasant twitter brightens even the darkest, coldest days. By contrast, willow ptarmigan are supremely adapted to the snow and cold. Their cousins, spruce grouse, seem to be drawn to wood smoke. Cheeky gray jays are quickly drawn to anything edible, and daily justify their reputations as camp robbers. Ravens steal even more.

The winter woods, though silent, often show signs of bird life. Alder cone fragments on the snow indicate hoary redpolls; bark chips around the base of a dead spruce speak of the visit of a northern three-toed woodpecker. And spruce cone scales around the base of a living tree show that white-winged crossbills are in the neighborhood.

Great horned owls frequently reveal themselves by their distinctive hooting calls. Boreal, great gray, and snowy owls are far less abundant. Toward spring these meat-eaters are joined by goshawks and peregrine falcons, which make themselves unpopular by robbing ptarmigans and hares from the peoples' snares, and later by short-eared owls, marsh hawks, and golden eagles.

Birding begins to get exciting in late April when the first white-fronted and Canada geese are heard calling overhead. Every day in May there are more new arrivals. Some, like gray-cheeked and Swainson's thrushes, are quiet for the first few days after arriving, while others seem to arrive in full song. It is interesting to notice how the dawn chorus changes as the spring ripens: fox sparrows, juncos, and tree sparrows may dominate one week; robins, ruby-crowned kinglets, and yellow warblers the next.

During spring migration coastal species such as pomarine jaegers, oldsquaws, harlequins, and scoters are most likely to be seen. A few wandering tattlers are spotted every spring, but a few years pass between sightings of bar-tailed and Hudsonian godwits. Asiatic oddities such as wheatears, and white and yellow wagtails also make it up the Kobuk valley from time to time.

Many birds are far more easily detected by sound than by sight, including olive-sided flycatchers, Say's phoebes, flickers, alder flycatchers, blackpoll warblers, and Lincoln's sparrows.

Lesser yellowlegs, which are very noisy whenever a person is in their territory, are called by the Eskimos the "goose's watchdog." Natives consider it bad luck to have a golden-crowned sparrow near camp, and hear in its plaintive three-note call the Eskimo word for "I'm crying." It is considered *very* bad luck to find the nest of a gray jay, spruce grouse, or Wilson's (common) snipe.

Waterfowl provide many a meal in springtime, when the lovestruck birds are often in the air and are easily taken. Pintails, wigeon, mallards, sandhill cranes, and geese are all welcome in the stewpot. In days gone by the people used to capture flightless, molting geese and their goslings in roundups near tundra nesting ponds.

By midsummer the birds are singing less and less, and the young of the year are on the wing. Most conspicuous are the great orbs of bank swallows that buzz and rattle above the marshes, chasing mosquitoes:

By freezeup the summer migrants have gone, except for the occasional rusty blackbirds that find scraps in the dog yard well into October. Then they too go south. ☐

A male spruce grouse, in full breeding plumage, does his best to catch the eye of any nearby females. Natives in the Kobuk valley consider it bad luck to find a spruce grouse nest.
Doug Murphy

FISH

Bob Uhl

Fish of many species found in Kotzebue Sound and adjacent waters have been the real people-sustaining harvestable resource over the years. Fish, though often not as preferred for a steady diet as caribou or muktuk, do seem always to be available in one species or another in nearly all inhabited living sites. Dried fish, frozen fish, aged fish, cooked fish, pickled fish, smoked fish, fish put down in oil, fish eggs, fish heads, fish livers, fish stomachs are in some form found daily in the diet of most residents.

The one major money-making industry involving most Kotzebue residents is a million-dollar commercial chum salmon fishery.

What is the most important species? An old-timer once said, "If the Lord had not placed the lowly tomcod in Kotzebue Sound, the Eskimo culture would have perished many years ago."

Tomcod, or more properly saffron cod _(Eleginus gracilis)_ are not beautiful, nor are they especially nourishing though in late summer and fall they eat pretty well on surf-killed shrimp, crabs, and small ocean fish. The importance of tomcod is that they are there when residents need them. They winter in brackish water, in river estuary zones, and fishermen need only make a hole in the ice in the proper zone to catch multitudes with a

Chum salmon hang on racks to dry at the village of Kobuk.   John and Margaret Ibbotson

shining gig just off the bottom. In days past when no other species could be found to feed dogs or people, fishermen survived on this little fish weighing up to two pounds. Reports indicate that arctic char and sheefish feed heavily at certain seasons on tomcod. Spotted seals, ringed seals, and yearling bearded seals, and beluga whales, eat great numbers of adult and fry cod.

In contrast to unlovely tomcod is the well-proportioned sea run arctic char _(Salvelinus alpinus)_ with its bluish-green back; silvery pink, red-spotted sides and white-trimmed fins. Having a high fat content, char are a treat turned into steaks or baked whole. Rod-and-reel fishermen have good reason to appreciate this 25-pound fish because it strikes suitable lures readily once it gets into fresh water. Cooked char livers mashed to a paste and mixed with a large bowl of ripe blackberries _(Empetrum nigrum)_ is a Kotzebue Sound food specialty that could compete with any epicurean delight.

Kivalina lies at the mouth of the most easily exploited large river with a dense char population, and is famous in the region for its fat arctic char. The Noatak River has a greater population of char as it is a much larger river, and the villagers at Noatak use large quantities of the fish.

Char overwinter in fresh water, and some populations run out into the ocean at spring flush in early June, and return on the heels of

the salmon run in mid-August after feasting royally on small ocean fish and shrimp. The out-going fish in June are generally very poor cooking quality. Incoming fish have a very high oil content and are superb, cooked or frozen.

The only fish of the region to rival the char as a table fish or a lure-taker is the shee _(Stenodus leucichthus)_. Shee are large (to 60 pounds) predatory fish living exclusively on live smaller fish or other live aquatic life. Much of a shee's life is spent in brackish water.

Shee spawn in the upper Kobuk and Selawik rivers. Selawik Lake and portions of Hotham Inlet are home for a large portion of the NANA-region shee population. In late winter and early spring these fish gather in huge schools, and woe to any small whitefish, tomcod, herring, smelt, or even pike or sculpin that might be in their path. This schooling made it possible for groups of fishermen to follow schools of shee for many days, even under four or five feet of ice, with techniques and equipment developed in prehistoric times. People and dogs starved to death when no school of fish could be found in February, March or April in days long past.

Shee, in months of ice cover, may get as far toward salt water as the village of Kotzebue. Large quantities are taken in fall netting operations between Lockhardt Point and the northwest corner of Hotham Inlet. A limited commercial fishery is allowed here. Early

ABOVE — *Only arctic char rivals sheefish as a table fare and sportfishing challenge. These large, predatory fish live exclusively off live smaller fish or other live aquatic life.*   Ken Alt

LEFT — *Howard Odell (right) helps hold this 48-pound sheefish which Dave Duncan (left) caught near the mouth of the Selby River while on a raft trip down the Kobuk River.*
Dick Zeldenrust, reprinted from *ALASKA*®magazine

BELOW — *A high fat content makes arctic char especially suitable for filleting or baking. These fish readily strike appropriate lures when they enter fresh water.*
John and Margaret Ibbotson

spring hooking with hand lines takes place in the much wider full reaches of Hotham Inlet and Selawik Lake.

Flesh of a large, 15- to 20-pound shee is superb food, but much unlike the pinkish meat of the arctic char. Shee flesh is white, firm, and mild-flavored.

Chum salmon, here in the farthest north river system suitable for their development, are the big money maker for many people of the region. Two important facts have made this possible. Though the salmon are at the northern limit of their range, living conditions here prove satisfactory enough that the quality of chum is very high. The second factor is the timing of the run. The run is late, and occurs at a time when salmon on the rest of the North Pacific coast are at a low ebb. Thus, on the fresh fish market Kotzebue chums bring premium prices.

Commercial salmon fishing was pioneered in the area by John Backland of Seattle who in 1912 built the Midnight Sun Packing Company on the site now occupied by Arctic Lighterage. He worked the operation through 1915, with only two traps and very few employees, and

ABOVE — *Commercial salmon fishing in Kotzebue Basin began in 1912 when John Backland of Seattle built the Midnight Sun Packing Company facility at Kotzebue.*
Nichols Collection, Courtesy of Mark Ocker

RIGHT — *Faith Moyer of Kobuk splits chum salmon with an* ulu, *an Eskimo women's knife.*
John and Margaret Ibbotson, reprinted from *ALASKA* ®magazine

the operation continued to be listed in fisheries reports until 1919 although there was no further pack.

The present commercial salmon fishery began very late compared to the rest of the state (1962), and has fluctuated much between very high and very low years for fishermen. Nevertheless, it has become a million dollar a year industry, and promises a brighter future as more information on biology and a fisheries enhancement project are put into operation.

Subsistence use of chum salmon at Noatak and Kobuk villages is considerable, and is a necessary part of their life style. Chums do not have much to offer the hook-and-line fisherman.

Though there are several species of whitefish in the region that have some local use, two

A commercial fisherman sells his chum salmon catch at Kotzebue. Even though Kotzebue Sound is the northern limit of their range, chums from this fishery bring high prices because of their high quality and because their run culminates when other salmon runs along the North Pacific coast are at a low ebb.
Dave Sweigert

species are by far the most important. In coastal habitats the Alaska whitefish *(Coregonus nelsoni)* is the most used species being superb for drying or freezing. Fat individuals make a good table fish.

Broad whitefish *(Coregonus nasus)*, less inclined to enter salt-tainted water, is a minor species in coastal areas but of major importance in the river systems, especially the Kobuk and Selawik.

Grayling and great northern pike, two species that have some subsistence use and are a favorite for rod-and-reel fishermen, generally speaking are fish of inland waterways: the grayling in mountain streams or larger rivers, and the pike in lowland rivers, lakes, and sloughs. The Kobuk and Selawik delta areas have huge populations of pike as do the Noatak flats just downriver from the village.

Burbot or mudshark *(Lota lota)* is another fresh-water fish much appreciated by people of the land for its good liver and tasty flesh. This species is a fresh-water cod that runs to 40 pounds, and readily takes a lure, especially at night.

Eskimo women from Ambler seine for whitefish — a subsistence diet staple — along the Kobuk River in September.
Robert Belous, National Park Service, reprinted from *ALASKA* ®magazine

Rainbow smelt and herring are abundant along the coast, and current studies are bringing to light more interesting facts on these tasty species that overwinter on the saltier side of the transient brackish zone. Shee, char, marine mammals, and people use these oily fleshed plankton eaters.

An interesting, exclusively coastal fish is the

arctic cod *(Boreogadus saida)* called *Kahlauq.* These are small, 6- to 12-inch, bluish-black, big-headed fish that can appear in unbelievable numbers in October at various Kotzebue Sound coastal locations. Although very scarce near shore the rest of the year, by October arctic cod are so numerous they make black-looking patches in the blue water as the schools move slowly along.

Seals gulp down the cod; glaucous gull yearlings gorge themselves, stand on one leg for awhile, then gorge again. Young eiders of several species do the same, and still, when there is a slight onshore chop to the waves and a narrow trough in beach gravel during freezing weather, many thousands of tons of arctic cod can be deposited live by waves on the beach gravel where they immediately freeze. Area residents can look both directions down the beach at dawn and see a three-foot-wide ribbon of fresh frozen arctic cod.

When eaten frozen, arctic cod have very soft, chewable bones; a creamy, tasty flesh; two half-cigarette-size roe skeins, and a deliciously oily liver. They are also delicious fried. Such tremendous numbers do not happen every year but it is indeed a spectacular happening when they do.

For the angler who has met every fishing challenge, the Kotzebue Sound region holds yet one other challenge that might prove diffi-

Salmon roe becomes food for village dogs at Kobuk village, a small settlement on the upper Kobuk.   John and Margaret Ibbotson

cult to meet. There is a rare fish that has occurred often enough over the years to have acquired an Eskimo name. No English or Latin names are known, and until recently the fish was simply a mystery among local residents. Now there seems reason to believe that the mystery fish is not a separate species, but a hybrid that has been found in Siberia when shee and Bering cisco *(Coregonus laurettae)* spawn over the same stream-bottom area. The result is a larger fish than the cisco. It is shee-size with a mouth of cisco proportions. When cooked, it has the white flaky texture of shee combined with the sweet, extremely oily flesh typical of Bering cisco.

Each season commercial and subsistence fishermen look forward to change. For the commercial fishermen, a site has been chosen and preliminary work begun on the lower Noatak River for a chum salmon hatchery enhancement program by the Alaska Department of Fish and Game. If this project works successfully, chum runs might not only be increased every year, but fluctuation in egg yield and maturation might also be smoothed out to produce a more consistent volume of harvestable fish. With the large number of limited entry permits and the amount of gear fished in the sound, some assurance of more salmon is certainly good news to commercial fishermen in an area that at present has only one species to commercially exploit.

Selawik built a community fish-curing facility with commercial potential in 1980, and other isolated sites may well become interested in commercial fishing in the near future.

The possibility of a commercial herring fishery for the sound has been much discussed, and finally in 1980 state biologists actively compiled data to determine the idea's feasibility.

For anglers there is in the works an in-depth arctic char study that should aid understanding this fish's life pattern. Fish and Game personnel are investigating and tagging char

A favorite of rod-and-reel fishermen, northern pike prefer inland waterways, especially lowland rivers, lakes, and sloughs. Kobuk and Selawik river deltas and the Noatak flats downriver from Noatak village shelter huge populations of northern pike.   Manya Wik

on the Kivalina, Wulik, and Noatak rivers, as well as at coastal sites between the rivers.

Some mysteries remain in understanding the other major sportfish, the shee. Investigations continue, but it seems apparent that the basic stock and area of production is so limited that commercial shee use will continue to be limited and monitored closely.

Kotzebue Sound's abundant fish resources will remain a sustaining factor for its people and may be a bit of insurance. Residents have been hooked on gasoline and stove oil for less than 50 years. Before that — for ages — fish and wind, directly or indirectly powered, lighted, and warmed everything.   □

The Pike of Springtime

Ole Wik,
photos by Ole and Manya Wik

Editor's note: *A similar version of this story first appeared in The Bass & Pike Issue of* Gray's Sporting Journal, *Volume Four, Issue 4, July 1979.*

As the Kobuk winter deepens, a quiet change takes place beneath the thickening, snow-dimmed ice of tundra lakes. Without light, aquatic plants stop producing oxygen, and without oxygen, fish cannot live. As the water in the lakes begins to go dead, fish drift down the slough systems toward more favorable wintering places. Some travel all the way to the major rivers, while others take refuge in the few lakes that for one reason or another remain sweet right through breakup.

Our Eskimo friends told us about one such lake during our first winter in the valley. They said that little ducks sometimes dived beneath the surface of the lake, never to reappear — victims of the large pike that lived there. Hooking, they said, was best in the month before breakup. And so, late that first spring, we hitched the dogs and set out for the lake.

We had a first-class spoon-type ice auger, and it bit through the ice with great promise. But soon the crank was hard against the surface of the ice, with better than a foot yet to go. This meant that we had to chop out a basin large enough to accommodate the full sweep of the crank, and then kneel awkwardly, butts high in the air, to complete the hole.

After about an hour of this we broke through the ice... and hit mud. This was puzzling. We drilled another hole, farther from shore, and got mud again. From the third hole we got water... but no fish. By this time we had little doubt that we'd somehow gotten turned around, and were on the wrong lake. A week or two later we got together with our Eskimo friends and straightened out the confusion, but by then the season was too far advanced for cross-country travel.

The next spring we went out again, and that time we found the right lake. We were in the process of rediscovering the sheer effort involved in putting a hole through five and a half feet of ice when we happened to notice fresh bear tracks along one edge of the lake. That was all the excuse we needed. We packed up our tackle, still dry, and set the dogs on the trail of a different sort of dinner.

Ten more springs passed, and ten times I thought about the lake. Why did Eskimos insist that the lake was unique? One year I made up my mind to find out. I sent for a good screw-type auger and a ten-inch extension. I cut the extension in half and welded in another 14 inches of rod, giving a unit that, fully assembled, stood more than seven feet tall. I was certain it would handle any ice in the valley.

The following April we hitched up the dogs, loaded the sled, and mushed downriver to our spring camp, as we do every year. I got up early the first morning in camp and set out alone across the tundra for the lake. Wind clouds stood like lenses over the summits of the mountains, and *nigiqpaq*, the North Wind, swept unhindered across the valley, fluttering the tail of my parka before hurrying on. By now I knew every birch knoll, every tree-rimmed slough so well that I found it hard to recall the time when these lakes had all looked the same to me.

Patches of bare ground were already visible on the tundra, and the sun stood well above the horizon to the northeast, speaking of springtime. But the lake itself was still covered with hard, sculptured snow dunes, and the wind spoke the language of winter. Though I wanted to rest, it was too cold to stand still for long, I quickly assembled the auger and picked a spot for my first hole.

The first few turns felt awkward, since the crank was at the level of the top of my head; but as the blades bit through the ice and the hole deepened I was able to get my full power into it. I watched the chips pile up as first the blade disappeared down the hole, then the extension, and then the final joint. By this time I was on my knees, and the crank seemed as if it, too, would soon jam against the ice. But all at once the blade broke through, and sweet, blue water gushed up to fill the hole.

I cleared the hole of ice chips, readied a spoon, and lowered it down the hole. The April sunlight, penetrating the ice, was bent and concentrated by the walls of the hole, so that the lure flashed with unexpected brilliance as it sank toward the darker waters below.

As I jigged, I gazed at my surroundings. The lake itself was almost a mile across. On its banks stood a few groves of healthy white spruce, flourishing in soil well enough drained to hold the permafrost at bay. Behind these stood a few scraggly, struggling black spruce, capable of surviving in poorer soil, and a few graceful birches on isolated knolls. Beyond lay nothing but tundra, sweeping to the mountains that notched the horizon in every direction.

The minutes passed without action. As much to get warm as to explore, I moved farther along the shore and put down another hole. This time I made some measurements, and found that my auger went through just under six feet of ice in seven minutes. Still there were no fish, so I kept going.

At the fifth hole, in 30 feet of clear water, I felt that first tap. I'd had a strike. Within a minute the fish returned, and I was leaning over the hole, and retrieving my line.

Up came a fat, shimmering *qallusraq,* a small member of the whitefish tribe. Suddenly I remembered the story of the two old women who had camped at the lake long ago, just after the ice had gone out. They had strung a net near the outlet, and had caught masses of whitefish so fat that they wouldn't dry properly. The women dug a cache hole, stored the catch against the permafrost, covered them with moss for insulation, and returned in the falltime to retrieve the fish for dog food.

ABOVE and UPPER RIGHT — *Outfitted with a screw-type auger into which he had welded an extension rod, Ole Wik drills holes through ice several feet thick in search of tasty pike.*

RIGHT — *A northern pike is hauled up through a hole in the ice.*

Things were looking up, for now I had bait. I cut a minnow-sized flap of flesh from the fish's belly, put it on the hook of my spoon, and started to jig again. Within minutes a sleek, glistening northern, all mouth and teeth, came thrashing up through the hole and lay green, gold and glossy white against the sky blue ice at my feet.

Satisfaction. How many men in ages past, I wondered, had stood upon this very lake, clad all in furs, gazing in thankfulness at the first fresh fish of the season? Could this lake, these tundras have looked any different a thousand years ago?

I scaled the whitefish, rinsed the scales into the hole, and watched them spiral down the tunnel past my line. Up came another pike, then another whitefish. Cold now, I made the rounds of the other holes, jigging for a while in each, and then I put down a few more holes. I

UPPER LEFT — *Manya Wik prepares pike for drying.*

LEFT — *Strips of northern pike hang to dry.*

ABOVE — *Kalle Wik pulls a bundle of pike across the ice, while the dogs, their noses working overtime, follow behind.*

had caught ten fish — enough, with rabbits and ptarmigans, to hold us until we could return with a proper camp.

By the time my wife Manya, son Kalle, and I set out for the lake a week later, the first of the warblers were flitting among the swelling buds on the willows, and we could hear the mysterious wind song of snipe overhead. Much of the tundra was now completely bare, and I had to jog ahead of the sled, winding from one wind-packed snowdrift to the next, picking a route that would give the easiest pulling.

Lakes which lay beneath hard-packed snow a week earlier were now covered with a deep layer of grey-blue slush, so we followed the sloping snowdrifts that still ringed the banks. Our fishing lake alone, of all the many we saw that day, was free of slush, and when we drove the team out onto the ice, we saw why.

Ice belongs on top of water, not the other way around, and the meltwater had found its way through my fishing holes into the lakes. Melted-out gullies fed into each of the holes, which were now twice their former size. Responding to the inflow of water, the ice had risen. This gave the surface a definite bow, since the ice was still frozen down all around the shoreline. We could plainly see that the center of the lake was higher than the edges, so that meltwater from now on would tend to collect in a moat right next to shore.

We made camp on a gently sloping snowdrift at one edge of the lake, where some spruce trees would screen us if the north wind began to blow. By now the season was too far along for snowmobile travel, and we knew that we would have no visitors. Several hundred square miles of wilderness would be ours alone for perhaps a week, until the snow bridges across the slowly filling tundra sloughs threatened to become unsafe even for the dogs. Then we would have to make our way back to our main camp over what little snow still remained.

We made good use of the time, and of the new auger — which made it possible to do a great deal of exploration with little effort. My experience with pike is that they tend to hit right away, almost as soon as the lure goes into the water, so if I didn't find action in the first few minutes, I'd move on and drill another hole. I'd jig there for a while, and then make the rounds of all the other holes. If I caught a fish in any one of them, I'd make the entire circuit again; if not, I'd go drill some more.

In this way we gradually developed an array of holes that gave us a feeling for the contour of the bottom and for the kind of water that the fish liked. We found that the best fishing was unquestionably in the shallow water near the outlet of the lake. Our most productive hole, in fact, was in a spot where only two feet of water separated the ice from the mud. We called this the "hot hole," because it produced so much better than others as little as ten steps away.

When Manya cleaned the first day's catch, she found that we were catching males and females in roughly equal numbers, and that the females were loaded with eggs. Pike leave their wintering lakes as soon as the ice goes out, and then spawn along the grassy edges of the sloughs. We reasoned that the fishing was especially good at the outlet because the fish were gathering there, ready to leave the lake as soon as the dead water in the slough was flushed out by the spring runoff.

Since it was so easy to drill holes, we decided to explore some of the other lakes nearby. We loaded the sled early one morning, before the sun softened the snow, and

crossed over to another lake system. The auger brought up yellow-brown water, clogged with bits of flocculated iron that signaled that there was no free oxygen left in the lake. We crossed a stretch of tundra to another lake, and then another, always with the same result.

Gradually it dawned on me why a few lakes had fish while most others were dead. All these tundra lakes are linked together like beads on a string, draining from one to the next through connecting sloughs. Very likely the shallowest lakes and the sloughs would be the first to go dead as winter progressed. The bad water would then spread to all the other lakes downstream. The only lakes that would stand much chance of remaining sweet through the winter would be those without inlets, either at the very heads of the slough systems or else off to one side. Ours was just such a lake; the nearest one like it lay about four miles farther back from the river.

These particular lakes would act as accumulators in wintertime, drawing the fish populations of the sloughs and several nearby lakes. In other words, the fish we were pulling up through our tiny array of holes really represented the produce of a number of lakes, temporarily concentrated in an unusually favorable spot. Like the Old Time People before us, we had made camp at a choke point where a migration had produced, for a while, an abundance of food.

We returned to the lake, content with what Nature might give us. Manya and I would move from hole to hole, pulling up a fish from time to time, and Kalle would busy himself scooting the dogsled around on the ice, picking up the fish that lay beside the various holes.

In all our days on the lake, I never did land

one of those duckling-eating monsters that our friends had spoken of. But I did ensnarl one long enough to see what they looked like. The fish, lightly hooked, hadn't been able to shake free because a loop of leader had tangled in one of its jaw tines, and I played it for a few minutes. At one point it lay sideways against the bottom of the ice, completely blocking the six-inch hole. I could see neither its back nor its belly — only a wall of pike skin. Finally it flipped over, dropped the loop of line, and flashed away. No matter; the smaller fish are better for drying anyway.

As the days passed and the sloughs slowly filled, water began trickling into the lake from its outlet. If anything, the scent of slough water seemed to draw even more fish to our holes. But one afternoon a snow dam somewhere up the slough system let go, and brown water suddenly began pouring into the lake. Within minutes the water in our holes changed color, and the fish quit biting altogether.

Our hours on the lake were now numbered. The incoming water was lifting the ice in the middle of the lake more and more, and the moat around the edges was deepening fast. We had to get off the lake while a few of the larger snowbanks still provided ramps from the lake up to the land. In some parts of the moat, the water was already hip-deep.

We struck camp, taking care to cache the fish-rack poles for next year, and headed back toward our base camp. The river would break up in a week or so, and the dogs, already shedding their winter fur, would begin their long rest.

The lake, five miles from the river over increasingly soggy tundra, would see no more human visitors until snowtime. But its pike, dried in the cool breezes of late May, would give us lunch for half the summer. □

THE RISE AND FALL OF REINDEERING

Long before the coming of white men, Alaska Eskimos attempted to buy live reindeer from their Siberian neighbors but the Siberians, who depended on their fine deer pelts as a staple for American trade, wisely refused to sell.

Caribou, a close cousin of reindeer, generally served Alaskans almost as well, providing skins for clothing and iron-rich meat, but just before the turn of the century, the wild herds all but vanished from northwest Alaska. Some blamed the caribou's disappearance on the influx of whalers and miners and the introduction of firearms, while others believe the animals simply shifted their migration pattern to the east. In any case their scarcity proved a hardship.

In 1890 Sheldon Jackson, a Presbyterian missionary who headed the Bureau of Education reported to Congress on the "destitute condition of the Alaska Eskimo," and arranged for the introduction of a bill asking for $15,000 to establish agricultural experimental stations for the introduction of reindeer. Jackson became such an enthusiastic advocate of reindeer husbandry that when legislation failed, he raised $2,146 in public donations, personally importing 16 deer to the Aleutians in 1891 and 171 more to Teller on the Seward Peninsula the following season.

The Aleutian reindeer quickly disappeared and Siberian herders, brought over to introduce reindeer husbandry in Teller, proved unsatisfactory, but Jackson continued to lobby Congress, winning a $6,000 appropriation in 1894 and annual funding thereafter in ever increasing amounts. The Russians placed an embargo on the exportation of deer in 1902 but by then, Jackson had purchased 1,280 animals and the transplanted herds were rapidly expanding.

The thrust of Jackson's program was to bring economic stability to the Eskimo population, not only with a supply of meat but with a means of entering the cash economy; and an ambitious apprentice system was established whereby Eskimos working five years could obtain the nucleus of a small herd.

Reindeer were introduced at Kotzebue in 1901 with the loan of 95 deer to the Friends Mission which was to take charge of Eskimo training. Alfred Nilima, a Laplander with much experience in deer husbandry, was hired to assist the missionaries, married into an Eskimo family, and built up a sizeable herd for the region.

Reindeer were likewise established at Kivalina and Deering in 1905 and Jackson's reports to Congress grew increasingly enthusiastic. "A change from the condition of hunters to that of herders is a long step upward in the scale of civilization," he proclaimed. And, not only were Eskimos being brought into the system, but other needs of the area were being met as well.

With due publicity Jackson rushed reindeer to starving miners on the upper Yukon in 1898 and, although the herd arrived almost a half a year after the fact and miners had survived on local fare, another herd was marched overland with great hoopla to starving whalers stranded by the northern icepack at Barrow.

Jackson's early reports also contain enthusiastic accounts of the introduction of sled deer, an innovation he predicted would soon replace dogs as local transport.

Congress shared Jackson's enthusiasm, appropriating $207,500 for the fledgling industry from 1894 through 1904, but some congressmen had second thoughts, and in 1905 special investigator Frank Churchill was sent north to assess the program.

Churchill reported that contrary to Jackson's estimates, only a few Eskimos had gotten into the new program.

"As yet, comparatively few Natives appear inclined to take up deer raising when left to themselves, as it means regularity of work of an irksome character which is distasteful to them."

had killed reindeer, to "put them in irons and keep them awhile on board, giving them as much of a scare as possible. We must do something to cause them to leave the reindeer alone."

Since the Lapps, hired by Jackson to train Eskimo herders, were allowed by contract to kill deer for their own use, the ban against Natives doing the same seemed unjust to some. And the contracts apprentice herders were required to sign with herd supervisors were varied and complicated, often requiring the men to take delayed payment and detailing numerous minor infractions for which an Eskimo could be fired on the whim of a supervisor.

Even more damning was Churchill's examination of herd ownership. The Reverend

BELOW — *Noorvik herders arrive at a reindeer fair, bringing Old Glory and their own banner with them. These fairs, which included competitive events and trading, attracted villagers from throughout the Kotzebue Basin.*
Lomen Family Collection, Archives, University of Alaska, Fairbanks

ABOVE — *Lapp reindeer herders and their families cluster near a sailboat they used to travel up and down the Kotzebue coast. One of the first Laplanders brought to the area to show local people how to handle the reindeer was Alfred Nilima who arrived near the turn of the century, married an Eskimo woman, and stayed on to build a substantial reindeer herd.*
Courtesy of Mrs. Fletcher Gregg

Nor did benefits of the industry appear to be many for the Natives. Despite Jackson's numerous press releases on feeding starving Eskimos, Natives were not allowed to kill reindeer for their own use and deer meat was not included in the weekly rations of herders. In fact, in 1897 Jackson urged Captain Francis Tuttle of the *Bear* to arrest some Eskimos who

Jackson had long drawn two salaries, he pointed out, one as superintendent of the Presbyterian Board of Missions for Alaska and a second as education commissioner. And the educator blatantly favored religious interests.

In an 1896 reindeer report Jackson had maintained, "The missionaries are the wisest and most disinterested friends the Natives have," insisting the churchmen could best direct transfer of deer ownership from government to Natives as the Eskimos learned to assume responsiblity.

"That they have done this to some extent is true," Churchill wrote, "but various reports of natives having deer is not very considerable, while the herds accumulated and now claimed as property of the missionaries constitute a very large part of all reindeer in Alaska."

Of a total of 732 deer at the Kotzebue station that year, Churchill found 310 belonged to the Friends Church; 370 to Nilima, the Lapp herder; and only 47 to Natives.

Odds were better at Deering where Karmun, the head Eskimo herder, owned 318 animals; two of his assistants, 25; and the mission 136; however, Churchill also was concerned with the monopoly of single, enterprising Eskimos and argued that successful herders like Karmun should not be backed by a $100 annual stipend and rations from the government.

Churchill questioned the propriety of giving government herds to the missions and voiced concern that now the reindeer business was proving lucrative, it would attract even more ambitious whites.

"It is believed the proper course from now on is to gradually get the deer into the hands of the natives and, so far as possible to allow no white man, under any pretext, to buy or control female deer," he warned.

The impact of this investigation is not certain. Congress continued to support the industry, but shortly thereafter Jackson resigned his position and by 1918 herds were owned 69% by Eskimos, 3% by the government, 5% by the missions and 23% by Laplanders or others.

This was the heyday of the reindeer

C.B.H. Inn.

industry. The number of deer in Alaska was estimated at 100,000 divided into 98 herds with ownership distributed among more than 1,500 Eskimos.

Walter C. Shields, reindeer superintendent from 1910 until his death in the flu epidemic of 1918, instituted annual reindeer fairs featuring competition in herding skills and races that brought together herders and their families from throughout the region. There was pride and status in being a reindeer man.

However, just as Churchill had feared, white men gained increasing control over the industry and Eskimo owners, whose operations were for the most part small, could not compete with well-financed companies like Lomen Brothers which owned trading posts and transport as well as stock.

When the local meat market declined with the pull out of miners around World War I, the Lomens began to promote stateside; developed a huge cold storage plant (using natural underground ice deposits) out at Elephant Point; built their own railway to reach its shipping facilities; and drastically lowered meat prices.

Eskimos who wished to complain of monopoly faced a member of the Lomen family who sat as district judge, and bitterness began to grow. The Reindeer Act of 1937 restricted the holding of domesticated reindeer to Natives, but by then the industry was pretty much dead.

Caribou again roamed the tundra offering readily available meat to hunters; luring whole herds of reindeer into the wild. Wolves were

Walter C. Shields (standing in dark cap) became reindeer superintendent in 1910. Since many advocates of an expanded reindeer industry argued that sleds pulled by deer were just as feasible as sleds pulled by dogs, Shields planned a journey around the Kotzebue area by deer sled. Sitting on the sled are (left) Miss Hawks, a teacher; and Mrs. Louise Nichols, a missionary. Nichols Collection, Courtesy of Mark Ocker

an increasing menace. Some say the range was about to give out. And there was little market for reindeer products.

By the time NANA Regional Corporation decided to invest in the business as a hedge against declining subsistence sources such as caribou in 1976, there were only two small herds of reindeer left in the area. □

143

RETURN OF THE REINDEER

Lael Morgan

Snow squalls obscured visibility, but pilot Doug Sheldon needed only occasional breaks in the weather to pick his way around Kotzebue Sound to the Seward Peninsula and down the tundra valley to rambling Kiwalik River.

In a rare glimmer of sun, he pointed out the reindeer herd foraging placidly through the snows below and, beyond, gravelly tailings left over from mining operations led the way home.

Another squall engulfed us and, more by feel than by sight, Sheldon eased his two-seater Piper Cub in for a feather-soft, touch down on a huge dirt strip.

His wife, Tessie; grandson, Ula Bear; daughter-in-law, Tina; and a horse were there to greet us. Smoke puffed from several chimneys which was in itself extraordinary.

The former ghost town of Candle is making a comeback. For starters it has one of the best airstrips in the area, large enough to take a four-engined Hercules. There are currently 12 permanent residents in the wintertime. And the town is back on the mail run again with its own zip code, 99728.

Candle began just after the turn of the century as a gold mining camp, named for the candlewood willows which are as close to real trees as grown in these parts. A post office was opened in 1902, and photos shortly after show false-fronted log businesses, and a jail and U.S. Deputy Marshal.

Around 1910 the population crested at 204, but the settlement remained viable until fire burned its heart out in 1966.

The reason for its revival is the same as for

BELOW — *Doug Sheldon (left) and Bud Williams try their hand at reindeer herding from horseback near Candle. Williams and his wife Eunice came to the Aleutians to work for a cattleman, and were lured to Kotzebue Basin when NANA decided to experiment with horses and dogs to herd reindeer.* Lael Morgan, staff

With pride, my hostess led me on a tour of the town and Hollywood, a suburb across the stream which had escaped the fire and still featured an enclave of mining buildings, old and new.

On a neighboring hill deserted Fairhaven Hospital still stood, nearly as straight as it had been when it was dedicated many decades ago. Its name, still legible on the wind-buffed sign, was that of the mining district, forgotten now by all but a few old prospectors. Beyond, in the protection of a muted spruce, was the Candle cemetery with ornate tombstones cleverly crafted from welded iron.

With a roar, the only active automobile in town hurried by. Fred Weinard and his wife Mary were moving from their camp at the mine to their winter home in town, the Covenant Church which they had occupied since their house burned in the 1966 fire. Except for the steeple, the former place of worship made a conventional and comfortable home.

Weinard's dad had immigrated from Sweden to southeast Alaska, then had come to Candle to work for Seattle interests as superintendent of Kiwalik Mining Company. Weinard's mother had been running a hotel in town when the couple met.

"I've been here all my life... a mining mechanic. When Arctic Circle had the company in the 1940s and 50s there were two dredges, over 100 men working at the time," the old-timer recalled. "Now there are no big nuggets. Just spots here and there. Pretty small."

Other permanent residents, besides Fred's son Brian, who also worked at the mine, were

its founding — gold. With the price up, owners of mining claims in the area have taken a second look at ground that was thought to have been played out. And some, like Fred A. and Mary Weinard, never gave up on Candle anyway.

There is no reason, though, for miners to linger in the isolated spot in wintertime for prospects freeze up fast here. What makes Candle active all year-round is reindeer for NANA Corporation has made Candle headquarters for its growing herd.

Sheldon, a mechanical wizard, had long worked as maintenance man first for the Kotzebue school system and then for NANA after it came into being in 1972, but essentially he was a man of the tundra and his wife Tessie, who spent all her young life in Candle, longed to return.

"I decided I might as well be a reindeer herder," Sheldon recounted. "My bosses at NANA were surprised to say the least — and not too pleased. But I took a cut in wages of $10,000 to get this job."

Tessie's father long served as U.S. Commissioner and postmaster of Candle and her grandfather, Alfred Nilima, had been a herder here, recruited from Finland by the government to teach Eskimos the techniques of raising reindeer.

Elephant Point, on the nearby coast, at one time served as headquarters for the Lomen Brothers' gigantic reindeer operations. Frank Whaley, who had flown for the Lomens in the days when herds on the peninsula numbered 350,000, told me that a great underground storage area that could refrigerate 10,000 deer carcasses had been built there.

Candle, about 40 miles to the west, was the nearest fair-sized town and a natural place for families of the herders to gravitate. Tessie's old family photos depict them as a handsome, hardy lot, posed by a small sail boat by which they commuted.

Reindeer forage on the tundra near Buckland.
John and Margaret Ibbotson

Eunice and Bud Williams, ranchers who came to the Aleutians to work for a cattleman and were lured north when NANA decided to experiment with horses and dogs for rounding up reindeer.

The experiment was a bold gamble. Traditionally reindeer were herded on foot. Modern day Eskimos use snow machines in winter and planes or helicopters in summer, but both methods are cumbersome, noisy, and keep the herd stirred up.

Horses were not new to the tundra. In fact, a barn which once housed 27 horses still stood behind Sheldon's house, a relic of the past when the beasts were used to haul freight. But horses had never been used for reindeer herding because old-timers believed they just wouldn't work.

The Williams had a remarkable way with animals, however, and in short order they had learned to ride right into the midst of a grazing herd without startling the deer. And they had also discovered they could move large herds efficiently with the help of a couple of dogs.

Williams' daughter, Tina, had come out to visit the previous summer, and stayed on to marry Sheldon's son, Joe, a herder and artist, which brought the two families close together. And while some Eskimo herders resisted the idea of playing cowboy, the Sheldons were willing to give it a try.

Their first and only horseback riding lesson had left much to be taught, Doug admitted with a grin, but he was game to try again, and so was I. The herd was too far away to reach easily on foot, and there was not yet enough snow for a machine. If I was going to see the deer, horseback was the only way to go.

Thin ice covering the first river almost did us in. Our horses, realizing they were in charge, saw no reason to follow Williams across, and Sheldon and I spent some time traveling in circles.

"Let the horse know you're boss," Williams suggested. I responded by giving the creature enthusiastic kicks with my snow machine boots which was rather like flailing it with balloons. Doug, who tried to reason with his horse in English and Eskimo, had little better luck. He was, after all, an airplane pilot.

Finally Williams returned, and got us going again. It was a long ride punctuated with snow squalls, but after a while fear and pain gave way to hope that we would survive to see the reindeer and eventually we made it.

The animals were spread out on the tundra as far as the eye could see, and although we startled them due to the novice riders in our troop, Doug and Bud managed to ride within working distance of them.

The trip home was one of the most beautiful I have ever experienced. As we headed along the riverbed to Candle it began to snow in earnest; huge, flowerlike flakes which frosted

ABOVE — *NANA officials cut horns from a reindeer during the first reindeer roundup in recent times in Kotzebue. Horns are processed into medicinal compounds in the Orient.*

LEFT — *John Schaeffer, executive director of NANA and a strong supporter of the reindeer industry, strokes a pet deer at Kotzebue.*

Both by Lael Morgan, staff

the red-leafed willows and turned the world around us to softly focused pastels.

That evening Doug fired up a small electric generator and the Williams came over to show us movies that Eunice had made the previous summer of Bud and their daughter working large herds of deer with their dogs. It had been the first season for man and beasts, and I was amazed to see the ease with which Williams handled the large herds. No wonder Sheldon was willing to suffer the indignity of riding lessons.

There was also footage of Sheldon and others trying to train a stubborn young deer to harness which was better than any slap-stick

comedy I had ever seen. Old-timers had used sled deer as Eskimos used dog teams and Russian herders still rode them, but NANA's early training sessions were not too smooth.

Still, NANA Corporation had come a long way in a short time. The corporation went into the reindeer business in 1976, more for the meat than the money, for the area's caribou herds were then declining and hunting had become a concern of subsistence users.

Although the Native corporation fielded many multi-million-dollar investments, reindeer was a low budget item. I had watched their first round-up when Native leaders and office staff — all inexperienced and soft from too much desk work — pitched in to dehorn the fledgling herd of 800 animals.

This first attempt at wrestling reindeer was as funny as the sled deer training films, but the young Eskimos had learned quickly and well. Today NANA's herd numbers 7,000 to 8,000 head, brings in about three-quarters of a million dollars annually (mainly through the sale of horns which oriental buyers believe have medicinal qualities) and employs 15 people full time.

There are problems. Skins of the animals cannot be used commercially because of damage done by warble flies, but working with scientists, the Eskimos are controlling pests.

Growth of the herd, currently the corporation's major concern, will be governed by range land leases, and there is considerable debate about how many deer available land can accommodate. But Sheldon and NANA executive director John Schaeffer dare dream of a 10- to 20-million-dollar reindeer industry that will someday serve as a mainstay for village life. ☐

►*Since the writer's tour of the reindeer camp in late 1979 Doug Sheldon has resigned from the NANA reindeer operation but headquarters is still at Candle and the thrust of the operation remains the same.*

ARCTIC GARDENING

Tony Schuerch

Tony Schuerch, a native of Kiana, received his bachelor's and master's degrees from Brigham Young University. He is deeply involved in the economic development of northwest Alaska, and is president of two companies; Kobuk Valley Educational Services and Arctic Jomax Construction, Inc.

We Inupiat are traditionally hunters and fishermen, not farmers. There is no evidence that our people ever cultivated crops before the coming of the white man. The closest the Inupiat ever came to that was gathering wild edible plants. It came as a surprise to many people to learn that even the most traditional of our villagers are accepting gardening with such enthusiasm. Still, it should not have been surprising. As one elderly villager told me, "All my life I have to travel to get food. Now I just get it by my house."

The story of gardening among our people began with the coming of the first white men who settled here near the turn of the century. Miners, missionaries, teachers, and traders often brought seeds with them to plant in the summer. Our people were fascinated, and very soon were gardening themselves. Some of these early gardens were quite successful. But most of the white people were transient, and soon moved on. Eskimo gardeners, meanwhile, did not have the knowledge and experience to know what to do when they encountered problems. For example, few of them understood the need for continued fertilization. They watched their crop yields diminish yearly as they continued to garden

Tony Schuerch (left) passes bags of potatoes to residents of Ambler after the fall harvest.
Curtis Dearborn

149

An Eskimo gardener plants his crop at Ambler on the Kobuk River north of the arctic circle. Prior to the Marston Gardening Project land in northwest Alaska was considered unsuitable for gardening. But efforts of local gardeners have shown that with patience and the proper knowledge and equipment the land can produce a wide variety of crops.
Curtis H. Dearborn, reprinted from *ALASKA*®magazine

on the same plot, until eventually it was no longer worth the time and effort to plant a garden. Chemical fertilizer was unknown. Organic fertilization was vaguely understood, but since the ground is frozen for eight months each year, composting can only take place during the short summer season.

Some of these early gardeners learned they could get better crops if they relocated their gardens every few years. But cultivating new ground in the tundra sod by hand is a back-breaking task. Tundra topsoil is usually peat, which in its undisturbed state lies in rubbery layers matted together. One disgruntled gardener compared his ground-breaking efforts to "trying to pulverize wet moosehide with a shovel."

As a child growing up in Kiana, I observed quite a number of families raising gardens. But

when I returned home with my family in summer 1976, there were probably less than eight Native families growing gardens in the entire region. Nearly all of these were older people whose efforts were not being noticed or copied by the younger generation.

My wife and children and I had gardened down south, both to supplement our food requirements and for recreation. We were amazed at how easy and enjoyable gardening could be, if one had the latest equipment and materials. We determined to try gardening when we returned to the Arctic.

Photographer Tommy Ongtooguk holds one of the huge cabbages for which Alaska is renowned at a garden in Ambler.
Courtesy of Tommy Ongtooguk

In Kotzebue I began trying to gather information on gardening in the Arctic. Although Alaska agriculture was being promoted at the time, virtually nothing had been researched on agriculture in the Arctic. While visiting Fairbanks on business one day, I went to the Cooperative Extension Service offices to get some help. There someone gave me the name of Muktuk Marston as a possible funding source for an arctic gardening project. Marston, as the organizer of the Alaska Territorial Guard, was a living legend in Alaska. He had spent years pursuing a dream of getting his Eskimo friends to garden and farm, with very little success. I wrote to him asking if he would be interested in funding a small experimental project in village gardening. Marston had his wife Elsie respond favorably to my letter, and soon we had $5,500.

Soon after, I contacted Native leaders in three Kobuk villages to try to get some interest. One person responded, Art Douglas of Ambler. He invited me to bring the project to the village and promised local support.

In June 1977 my son Matt and I arrived in Ambler with a load of fertilizer, fencing, seed, bedding plants, a new power tiller, and all our camping gear. At first we felt some misgiving, wondering how we would feel if things did not work out. But we need not have worried. Ambler people welcomed us, and allowed us to try out the tiller on their proposed garden spots. We were all surprised and delighted at the speed and ease with which the tiller made pulverized seedbed out of tundra sod. The people had never seen chemical fertilizer before either, and expressed some misgiving about it. They did spread the fertilizer on their gardens, however.

Gardening seemed to become a family activity, involving both men and women. I had been afraid that the men who took great pride in their ability as hunters would consider gardening to be demeaning. But to my surprise the most successful and renowned

Tommy Ongtooguk June 12, 1991

LEFT — *Robert Cleveland tills the soil of his garden plot at Ambler.*
                                    Tommy Ongtooguk

BELOW — *Harry Tickett washes turnips from a Kobuk valley garden at Shungnak.*
                                    Tommy Ongtooguk

hunters became the most successful and enthusiastic gardeners. It was they who asked the most questions, and were most concerned about getting maximum production. Only later did I realize how closely related subsistence living is to gardening. In fact, villagers often refer to gardening as subsistence farming.

Successes at Ambler gave us the confidence to expand the project to other villages, and since then it has been difficult to keep up with the interest and demand from other villages for a gardening project. The first year in Ambler we saw about 25 gardens. The second year we expanded the project to include ten villages which produced about 250 gardens. The third year the project served 25 villages and produced about 550 gardens. In summer 1980, the project was in 35 communities from Naknek to Noatak, in four regions of western Alaska. Between 700 and 800 gardens were grown.

Despite the fact that more than 95% of the Native gardeners had never gardened before the project came to their community, they were nearly all successful. Nearly all vegetable varieties did well. People grew beets, broccoli, Brussels sprouts, cabbage, carrots, cauliflower, celery, chives, collards, kale, kohlrabi, head and leaf lettuce, mustard greens, onions from sets, parsnips, peas, potatoes, radishes, rhubarb, summer squash, swiss chard, and turnips. In addition to these cool weather crops, a few gardeners grew cucumbers, beans, tomatoes, strawberries, and pumpkins, all of which were marginal. Although the gardeners are continually surprising themselves with the variety of crops that can be grown, there are limitations. This is, after all, still the Arctic, and it is probably safe to assume watermelons will not become a major crop here. In addition to vegetables, Eskimo women show a high interest in growing flowers. Certain varieties do very well in the Arctic.

The gardening project is really more an *effort* than it is a *program*. It has no full-time professionals, and is aimed at simply making things easier for those who want to garden. Through the Marston Foundation and Brigham Young University, tillers, seeds, fencing, and

Tony Schuerch surveys his crop of pumpkins in his garden at Kiana on the Kobuk River. (The pumpkins later ripened in storage.) In addition to pumpkin, lettuce, radishes, onions, peas, turnips, potatoes, several other vegetables and flowers are cultivated in Kotzebue Basin.
Curtis H. Dearborn, reprinted from *ALASKA*®magazine

The Wik family of Ambler used the project rototiller to prepare the soil for their garden plot. "Now that we've tested various sites, we're ready to enlarge the garden and really go to town gardening," says Manya Wik who took this photo of one season's efforts.

sense, and have proved to be very resourceful. When they experiment and succeed, as they often do, the credit is theirs, and they share the newly gained knowledge with their neighbors. When we are asked, as we frequently are, if we have an experiment station, we jokingly reply that we have 700 of them this year.

Of course, with this amount of interest and activity in gardening, there were bound to be a few foresighted and outstanding individuals who began to envision long-range social and economic development opportunities. Grant Ballot is one of these. A talented and energetic young leader from Selawik, he envisioned the development of farming there. But since Selawik is located in a swampy area, he and other local Native leaders decided to develop an agricultural site 15 miles north, on the south slope of the Hockley Hills. Ballot obtained a state legislative appropriation of $412,000 for his village, and planting is now in full swing. "Our goal," says Ballot, "is to become self-reliant in food production. We need an alternative to government dependency and a supplement to subsistence." Rural Venture, Inc., a development corporation centered in Minneapolis, has been contracted to furnish professional planning and development expertise.

The first farming effort, however, is taking place in Ambler, where the project first began. It is being operated as a private enterprise on NANA lands and on the Native allotment of Nelson Griest. Griest, who was raised in the old nomadic Eskimo tradition, never saw a white man before he reached young adulthood.

fertilizer are donated for the use of each village. Wherever possible, the people are asked to buy seeds and fertilizer at cost to encourage self-reliance and independence. Village gardeners do best when someone is available to visit them in the early spring to tune up and make repairs on the village tiller, bring in new seed supplies, and hold a community meeting to teach and motivate the would-be gardeners. Gardening is still new enough so that most families need some encouragement to get started. Always, we encourage the gardeners to experiment with new methods and new varieties. Arctic gardening is new enough so that there are no real experts in it yet, and we all are learning together. Every year some enterprising gardener discovers something that we did not know before.

Perhaps one of the most humbling experiences came that first summer in Ambler, when I had brought Dr. Curtis Dearborn, research horticulturist, into Ambler to evaluate our crops. Earlier in the year we had told the people not to bother trying to grow tomatoes, as it could not be done without a greenhouse. Walking beside the home of one of the gardeners, Dr. Dearborn remarked on the fine looking tomato plants in Ike Douglas's front yard. I told him I didn't know Ike had planted tomatoes. Later, when we saw Ike, he denied planting any tomatoes. Dr. Dearborn then directed us to three tomato plants nearly overgrown with weeds, one of which had ripe fruit on it. While all three of us stood there wondering how they got there, Ike's wife came out of the house and asked us what could be so interesting in the area where she dumped her kitchen garbage scraps. Those wild tomato plants reminded us of how little we know about just what the limits are of arctic gardening.

Some people have expressed surprise that we would encourage inexperienced people to experiment with new gardening methods. But Inupiat are full of ingenuity and common

Since the gardening project began, he has been motivated to farm commercially, but had neither the equipment nor the resources to do so. In spring 1980 his dream became a reality when Control Data Corporation of Minneapolis donated $90,000 worth of tractor, implements, fuel, and support services to help him get started. Under the example and instruction of Pete Christenson of Fairbanks, Griest became a capable operator and mechanic, and cleared forty acres of land in the spring and summer. Although prudence would dictate that he wait a year for the ground to warm up before planting his first crop, he went on to plant a large test crop of potatoes right away. It was an unusually poor year, with the first killing frost on the last day of July. Nevertheless, he managed to harvest 1,100 pounds of potatoes, most of which he sold. As nearly as we know, he is the first Eskimo farmer in Alaska's history. With this taste of success, he is now planning a full-blown effort in potato production for next spring.

Having heard of these efforts, Brigham Young University's Dr. Dale Tingey collected and shipped 50,000 pounds of fertilizer for Selawik and Ambler. It is now safely in storage in these communities, ready for application in the spring.

In summer 1980, for the first time, carefully monitored test plots of grain were planted in several locations in the Kobuk valley by Dr. Frank Wooding of the University of Alaska. As a result of these tests, Dr. Wooding has confirmed that barley can be ripened in the Kobuk valley, and possibly oats and wheat in a good year. At this time it is impossible to say what these developments will lead to, but there is talk of feedlotting reindeer and bringing in sheep and goats.

We could never have imagined back in spring 1977 just what would result from our little agricultural experiments. But one good thing leads to another, and Inupiat are quick to recognize a good thing. Our Native corporation leaders have placed their support and encouragement behind the agricultural efforts. In a recent news article, NANA President John Schaeffer is quoted as saying, "Right now we import almost all of our food. But if we can grow our own foodstuffs, we can significantly reduce our dependence on imports."

We Inupiat have always loved the land, and today as yesterday, our survival and security depend on it. But now we are discovering the land is much more valuable than to chase game over, or to camp on, or to dig minerals out of. We are learning that in exchange for an investment of care and labor, the land will produce wonderful foods which were unknown to our people not long ago. By learning to farm, we are insuring that future generations of people here will not only survive, but will prosper as well. ☐

ABOVE — *Elsie Marston, widow of Colonel Marvin "Muktuk" Marston, samples kale from Joyce Denslow's garden at Ambler. In the foreground grow chard and Brussels sprouts.*
Barbara McManus

RIGHT — *Barbara McManus displays some of the bountiful harvest from her garden at Ambler. For vegetable lovers there is plenty of turnips, kohlrabi, cabbage, lettuce, potatoes, and onions.*   Courtesy of Barbara McManus

ARTS AND CRAFTS IN THE KOTZEBUE BASIN

Dorothy Jean Ray, photos by Dorothy Jean Ray, except as noted

An authority on Alaska Native art, Mrs. Ray is the author of several books on her favorite subject. The latest, Aleut and Eskimo Art, *is due off the press soon. In 1947 Mrs. Ray made a three-month prospecting trip to the head of the Noatak, and in 1961 she canoed down the Reed and Kobuk rivers. An Alaska resident from 1945 to 1954, Mrs. Ray now lives in Port Townsend, Washington.*

The arts and crafts of Kotzebue Sound and its two important tributaries, the Kobuk and Noatak rivers, were generally similar during the 19th century, but there were significant differences that set them apart. Kobuk and Noatak people neither carved ivory nor made wooden masks, both of which have become widely associated with Alaska Eskimo art; in contrast a number of ivory and wooden objects have been collected from "Kotzebue Sound."

The provenience, "Kotzebue Sound," included objects made by people living in a large area extending from northern Seward Peninsula to Kotzebue as well as by Eskimos from distant villages such as Point Hope and Wales. The Kotzebue trade fair of the 18th and 19th centuries brought together hundreds of "foreign" Eskimos annually for trading, fishing, and hunting the white whale. After American traders and expedition ships began stopping at the huge encampment during the second half of the 19th century (on August 22, 1884, Lieutenant J.C. Cantwell estimated that the camp contained 1,400 Eskimos), the people began offering artifacts for sale. Therefore, it is probable that some of the objects collected at "Kotzebue Sound" and now labeled as such in our museums, actually came from other places. The first objects ever illustrated from northern Alaska, however, were collected at a summer camp on the southern shore of Kotzebue Sound at Goodhope Bay, that is, the northern shore of Seward Peninsula. These ivory sculptures and drill bows were sketched by Ludovik Choris, the artist of Otto von Kotzebue's expedition.

People of the two rivers had a rather limited inventory of arts and crafts objects compared to coastal Eskimos. They did not hunt walrus (there was actually little walrus hunting even in Kotzebue Sound) which may account for the small amount of worked ivory in both prehistoric and historic times. They were able to obtain ivory tusks, however, from traders at the Kotzebue fair, yet they chose not to use ivory for their tools or art work.

Few objects were collected from the Kobuk and Noatak inhabitants, especially during the early souvenir trade, because they lived off the beaten path of the usual ships and traders. The souvenir business grew to immense size after the discovery of gold near Nome in September 1898, but the hundreds of prospectors who were lured to Kotzebue Sound and the Kobuk River by fraudulent reports of gold several months before the Nome gold strike found few, if any, artifacts to buy from the Eskimos who visited them on the banks of the Kobuk during the winter of 1898-1899.

The impression that Kobuk River arts and crafts were "unEskimo" because of the lack of ivory objects and masks was further strengthened by the use of two unusual materials, nephrite (the Alaska variety of jade), which was found in Alaska only north of the Kobuk, and birch bark, which was generally associated with Athabascan Indian crafts.

Many nephrite tools dating from the 16th century A.D. have been found in the Kobuk area. These tools were aboriginal trade items, about which early explorers to many parts of Alaska remarked. During the 19th century, simple ovate pendants of jade were popular amulets for curing illness all along the coast of western Alaska.

It is somewhat of an anomaly that this valuable material was traded afar when, according to Cantwell, the Eskimos avoided the Jade Mountains, the principal source of nephrite, because of their resident malevolent spirits. But J. Louis Giddings, the archaeologist, was told by the Kobuk people in 1940 that their ancestors had walked from Onion Portage — now a famous archaeological site —to the Jade Mountains, apparently without fear of any kind, to get "as much jade as they wanted." They then cut it into chunks with slabs of sandy schist, wearing it down to the required shape on a piece of sandstone.

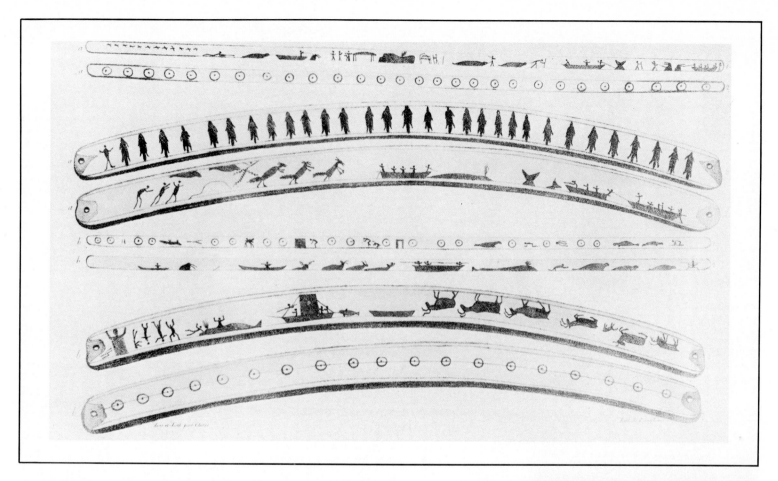

Very little jade was worked during the early part of the 20th century, but in 1952, the Indian Arts and Crafts Board of the U.S. Department of the Interior in cooperation with the Alaska Native Service, established the Shungnak Jade Project, hoping to provide a source of income for Eskimos from the sale of jade jewelry and other objects. In 1953 and 1954 they set up a summer shop in Kotzebue where there was a good tourist market. Eskimo craftsmen produced and marketed objects such as bookends, gavels, crosses, earrings, rings, tie clasps, bracelets, and pendants

ABOVE — *Ludovik Choris, artist of Otto von Kotzebue's expedition in 1816, sketched these ivory sculptures and drill bows.*
From *A Voyage of Discovery, into the South Sea and Beering's Strait . . . in the years 1815-1818,* courtesy of Dorothy Jean Ray

RIGHT — *Workers of the Shungnak Jade Project made this seal-shaped nephrite earring.*

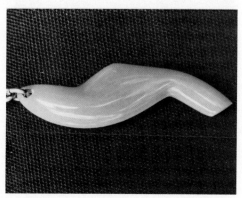

in a range of nephrite colors from light to dark green. The earring shaped like a seal in the illustration is made from an ashy light-green jade. When I visited the project in Shungnak in

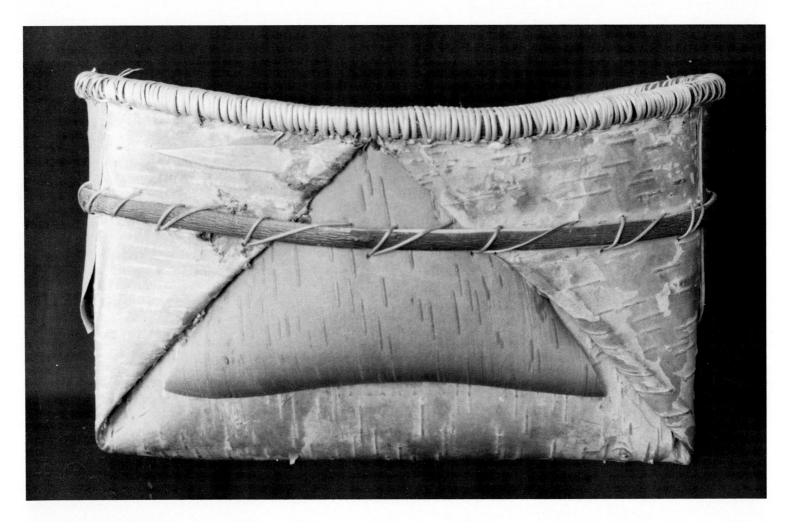

1961, it was near abandonment. The jade had proved to be difficult to work, the overhead was too costly, marketing problems had not been solved, and the participants' interest had waned — in an area where carving had never been emphasized anyway.

Jade has had a revival, however, and is now one of the projects of the NANA Regional Corporation in the spacious workrooms of the Museum of the Arctic in Kotzebue, established subsequent to passage of the Alaska Native Claims Settlement Act of 1971. With better machinery and successful financing, the workmen turn out a variety of products, including table tops, lamp shades, and mosaic designs from nephrite mined on the Jade Mountains, which the corporation purchased from a private owner.

Although the Kobuk people did not use the standing or drift spruce of their area for masks, they had mastered the techniques of making birch bark platters, baskets, and watertight

Susie Stocking of Kobuk made this birch bark basket in 1961. The rim is lashed with smooth split spruce root.

canoes. Cantwell, who explored the Kobuk River in 1884, remarked that the upper Kobuk birch bark canoes, eight to ten feet long and waterproofed with melted spruce gum, were "of most exquisite design."

Fragments of birch bark baskets date back to the 13th century A.D., and baskets in both traditional envelope style and of innovative designs are made for sale today in Ambler, Kobuk, and Shungnak. Envelope-style baskets that I bought in 1961 at Kobuk were made on the same pattern as those photographed in 1928 by Edward S. Curtis, and illustrated in his *North American Indian.* One of the new designs is an alternating light and dark diamond motif made with the outer white birch bark and the underside of the bark which is brown when collected in early autumn. Kobuk and Noatak women did not make twined or coiled grass baskets.

The people of Kotzebue Sound and tributary rivers used natural substances rather than carved objects for dancing finery and amulets. For ceremonies they preferred to wear heads

An alternating light-and-dark design decorates this birch bark basket made by Florence Douglas of Shungnak in 1967. The light comes from the white outer birch bark, the dark from the underside of the bark which is brown when collected in early autumn.

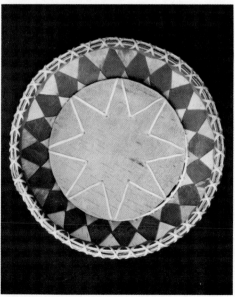

and wings of animals and birds instead of masks, and for amulets they used natural objects thought to have specific magical properties, although they did make some carved ivory and wooden amulets. Beads, which were luxury trade items in the early 1800s, were also used as amulets, a large bead often costing as much as a whole fox skin. Women strung tiny seed beads purely as ornamentation in their ears or hair.

Edward W. Nelson, the author of the monumental book, *The Eskimo about Bering Strait* (1899), tried to collect as many objects as possible when he visited Kotzebue Sound in 1881, yet, compared to his collections from other Eskimo areas, it is quite small. His attempts to collect charms and amulets met with failure. One charm especially intrigued him — a wooden object in the shape of a strange, tusked animal, which held a beluga (white whale) from a row of teeth placed beneath it along the entire length of its abdomen. He collected other fine specimens, however, which are now in the Smithsonian Institution: an arrow straightener made of ivory in the shape of a caribou lying down, engraved drill bows and bag handles, and needle cases with delicate sculptures of animals on the sides.

Despite the meager production of sculpture of any kind from the rivers, Lieutenant George M. Stoney, another Kobuk River explorer, collected an unusual and artistically splendid figure of a woman made from a gray stone in 1886. Only 3³⁄₁₆ inches high and less than a quarter inch thick, it is unique in both material and style, and only its tattoos and markings on the chest indicate that it is a woman. This piece possibly was made especially for Stoney when he was living at Fort Cosmos, near the present village of Shungnak during the winter of 1885-1886.

Stoney had also commissioned a man to engrave a walrus tusk with the names of the expedition's members as well as typical

A stone figure of a woman, 3³⁄₁₆ inches high but only ³⁄₁₆ of an inch thick, was obtained by Lieutenant George M. Stoney near Shungnak in 1886.

Eskimo activities, although he did not mention it in his writings. The engraving appears to have been done by the same hand that engraved two ivory pipes, also collected by Stoney supposedly at Kotzebue Sound, and illustrated by both Nelson and W.J. Hoffman. However, I believe that Stoney mislabeled the pipes because the subject matter and style of engraving were much more like those that came from the Saint Michael area than from Kotzebue. The majority of pipes and engraved tusks made from the 1870s to the 1900s came from Saint Michael where traders provided walrus tusks for carving.

Kobuk and Noatak peoples dressed in special, fancy fur clothing for dances and other ceremonies, but early visitors to the area invariably remarked that their designs and trim were not as elaborate as on the coast. The women, however, especially around Kotzebue, were as skilled in sewing as their coastal relatives, and when the Nome Skin Sewers Cooperative Association was active in Nome during the 1940s and 1950s, people from this area sent slippers and mukluks to be sold on consignment. Mrs. Emma Willoya, manager of

ABOVE — A ptarmigan-quill belt decorated with the words "Hugo Eckardt Mining Man" was in the Kotzebue museum in 1973.

RIGHT — In 1968 Mamie M. Beaver crafted this Easter card for her friends Mable and David W. Johnson.

the Skin Sewers, told me that the women of Kotzebue sent her the best hard-soled (from oogruk, or bearded seal) slippers of all the villages. At the present time there is a renewed interest in sewing fur parkas, especially fancy ones, a trend that is evident among all Alaska Eskimo women who still know how to sew furs.

One of the unusual arts of this area is ptarmigan-quill weaving, usually in the form of belts. John Murdoch, the scientist, first noticed these "feather belts," as he called them, at Point Barrow in 1881, and though he said that they appeared to be "peculiar to the Point Barrow region," others are known to have come from Kotzebue, Noatak, and Noorvik. (The Alaska State Museum in Juneau has quill belts from both Point Barrow and the Noatak

River from the 1920s.) According to Murdoch, they were worn only by the men, usually with an amulet suspended from the back.

In the 1950s, several women of Noorvik revived this craft and produced a number of belts and napkin rings. The attractiveness of the design stems from the contrast between the black tail quills and the white wing quills, which are woven on a nine-strand warp, one heavy middle sinew braid flanked by four strands on each side. They are rarely made now because of the difficulty of obtaining and preparing the quills, and a request I made in 1976 to have a napkin ring made was still unfulfilled in 1980.

Pottery making was of importance in prehistoric times in all of this area. However, like the Eskimos of Alaska generally, they did not make high-grade pottery, nor did they decorate it attractively. In 1881 at Hotham Inlet, Nelson sketched a tall pot with slightly flared and scalloped rim, with short, straight marks incised in rows down the pot vertically. There, at the summer camp, he saw many such pots, which varied from two- to three-gallons capacity. As late as 1928, Curtis saw both stone and clay lamps and "Swedish oil stoves" used for cooking and heating at Noatak.

Kotzebue has been a center for Eskimo arts ever since non-native traders settled there, drawing artisans from distant places. For

ABOVE — *Calvin Oktollik made this ivory swan for a bola tie in 1973.*

BELOW — *Abraham Howarth made this sled from a caribou jaw about 1968.*

RIGHT — *Johnny Evak, Sr. carved this whalebone billiken, about nine inches tall, about 1972.*

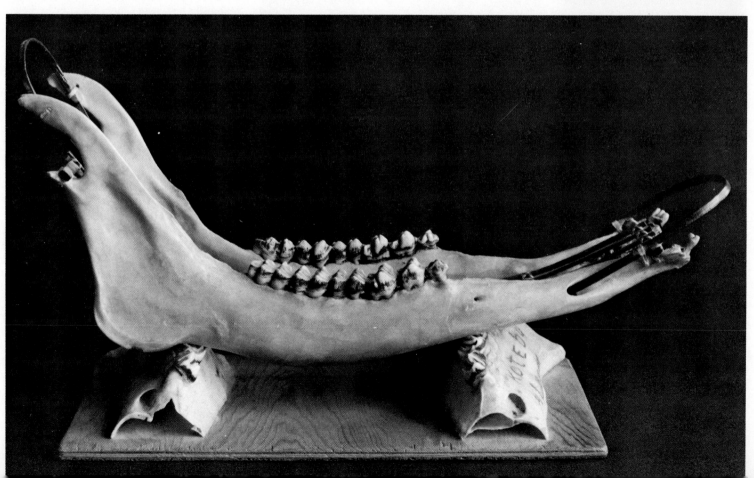

One of the most renowned doll makers in Alaska history, Ethel Washington crafted this pair about 1955.

example, some of the Diomede Islanders occasionally chose to go to Kotzebue instead of Nome for a summer of carving ivory and making fur slippers. A number of people from other villages have also come to live permanently in Kotzebue. The provenience, "Kotzebue," has therefore continued to be a term that encompasses objects made by people both originally from Kotzebue and outlying villages.

The list of producing artists over the years is too long to give here, but illustrations of a few creations will give a small idea of the variety of objects that have come from Kotzebue: the exquisite bird made for a bola tie by Calvin Oktollik in 1973; an Easter card made by Mamie Beaver for her friends, Mabel and David W. Johnson in 1968; a "sled" created in the 1960s from the jawbone of a caribou by Abraham Howarth, who had been a member of the famous relief party to Wrangel Island on the *Donaldson* in the early 1920s; an outsize billiken made from whalebone by Johnny Evak, Sr., about 1972; and two dolls made by one of the most renowned doll makers in all of Alaska history, Ethel Washington, about 1955.

Birch bark baskets, jade objects, and cloth and fur articles now form the bulk of present goods for sale, but one can always find a few ivory and stone carvings and pen and ink drawings in the Kotzebue stores. For the people themselves, the traditional bentwood buckets, clay pottery, sandstone lamps, woven willow bags and nets, mountain sheep horn ladles, snowshoes, bark canoes, and grass matting have given away to metal pans and ladles, crockery, electric light bulbs, nylon netting, commercially made snowshoes, wooden boats with outboard motors, and plastic sheeting. □

Jade

Photos by Lael Morgan, except as noted.

Early explorers noted Alaskans made wide use of only one precious mineral — jade. In 1778 Captain James Cook reported "greenstone" was used here as a cutting element for tools and weapons and for occasional ornaments, but outsiders needed another 100 years to discover that the Kobuk area was the mineral's source. Not that Eskimos made any secret of the location of the mother lode. The deposit was so large they could afford to be generous and, unlike other aboriginal people, they did not hold jade sacred.

"The Innuits call it fire stone and say it is made in a very hot fire from some of the volcanic cones of their mountains," wrote naturalist E.W. Nelson in 1883. And, scientifically speaking, they were right.

Of course there were legends about the remarkable stone. One legend told that a Kobuk man once built an entire house of jade, beautifully lighted because of the green translucence of the mineral. Those who lived in dark sod houses coveted the jade enough to take it from him, and pieces of jade can still be seen far from the original source on a hill frequented now by berry pickers.

But Eskimos favored jade mainly because it was harder and sharper than anything else available to them. White man introduced more wieldy knives and axes of steel, but even these could not chip or scratch hard Kobuk jade.

How Eskimos worked jade remains a mystery. Old-timers remember it was sometimes polished by placing pieces in a seal-

NANA craftsmen designed this jade bear which was carved in the Orient.

BELOW — *This jade boulder appears as it would in its raw state in the mountains surrounding the Kobuk drainage where it was found.*

BOTTOM — *A sawed jade boulder from Dahl Creek in the Brooks Range shows the more familiar green of processed jade.*

Both by Steve McCutcheon

skin poke with sand, then tying the poke to a supple willow branch to be tumbled in a stream. The jade could have been cut using cottonwood sticks dipped in water with sand as an abrasive, but the process would have been long and laborious.

In 1885 Lieutenant George M. Stoney, guided by two Eskimos, pinpointed the Jade Mountains, and brought out samples of the gem for analysis.

Inserted here is his firsthand account as published 13 years after the fact in the U.S. Naval Institute Proceedings, December 1899.

Expedition to Jade Mountain

On my first visit to Hotham inlet I noticed that the natives had a great many implements made of jade stone, and one man had a piece in the rough state. I inquired where they had gotten it and was told "on the big river" meaning the "Putnam" for which I was searching. When I discovered the river, and again asked about the jade, I was told it was further up.

On my second visit, the mountain where it was said to exist, was pointed out from the river, but the natives refused to accompany me to it, saying that they would never return — that only the medicine men could visit it, and then not until after a long fasting. I tried in every way to get at least one of them to go but without success. One man finally pointed out to me the best route, and I decided to take one white man and go anyhow.

On reaching the mountain I saw a green stone in large quantities; but it was so tough that only with the greatest difficulty did I succeed in chipping off some specimens with a cold chisel. These specimens were sent to the Smithsonian Institution, but proved not to be jade. In conversation afterwards, Professor Spencer F. Baird, then at the head of the Institute, told me that if I could find the jade deposit it would be one of the great discoveries of the age. So on my third expedition I determined to make a special effort to find it.

On July 27, 1886, I left Camp Purcell, Pipe Spit, in the "Explorer" to visit the group of mountains which I had named Baird and find the jade stone. I went up the Putnam to the

point nearest the mountains, left the "Explorer" and started overland. The expedition consisted of myself, two white men, five natives, and three days' rations. The walking over the tundra was severe and the mosquitoes terrible both day and night. Owing to the recent rains the creeks were very much swollen and the party was obliged to swim across one. This stream, about thirty yards wide, was running at the rate of five or six knots in the middle with still water along the banks. I made a raft of theodolite legs and tent poles; and to make it more buoyant inflated our skin boots and tied them all around it. I then made a tow-line of all the odds and ends at hand, straps, ropes, etc. Those who could, swam over, temperature of water 38 F., the rest were rafted across, as were the stores, tied up in a rubber blanket. Later on, we forded another creek in water up to our waists. Much of the walking was through water knee deep.

On August 1, I reached the mountains and spent two days digging and looking for the jade. The entire spur of mountains was of green stone and amongst it I found the jade. I also found asbestos in the strata of the rocks. I saw only a few marks that indicated visits of the natives. I got a round of angles from near the top on one of the mountains. On the return, the coal vein discovered on my second trip, was visited. This coal was not good. Specimens of the rocks and coal were forwarded to the Smithsonian Institution. The road back was less irksome as the water had fallen so that all streams were fordable. August 3 I reached the "Explorer" and August 7 reached Camp Purcell, Pipe Spit.

Prof. Thos. Wilson, Curator, Division of Pre-historic Archaeology, U.S. National Museum, Mr. J.R. Bishop and Prof. Geo. F. Kunz, of New York, have taken great interest in this jade deposit.

163

Years ago Ray Heinrichs sent Kotzebue jade to German carvers with a number of design ideas. This mastodon is a product of that era. The piece is now owned by Mable Walsh.

Lieutenant J.C. Cantwell, a competitive explorer with the Revenue Service, also reported the location that year, but the find caused no excitement for this was the era of the great Alaska gold rush. Chinese and those from other distant cultures valued jade far higher than gold, imbuing it with lucky and health-giving properties and much admiring its beauty, but Americans had little use for it.

U.S. Geological Survey personnel studied the find in 1913 and again in 1930, but interest was marginal. And, according to the late Archie Ferguson who moved to the country in 1917 and stayed through the early 1950s, the jade had yet to make anyone rich, including himself.

According to Ferguson, the area was first staked in 1907 by trader Hugo Echardt and Harry Brown who ran a store and post office at Kobuk. Later the claims fell to Tom Berryman, a Kotzebue trader.

"He had that mountain staked but he didn't know what to do with it so he gave it up," Ferguson told the *Seattle Times* in 1955. "The next to win it was Walter Cohen. In 1925 B. Hanson took it over. The three men have since died and didn't get anything."

In 1943 Marvin "Muktuk" Marston heard about the mountain of jade and got Ferguson to fly him in. Prospecting alone two days, Marston discovered an enormous nugget which greatly excited him.

"The Major was pretty husky then and in his joy over his discovery he didn't realize how much it weighed," Ferguson recounted. "The tundra was soft and marshy with clumps of growth scattered all around. Marston slipped and slogged along, stumbling over the clumps

for about four miles. When he reached Kobuk he was nearly all in.

"Finally he dragged himself to the store and post office run by Harry Brown. Someone took his picture with the jade strapped to his back. They put it on some scales and Marston nearly collapsed. The rock weighed 165 pounds.

"Marston was near exhausted when I flew in for him four hours later but we loaded the jade on the plane and went back to Kotzebue. I heard afterward the rock was cut up and distributed to service men."

Early samples taken near the top of the Jade Mountains had proved of inferior quality, but in 1944 the U.S. Bureau of Mines found gem-quality stones around Mauneluk River.

The following summer Russell Havenstrite, owner of Arctic Circle Exploration, flew Walt Disney and a couple of bankers into the Kobuk, but failed to interest them in backing a jade venture, and Ferguson transported 22 tons of nuggets to Seattle, only to discover they did not bring enough to cover shipping costs.

The problem was the same as encountered by Marston. Surface jade came in the form of boulders — many weighing 20 tons. Quality varied from rock to rock, and there was no way to assess quality without dragging mammoth rocks through 14 miles of marshy timberland to the riverbank, then shipping them down to Seattle for cutting.

Some prospectors did get lucky. Eskimos who gathered smaller nuggets from local streams to sell in Fairbanks met with modest success. In 1947 freelance writer George Van Hagen and friend Harry Coleman of Chicago shipped out a 728-pound nugget that apparently made a profit, and Arctic Circle Exploration made headlines in Seattle by reporting theft of $1 million worth of jade from their warehouse. The estimate was later pared to from $20,000 to $60,000, and the missing jade

TOP — *Jade is almost as hard as diamond and few local artists will carve it. An exception is Rob Martin who does painstaking work for his own pleasure. He says he can't compete with cheaper Oriental labor on a full-time basis —these are the end products of many months of work.*

ABOVE — *A jade mouse trap is just the thing for the man who has everything. This one was designed by Rob Martin of Aurora Arts and Crafts.*

recovered with no charges filed, but the press helped establish a market.

Then, in 1952, Ferguson, a son, and two partners introduced a portable wire saw with which they succeeded in cutting boulders in the field. It was a first, Ferguson boasted.

"In a single day we cut a four-inch slab weighing 400 pounds. Doing it the Eskimo way would have taken nine days."

He did not elaborate on the Eskimo way, but that, too, was changing. In 1954 the Bureau of Indian Affairs in conjunction with the Alaska Rural Development Board, established a jade workshop in the village of Shungnak, equipping the workshop with 14 diamond saws. A similar facility was planned for Noorvik in 1959, however neither venture was long lived.

Jade made headlines again in Seattle in 1965 when the Oceanic Trading Company discovered a lively market in China, but takeover by the Communist government soon closed the door on that trade.

Gene Joiner, who also staked claims in the Jade Mountains, succeeded in getting an order from Juan Peron for a nugget from which a lifesize statue might be carved in memory of the Argentine's wife, Eva, only to have the dictator topple from power before the jade could be shipped.

The 15-ton boulder languished for some years beside the Kotzebue airstrip until Joiner thought he had the interest of a Japanese firm and shipped it to them in Seattle. When that deal fell through, John Haley purchased the prize and sent it north once again.

NANA Corporation's logo is etched on a piece of jade from their mine.

Ira Stewart's jade operation at Dahl Creek. The long-time miner benefits from a large airstrip which nets him lots of visitors. His summer home is like a hotel, he says cheerfully, but he often puts visitors to work and everybody is happy. These photos were taken by Jon Osgood, safety investigator for the Department of Transportation who happened on the claim during a flying vacation and enjoyed Stewart's hospitality.

Haley, a double amputee who pioneered the jade business in Fairbanks in 1968 and sold out to retire in 1974, took his business back last year (1979) and is delighted to vindicate Joiner for his faith in the nugget.

"It's the best jade that's ever come through this shop," he declared. "We've already used a ton and a half of it."

Stubbornly, Joiner continued to seek markets abroad — often with little better results than his Argentine venture. Mining alone or with a small crew, he became known as the jade king of the Arctic until, in 1976, he sold his 22 claims to NANA, the Kobuk area regional corporation established under the federal Native Land Claims Settlement Act.

The new owners have expanded Joiner's operation under the name Jade Mountain Products, building a small airport and a bunkhouse called Bigfoot Lodge at the mountain site and a $700,000 facility at Kotzebue to cut and polish large boulders.

A seven-man crew spends its summers prying up the valuable nuggets, then takes advantage of early winter freezeup to sled raw jade over frozen marsh lands to the Kobuk River for shipment to Kotzebue the next spring.

Another substantial mining effort is that of Anchorage photo dealer Ivan Stewart who bought an operation at Dall Creek from bush pilot Bill Munz and staked a few claims himself. Stewart employs four men including himself in summer and encourages visitors to the spread. He markets in Anchorage under the name of Stewart's Jewel Jade Mine.

Also in Anchorage is Aurora Arts and Crafts started by Bob Martin who now works with his son, Rob, a talented carver.

Ray Heinrichs, formerly of B&R Tug and Barge in Kotzebue, pioneered German markets and hired German carvers to promote Kobuk holdings he bought from Charlie Sheldon and Joiner. He now manufactures and sells jade products under the name of Kobuk Valley Jade working out of Girdwood, in southcentral Alaska.

Kobuk jade is nephrite — sometimes called true jade — and it comes in a variety of colors.

The Jade Mountains are a small range 3,350 feet high, which have an odd grassy appear-

LEFT — *Pete Schaeffer at NANA's Jade Creek with a boulder that has been field cut to test its quality.*

BELOW — *NANA workmen cut jade in the field at Cabin Creek, below the summit of the Jade Mountains.*

UPPER RIGHT — *NANA's Jade Mountain Products maintains a jade factory in Kotzebue. Here workmen grapple with boulders that have been cut for finishing.*

RIGHT — *Because of the size of the boulders it must process, Jade Mountain Products jade factory is cavernous. Here workmen prepare to move a small boulder to a cutting saw.*

Artists for NANA Corporation utilize the green translucence of jade in the design of these relief carvings of an Eskimo woman fishing, 6"x6". The work was done in the Orient from Alaska designs.

ance because of serpentine gravel which covers their peaks and upper slopes. Numerous prospectors, both Eskimo and white, hold claims in these hills and jade-rich areas beyond them, but NANA's operation is the most extensive and its holdings form an impressive U-shaped block covering the two main peaks and encompassing Cabin and Jade creeks which are both well-littered with the valuable rock.

Al Adams, NANA stockholder who was recently elected to the state legislature, utilized Jade Mountain Products to build this stunning fireplace in his new home. His daughter Michelle perches on the jade hearth to do some reading just before bedtime.

The first waves of miners to the Kobuk cleaned the area of many small nuggets, but mammoth chunks of jade remain because early equipment was not powerful enough to handle them.

Today's on-site cutting techniques enable miners to select only the best material, and modern technology can handle from 50,000-to 75,000-pound nuggets with comparative ease.

The supply of boulders on the Jade Mountains is adequate to meet developing markets for many years to come, and many suspect this is only the beginning. Although the subsurface of the Jade Mountains has yet to be thoroughly tested, it could well contain the most spectacular load of nephrite of them all. □

NANA designers created this jade eagle which was carved in the Orient.

MINERALS: A MODERN RUSH

Mark McDermott

A geophysicist, formerly with the U.S. Bureau of Mines, Mark McDermott now searches for mineral deposits throughout the North for Anaconda Copper Company.

A warm summer day lay lightly on the Kobuk River valley. The gentle breeze that stirred the spruce and birch trees covering Pardners Hill kept the mosquito swarm out of Rinehart Berg's face, if not out of his consciousness. It was 1948, and Berg was wandering through the Cosmos Hills, doing what he liked to do best. Prospect. On this day, however, he was not one of those whom Robert Service described as "men who moil for gold," struck by the "taint of the gold-dust." It was a heavier metal Berg sought. The federal government, in the wake of the Manhattan Project and Hiroshima, realized that uranium was needed, and in great quantities, to fuel the infant Atomic Age. The government offered a ready and available market to prospectors throughout the United States and prospectors like Berg swarmed the hills during the late 1940s.

Berg carried a Geiger counter, and poked around the old gold workings on Pardners Hill, abandoned by miners heading for the gold fields at Nome. Riny hiked up nearby Ruby Creek, and soon found a spot that made his

Rinehart Berg's discovery in 1948 of a substantial copper ore deposit led eventually to establishment of Bornite Camp in the Cosmos Hills in the Kobuk valley.
Kit Marrs

Mining camps at Red Dog and Lik (shown here) in the DeLong Mountains have been set up to explore massive outcroppings of lead and zinc minerals that occur nearby. John Shively

Geiger counter sing. As he investigated the area he had little inkling that his discovery would lead him to be a millionare a decade later.

Soon after his discovery, Berg began to scrape away the tundra and surface muck from the radioactive spot. To his amazement, he found not the expected yellow or black coatings on the rocks that spoke of a buried uranium deposit. Instead, the rocks were coated with a bright blue-green crust. Malachite green. Copper.

For the next few years, Berg worked his prospect — alone at first, then later with the help of hired Eskimos. He got a grubstake from John S. Bullock, a Kotzebue merchant, and started digging exploration pits and trenches. It soon became obvious that a bulldozer was needed on the property, but the only one available in the country lay at the bottom of the sound near Kotzebue, where the machine had been lost from a barge in an acci-

dent years earlier. Berg and helpers raised the bulldozer, refurbished it, and drove it up to Bornite the next winter.

In 1956 Russ Chadwick, of Bear Creek Mining a subsidiary of Kennecott, headed to the Cosmos Hills to see the Ruby Creek deposit he had heard about. Berg and Chadwick hit it off immediately, and Bear Creek soon had an option on the property. Bear Creek began a large scale drilling operation, and during the following years drilled more than 150,000 feet of exploratory diamond drill holes and employed dozens of men.

In 1964 Kennecott was convinced they had a major ore body in the Bornite deposit at Ruby Creek, and purchased the property from Berg and Bullock — for $3 million. Berg took his share and generously rewarded those of his friends who had helped him through hard times in the past. The rest of the money went toward his passion, prospecting.

That same year Kennecott announced plans to sink a thousand-foot shaft to explore the deposit underground. About 2½ thousand tons of equipment and supplies would be moved into Bornite that summer; the shaft was to be started that fall. But the Bering Strait was late in breaking up that year, and then a drought kept the river so low that barges could barely navigate. By October 1964 the equipment had reached Onion Portage, south of the Jade Mountains, and could go no farther. The equipment sat there until winter, when a cat train hauled it the remaining miles to Bornite. A year later the shaft was begun, and neared completion in August 1966. But Kennecott was not yet through its streak of bad luck.

At lunch time on October 27, 1966, workers 1,076 feet below the surface of Ruby Creek climbed into the cage that would take them to the surface. When all the workers reached the surface for lunch, a small dynamite charge was set off at the shaft's bottom — a routine procedure in excavating the shaft. But, unknown to the men, that one charge ruptured the floor of the shaft, and tapped an aquifer. Water rushed in and filled the shaft at the rate of 15,000 gallons a minute.

After lunch the workmen got in the cage, closed the gate, and headed rapidly down the shaft. Partway down they were tipped off by pumps gushing muddy water on one of the side levels, and they shone their light downward to see the cold dark waters rushing up to meet them. They frantically signaled the hoist operator, who managed to stop the cage in time. By nightfall the thousand-foot shaft was full of water. Although the shaft was pumped out and work continued for a few more months, the momentum was broken, and before long the Bornite Project languished.

In the decade that Kennecott worked actively on the Bornite deposit, from 1956 to 1966, the company initiated a major geochemical sampling program to find other deposits. Flying in old Bell helicopters, often without any base maps, Kennecott personnel sampled stream sediments throughout the western Brooks Range and analyzed mud for its metal content. Thousands of samples, when plotted on maps, indicated which drainages might have metal deposits upstream. Ironically, the Red Dog/Lik lead-zinc district was evident in the data, but because Kennecott was only interested in copper deposits at the time, the Red Dog deposit would wait another decade for discovery.

In 1968 Kennecott's regional program paid off. The Arctic deposit was discovered 15 miles northeast of Bornite in the Schwatka Mountains. Other deposits began to be discovered within the area, and it was soon obvious that a major copper-lead-zinc district was being defined. Arctic, Sun, Smucker — one after another major metal deposits were located in volcanic rocks trending east to west across the southern foothills of the Schwatka Mountains.

In 1973 only Kennecott and Sunshine Mining Co. had claims in the area, but things were about to happen quickly. Riz Bigelow and Dick Walters had worked for Kennecott in its heyday at Bornite. By 1973 both men had left, Walters heading Sunshine's exploration efforts in the western Brooks Range, and Bigelow working for WGM, Inc., a geological consulting firm. In early winter 1973 Walters flew to the Kobuk valley to move fuel for the coming field season. He found three helicopters flying staking crews up and down the mineral belt. In Walters' words, "It soon became apparent that it was their intention to stake the entire mineral belt." Bigelow, from his days with Kennecott, knew the potential of the area and was staking claims for Noranda LTD. Walters knew the ground as well — he had worked in the same area with Kennecott for years. Now, in late 1973, the two men slugged it out in the biggest staking war Alaska had ever seen. Both men knew the area, both knew what was at stake.

Throughout the winter of 1973-1974, helicopters flew crews up and down the Kobuk valley. In six months nearly 6,000 claims were staked. When the dust settled, Sunshine Mining Co. came out in a better position, because their staff could follow up on a regional geochemical survey completed in summer 1973. By the end of the 1975 season, WGM, Noranda, Anaconda Copper Co., Sunshine, and Kennecott had staked over 10,000 claims, and literally covered the Ambler District from one end to the other — a total of 300 square miles.

Activity in the district had barely died down when in 1970 Irv Trailleur, with the U.S. Geological Survey, landed at Red Dog Creek in the DeLong Mountains. Trailleur noticed several of the tributaries and parts of the creek were rust-stained, but he stayed only long enough to take a few samples. Had he hiked the creek, he would have come up on an area

Anaconda geophysicist Perry Eaton studies malachite-stained (copper) rocks in the Ambler River area. Mark McDermott

On the shores of a tundra lake in the Shungnak River valley sits Anaconda Copper's Shungnak exploration camp, a base from which geologists search for copper-lead-zinc deposits.
Mark McDermott

is in its infancy there, and the area has just begun to be evaluated.

Since Riny Berg hiked up Ruby Creek in 1948, over $100 million, and perhaps as much as $250 million, has been spent exploring the region to assess its mineral potential. Berg and Bullock's $3 million payment for the Ruby Creek deposit begins to pale in comparison to the mineral wealth that is yet to be realized from Kotzebue Basin. ☐

Sunlight obscures the top of an Anaconda drill rig in the Ambler River area. In the early and mid-1970s mining companies competed with one another in a rush to stake much of the Ambler District. By the end of the 1975 season more than 10,000 claims covering the Ambler District from one end to the other — a total of 300 square miles — had been staked.
Mark McDermott

where Red Dog Creek flowed over 100 feet of outcropping massive sulfides. Sphalerite and galena, the main ores of lead and zinc, were there in incredible abundance, exposed right at the surface. U.S. Geological Survey reports in 1975 started another claim-staking rush, led by Cominco-American Ltd., and WGM, Inc., for Houston Oil & Mineral Co. Two entirely new districts have since been defined — Lik/Red Dog; Drenchwater Creek, and others, a string of carbonate and shale-hosted lead-zinc deposits stretching more than 100 miles from Noatak National Preserve into National Petroleum Reserve-Alaska (NRP-A).

Mineral exploration in the districts has to deal with land withdrawals, changes of land status, and overlapping state, Native, and federal land claims. The Ambler District is situated in a window, completely surrounded by national interest lands. In fact, it was the publicity and efforts of the mining companies involved that kept the district open to exploration and possible future development.

Access to the districts is the key stumbling block to development at this time. Several proposals, including a rail or road link to the trans-Alaska pipeline corridor or Nome, have been suggested. Some of the more unusual options are flying the ore concentrate out in 747 cargo jets, or transporting the ore by hovercraft.

The Ambler District alone is estimated to contain $9 billion worth of copper, lead, zinc, silver, and gold at 1980 prices. The worth of Bornite, Red Dog and Lik can only be guessed at, but is certainly well in the billions of dollars. Tens of billions of dollars in metals lies buried beneath the lichen-covered hills of the DeLong and Schwatka mountains. Exploration

TRANSPORTATION

Although it was dangerous to venture out of known territory in early Eskimo times, Natives of the Kotzebue region apparently ventured widely, going as far west as Siberia, east into Canada, north to the arctic coast and south as far as their warring Indian neighbors would allow.

They traveled mainly by water; paddling large, open skin boats for long ocean voyages, whaling expeditions, or to attend trade fairs; and light kayaks for solitary endeavors like seal hunting and trips where portages were required.

Eskimos of the interior often fashioned canoes of birch bark caulked with pitch, and snowshoes were long used to cope with deep winter snow.

While archaeologists have found few signs of dog bones in their earliest digs and the first explorers failed to mention the animals, dog traction apparently came into wide use in the 1700s, and the size of teams increased as Eskimo drivers became more experienced. By the mid-19th century outsiders often remarked on large Eskimo canine populations, the howling of which could be heard for many miles over tundra and sea. The animals gave notice of invasion, and pulled sleds and boats.

The majority of researchers say sailing techniques utilized by Eskimos for their skin boats were introduced by outsiders who explored their coasts, but wind power was well on its way to replacement by steam when

the Kotzebue area was officially mapped and charted.

Handicapped by shallow seas, large vessels have always had to anchor off Cape Blossom, and passengers and freight have had to be lightered in with shallow-draft vessels. The early history of settlement is fraught with harrowing tales of wrecked barges and supplies lost in angry surf.

Before the turn of the century, few ships appeared on this coast except for whaling vessels bound for the high Arctic. The gold rush of 1898 briefly improved transport to the area, however, according to Alice Cook, a writer working with journals of Captain B.

A skin boat frame is loaded on a sled to be hauled 35 to 45 miles northwest of Kotzebue to Sealing Point about 1914. Natives caught seals and prepared seal oil each spring at the point.
Nichols Collection, Courtesy of Mark Ocker

Cogan. The captain, an enterprising whaler, formed Kotzebue Sound Mining and Trading Company and, with a couple of partners, purchased three old sailing barks and materials to build a stream launch, then began advertising transport to "Kotzebue Sound Country, the New Alaska Gold Field," at $200 per head.

The company's maiden voyage was made with the *Northern Lights* and the *Alaska.*

Water transportation was extremely important to early pioneers and Natives in the region. This photo, taken about 1913, shows a variety of barges and skin boats clustered together near Kotzebue. Nichols Collection, Courtesy of Mark Ocker

Stopping at Saint Lawrence Island en route, Cogan, with the help of passengers and crew, built the steam launch *John Reilly* which was destined to become the most famous boat of the era. On launching at Kotzebue Sound with 150 tons of freight from the deeper-draft *Northern Lights*, the *Reilly* went aground on a bar. According to passenger W. Alston Hayne, Jr. (whose correspondence has been compiled by his son and editor Alice Cook), the boat "stuck fast on a bar at the mouth of Hotham Inlet and remained there 24 hours despite all efforts to get her off. If a storm had come up she would have been lost."

But the *Reilly* survived to become stuck on numerous other bars. The winter of 1898-1899 the *Reilly* was frozen in on the Kobuk River and not expected to survive, but emerged to go on to glory. That spring hundreds of discouraged, sick and dying miners came downriver seeking passage outside, but one crew of five, led by Lewis "Chip" Lloyd, came out with a poke of gold and backed by John

Tallart, "a wily banker," hired the *Reilly* to take them and their supplies back to the gold fields.

Passengers not in on the discovery were kicked off the boat, and one named Brown quickly chartered prospector Sam Pepper's launch, *The Delight,* and followed the *Reilly* in hot pursuit. The *Reilly* gang outmaneuvered them, however, and seems to have been the only group that really struck paydirt in a big way.

Other well-known vessels of this era were the *Grace Dollar* which had the record time of 16 days from Kotzebue to San Francisco, and the *Penelope* owned by a group of Quaker miners which included naturalist Joseph Grinnell who later wrote about his prospects — both for birds and gold.

Probably the first regularly scheduled transport to the Arctic was that of Pacific Steam Whaling Company which established a base at Point Hope and other areas to the north in the mid-1880s and continued to operate for a decade; however this transport was apparently open only to whalers.

Early missionaries were usually forced to charter from Nome. About 1905 the Bureau of Education began to supply the sound on a regular basis, establishing a precedent that continues to this day with the annual sailing of the Bureau of Indian Affairs supply ship *North Star III*, although complaints of the government-subsidized service have long come from the private sector.

Regular mail service, instituted at the turn of the century, depended on government boats. Local dog mushers were contracted for inland delivery during the winter.

Advocates of the reindeer industry publicized mail delivery by sled deer but the public relations stunt was apparently abandoned

In 1945 Archie Ferguson, first to establish a major lighterage service in Kotzebue Basin, had the Kotzebue *built as his mail boat. However in 1951 the vessel got caught in the ice seven miles southwest of Kotzebue and was carried north with breakup of the ice the following spring.* Edith Bullock

BELOW — *Birch bark canoes traditionally provided water transportation for Eskimos and whites living on rivers or lakes. Willie Goodwin paddles this canoe at Onion Portage on the Kobuk in 1966. Mark Cleveland built the boat for Brown University's archaeological museum.*
Ken Ross

RIGHT — *Small planes, such as this one from Ambler Air Service, and dog teams enable Kotzebue Basin residents to reach even the most remote sites. Because of rising gas prices for snow machines, dog teams are regaining their traditional role in bush transportation.*
Anore Jones

after just a few runs because dogs had more endurance.

Frank Churchill investigated the reindeer industry on behalf of Congress in 1906, and outlined the economics of the mail business as well.

"Mr. Thomas (the Kotzebue Friends Church missionary) operates the mail route in the name of Albert S. Nilima (the Lapland reindeer herder) from Kotzebue to Shungnak, a distance of 150 miles, making five round trips for which he received $150 a trip. Thomas hires natives to carry this mail for $30 for each of the first two trips and $100 for each of the last three, by which it is observed that Mr. Thomas is also a very thrifty man."

In the mid-1920s Noel Wein started a flying service at Nome and shortly thereafter pioneered flights to the Kotzebue area. Archie Ferguson, one of his first passengers, was so enthusiastic about the new mode of transport that five years later he bought a Great Lakes Trainer for $4,000 plus $1,000 shipping, hired Chet Brown to teach him to fly, and started Ferguson Airways with his brother Warren. Many Selawik people recall Ferguson's as the first plane they ever saw and ultimately they named their airstrip in his honor.

Rival pilot was John Cross, a veteran of the Air Services Signal Corps who had flown with Jimmy Doolittle in Kansas City, then came north piloting first for Cordova Air Service, then Wien and trader Boris Magids out of Deering.

Later he built his own airline, pioneering a route from Kotzebue to Barrow, but duty in the Air Force during World War II interrupted the business.

Only recently retired with 21,300 flying hours logged to his credit, he keeps his radio on to listen for flight reports from son Milt who flies both helicopter and conventional fixed wing aircraft for the Kotzebue National Guard and for NANA Corporation. Three other Cross boys also fly, one commercially.

The first Eskimo to pick up flying skills was wolf-and-bounty-hunter Bert Beltz. His brother Johnny also became a well-known pilot. Friends recall Johnny flew for some years without a license because he feared he could not pass the FAA physical due to a bad back. Finally he had an accident which the FAA investigated and, to their credit, inspectors cleared his paperwork and allowed him to fly.

175

ABOVE — *In 1951 Louis Rotman and John Bullock formed B&R Tug and Barge to provide lighterage and marine freight services at Kotzebue. In 1975 the company was sold to Crowley Maritime which, as Arctic Lighterage, operates modern facilities including the barge, vans, and crane shown here.* Penny Rennick

LEFT — *River ice still clogs the Kobuk a few days before breakup as this bush family unloads their sled from their boat at spring camp.* Anore Jones

Other pioneers of the era were Holger Jorgenson, Art Johnson and Tom Richards, Sr., the first Eskimo to hold a commercial license and still in the cockpit for Wien.

Archie Ferguson was the first to establish a substantial lighterage service in the Kotzebue region, and in 1945 he built a 70-foot steel vessel named the *Kotzebue* to fulfill his mail contracts. In mid-November 1951 the vessel froze in the sound seven miles southwest of Kotzebue. Passengers and a barge of drummed petroleum products were saved, but the ship was carried north by ice the following spring and vanished.

In 1951 Louis Rotman, in partnership with John Bullock, formed B&R Tug and Barge to provide lighterage and marine freight services, and to act as wholesale distributor for Standard Oil of California. Rotman sold out a year later to Bullock's wife, Edith, and the company was incorporated in 1956 with stock divided equally between husband and wife except for minor holdings of Alice C. Connolly, head nurse at the Bureau of Indian Affairs Hospital, and Charles P. McGowan, FAA manager for Kotzebue.

The firm prospered, building the first docking facilities in Kotzebue and investing heavily in land, buildings, equipment and warehouses for its shore base. Soon the company contracted with the federal government to deliver to its installations along the arctic coast which had formerly been supplied by the Navy; then B&R moved into international waters during the Vietnam War.

Ultimately the company overextended and was bought in 1975 by Crowley Maritime which operates it today with a modern fleet of barges.

A two-mile state highway passes through downtown Kotzebue, and local vehicles run the gamut from speedy motorcycles to sedate early Plymouths. Penny Rennick

Problems in servicing the area remain basically the same as they have always been, however, in that the shipping season is extremely short, the sound and river network extremely shallow, no connecting roads exist, and all freight not waterborne must be shipped by air.

Regularly scheduled flight services connect Kotzebue to the rest of the nation, and the area is currently served by two major carriers and numerous bush operations. Village runways are being extended and many have lights for night landings, but bush flying in the Arctic still hinges on the weather and remains very expensive.

As for the future, it is uncertain at best. The state highway department's plans to connect Kotzebue Sound to the rest of the state have not been well received locally, although a road recently connected the isolated village of Kobuk with Bornite mining operations and a similar project is slated for Ambler.

Large federal and Native land selections pose right-of-way problems in the future, however, which may hamper development. □

HOPES OF A NATIVE SON

Willie Hensley was reared by traditional Eskimo grandparents who lived about ten miles from Kotzebue, migrating seasonally to hunt, trap muskrats, and fish on the Noatak delta. In summer they lived in tents, in winter, sod houses; a hard existence but, for the most part, a happy one.

When, occasionally, the family moved into town for a month or so, young Willie tried grade school and, despite the fact his attendance was spasmodic, he proved an exceptional student. Ultimately a Baptist minister who befriended him, got him to Harrison-Chilhowee Baptist Academy in Tennessee where he made first string football despite his light frame, did well in school theatricals, and became president of his class.

Later he attended University of Alaska, picked up a political science degree with a major in economics at George Washington University, Washington, D.C., and made a trip to Poland and Russia with the Experiment in International Living program.

Elected to the state House of Representatives in 1966, he introduced the topic of Native land ownership at a meeting of the Juneau Democratic Club in the cramped basement dining room of a musty hotel. Reading from a term paper, "What Rights to Land Have the Alaska Natives?," which he had written for a law course he had taken from Alaska Justice Jay Rabinowitz, he made a strong case that his forebears had never relinquished title — never lost any wars or signed any treaties — and went on to persuade fellow legislators to pass a bill honoring the concept, and giving the Native movement state backing.

He was a strong voice in organizing the Alaska Federation of Natives (AFN) and — with his cousin, John Schaeffer, and Robert Newlin from neighboring Noorvik — founded the Northwest Alaska Native Association (NANA) which functions today as his area's regional corporation.

Hensley lobbied Congress actively for passage of the Alaska Native Land Claims Settlement Act and worked with equal enthusiasm to win precedent-breaking concessions for his people in the Alaska lands bill. After losing a bid for U.S. House of Representatives, he helped organize the first Native-owned bank in the state — one of the fastest growing financial institutions in Alaska — and serves as president of its board. In 1980 he won an award for public service through the Rockefeller Foundation.

Yet despite this astonishing record of wins, or, perhaps because of it, Hensley has recently come to question the success with which his people will be able to maintain their cultures.

Willie Hensley was reared by traditional Eskimo grandparents and went on to become a leader in Native affairs throughout the state. Today Hensley is chairman of the board of United Bank Alaska.   Lael Morgan, staff

As keynote speaker for the ninth AFN Convention (1980), he spoke with concern for the retention of cultural identity, and voiced a fear shared by a growing number of Native leaders that although their movement has won most of its economic and political battles, it may ultimately lose the war of spirit.

"We've come a long way since 1966," Hensley reflected, "but as I view the situation, there has been a great deal of confusion as to what's happened to us. We were able to make

In a joint venture, NANA Corporation had built two oil rigs, the first in the state built by Alaskans. Here Willie Hensley (in three-piece suit) dances with NANA board members Vince Schuerch and Christine Westlake and with NANA dancers to dedicate the rig at a party in Anchorage.   Lael Morgan, staff

significant advances, simply because we put aside our cultural and historical differences and were able to move together in unity.

"Although we've had a major influence on Alaska — on how it is now and how it's going to be in the future — there's a great deal of confusion as to what we have created. I think there are many people — many of our own people — who do not understand why we fought so hard for the land.

"Basically, we did not fight for the land because it represented capital, or because it represented money, or because it represented business opportunities. We fought for the land because it represents the spirit of our people.

"What happened in the Land Claims Settlement Act should be understood if our main objective of survival is to be achieved. What I mean by survival is not just political survival or economic survival. I'm talking about survival of our tribal spirit, of our languages, our

culture, our self-respect. We should not be confused. The Settlement Act must be analyzed in light of two hundred years of American history — the end product of an effort to de-Indianize the Native population. The land which represents our spiritual homeland now rests in the corporation — a soulless entity that is designed for commercial purposes.

"We cannot look to corporate life or politics to fill the void of a century of psychological repression. Business and politics are not an

end. They are simply a means to the primary task of tribal renewal and survival. Our people have been misled to believe that to be an Inupiat or Yup'ik or Indian or Aleut is incompatible with successful survival in the modern world and this is a fallacy."

Painfully, Hensley traced the massive changes through which his people have gone since the Russian invasion in 1742; the coming of the whalers and miners with the destructive introduction of alcohol, the impacts of two world wars, highway and road construction, the influx of newcomers and with them the pressure for conformity to the standards of others.

"The fact is, Alaska's Native people — just as the Indian people in the 'lower 48' — have fought the same tide of assimilation, acculturation, individualization, and atomization," Hensley said. "This process has taken a toll on our spirit, on our identity, on our language and on our culture. We have alcoholism and drugs, dropouts, family breakup and crime in our communities because of the pressures we've had on us. We've almost lost the willpower to reassert our tribal identity and reconstitute our languages which are the expression of our spirit and who we are inside."

Hensley called upon the delegates to help rebuild their societies and focused on education as the place to start.

"Education has been viewed as the panacea — as a cure-all for Native people — but it also has been used by the government, in conjunction with religious groups, as the means of deculturizing our people," he charged.

"Our misled missionaries of education have been drumming into all our people the idea that you could not remain an Eskimo or Indian and still be educated. It is not true, and we should put to rest the thought that Native people are inherently ignorant. . . . I'm not saying that we should not be educated. Education is essential. . . . But we cannot continue to educate our children at the expense of their identity as Inupiat or Yup'ik or Indian or Aleut people."

Optimistically, Hensley pointed out that Native people have all the elements for successful future survival; a land base, capital, and some fairly experienced managers and politicians. But he suggested each group must develop a regional program to revive language and spirit of their people. Among stateside Indians, language and spirit are the concerns of tribal councils, he explained, but Alaskans have none.

"Unfortunately, our leadership has been confronted and had to deal almost entirely with only one aspect of the problem, and that is the economic aspect. The language of the Settlement Act which our leadership negotiated is dominated by economic considerations. It would be easy to be deceived and think that's what the act is all about. We have to realize that economics is only the surface, and that the hope for many other aspects of our culture and our identity are also in the Settlement Act."

This legislation, which is a monument to capitalistic thinking, directed Native groups to form 13 profit-making corporations with tribal members as stockholders. Land and money from the settlement (about $1 billion and 40 million acres of land) were vested in these business entities, and profits from them are to go to stockholders, just as would be the case with any major corporation like Coca Cola or IBM. And, just as in other corporations, these businesses are not allowed to squander money on cultural functions or social services, for if they do they are open to stockholder suit for unwise investment of capital.

Yet, while the majority of corporations have had trouble enough organizing to get a toehold in the business world, some have managed to concern themselves with social and cultural stockholder problems and still adhere to sound business practice.

Hensley's regional, NANA, has been among the foremost. Happily, most of its stockholders — even some younger than Hensley — once lived traditionally, and appreciate what was valuable in their past.

Early, the NANA board of directors passed a resolution stating priority for matters of cultural heritage preservation. The company has invested heavily in ventures that will employ stockholders on home ground. And often board meetings are scheduled to coincide with cultural events so that the travel budget can cover both economic and socio-cultural concerns at the same time.

An additional asset is the fact that NANA's villagers all speak the same language — not the case in many other regional corporations — and travel and communications are easier here than in other areas. The ties of family link many villages and a genuine concern for neighbors remains.

There is, of course, no turning back the clock. Changes have been coming fast, and will continue to assail old traditions. But the unique cohesiveness of the area serves, yet, to give Hensley and his fellow Inupiat hope that the best of their culture may remain intact. ☐

BELOW — *Residents of Noorvik gather for the first NANA stockholders meeting in 1974. Their village — pictured on the following pages — is the third largest village in the NANA region and was settled in 1915 by Eskimos from Deering. At the Alaska Federation of Natives convention in Anchorage in 1980, Willie Hensley urged Alaska Natives to remember the value of the land. "We fought for the land because it represents the spirit of our people," said Hensley.*

Below — Lael Morgan, staff; Overleaf — John and Margaret Ibbotson

Maniilaq's Vision

The coming of outsiders to northwest Alaska was no surprise to local Inupiat for around the turn of the 19th century a number of Eskimos, including the gifted seer, Maniilaq (also written Maniilauraq) had foretold it.

A new race, white men, would come into their land, Maniilaq said, and they would prove a mixed blessing. Some Inupiat would be made rich by them, others poor; and amazing changes would follow.

In the future, according to Maniilaq, it would be possible to travel upriver in a boat with ease without having to use a pull rope or paddle. Men would fly through the sky on iron sleds and speak through the air over long distances. Man would write on thin birch bark and a new kind of clothing would be introduced.

Maniilaq was born on the upper reaches of the Kobuk and it is not certain whether he was named for the mountains and river of his region, or they for him. He married a Noatak woman, and they had three children; sons Uqquutaq and Itluun and a girl whose name is not remembered. They lived for many years at the mouth of the Ambler River but like most of their contemporaries, the family traveled widely, following the game in season and going on long trading expeditions.

Unlike his peers, however, Maniilaq sought to introduce a new way of life, and took advantage of his travels to teach. He seems to have been an innovative thinker, and his philosophy was remarkably like that of Christian missionaries who were soon to follow in his wake.

Maniilaq's knowledge came not from himself, he claimed modestly, but from his father who lived in the sky and dressed in white. He was said to have counted the days and rested every seventh day, and to have encouraged the taking of a week during the Christmas season for rest and celebration.

To further distinguish himself, the prophet carried a pole or staff called a *napaqsraq* which he planted wherever he settled. Some recall the *napaqsraq* bore a flag on the day of rest, and when its owner was thinking and did not wish to be disturbed.

Early, Maniilaq was ridiculed for his seemingly impossible predictions, however time often bore him out and he began to acquire a following.

In his day, shamanism had a strong hold on the Inupiat. Maniilaq went out of his way to challenge its taboos, proving them false, and undercutting local witch doctors who demanded large offerings of food and furs in exchange for their prowess in grappling with evil.

One widely held fear was that if a person cut and tanned a caribou skin during fishing season he would die. Maniilaq deliberately broke this rule and survived, and also ate beluga meat with berries or roots without ill

The last boat in before freezeup breaks through the Kotzebue Sound ice. Lael Morgan, staff

effects, although this mixing of sea and land foods was likewise deemed lethal.

He predicted an end to the cruel belief that expectant mothers be isolated in snow houses to deliver their own babies, and similar taboos against young girls who were put away for a year and subjected to great hardship at the beginning of puberty. These practices would be ended when the *Iivaqsaat* or white people brought the gospel to the Natives, he said.

Vindictive medicine men naturally tried to kill him, but it was said that Maniilaq's soul was too bright to look at and that they could never harm him.

The fate of the prophet remains a mystery. Old-timers recall that his wife died at Sisualik and Maniilaq, himself, was last seen headed for the north slope to spread his message. Some say he died at Demarcation Point near Barter Island and that descendents of the adopted children of his son, Itluun, still live in that area.

The name lives on, not only in the memory of the old and with an adopted line, but in the minds of planners, for two of Maniilaq's predictions have yet to be fulfilled. One is that the village of Ambler will become an enormous city, and the second is that there will be two winters together with snow up to the treetops, followed by a spring breakup that will flood to the shoulders of the tallest mountains. A rich legacy of copper and other minerals near Ambler may, indeed, make the first prediction feasible, and those who believe the second are keeping a leery eye on the weather. □

A setting sun in March at Selawik brings promise of another day in Kotzebue Basin.
Barb Askey

ALASKA GEOGRAPHIC® Back Issues

The North Slope, Vol. 1, No. 1. Charter issue of *ALASKA GEOGRAPHIC*. Out of print.

One Man's Wilderness, Vol. 1, No. 2. The story of a dream shared by many, fulfilled by few: a man goes into the bush, builds a cabin and shares his incredible wilderness experience. Color photos. 116 pages, $7.95

Admiralty . . . Island in Contention, Vol. 1, No. 3. An intimate and multifaceted view of Admiralty: its geological and historical past, its present-day geography, wildlife and sparse human population. Color photos. 78 pages, $5.00

Fisheries of the North Pacific: History, Species, Gear & Processes, Vol. 1, No. 4. Out of print.

The Alaska-Yukon Wild Flowers Guide, Vol. 2, No. 1. First Northland flower book with both large, color photos and detailed drawings of every species described. Features 160 species, common and scientific names and growing height. 112 pages, $10.95

Richard Harrington's Yukon, Vol. 2, No. 2. Out of print.

Prince William Sound, Vol. 2, No. 3. Out of print.

Yakutat: The Turbulent Crescent, Vol. 2, No. 4. Out of print.

Glacier Bay: Old Ice, New Land, Vol. 3, No. 1. The expansive wilderness of Southeastern Alaska's Glacier Bay National Monument unfolds in crisp text and color photographs. Records the flora and fauna of the area, its natural history, with hike and cruise information, plus a large-scale color map. 132 pages, $9.95

The Land: Eye of the Storm, Vol. 3, No. 2. Out of print.

Richard Harrington's Antarctic, Vol. 3, No. 3. The Canadian photojournalist guides readers through remote and little understood regions of the Antarctic and Subantarctic. More than 200 color photos and a large fold-out map. 104 pages, $8.95

The Silver Years of the Alaska Canned Salmon Industry: An Album of Historical Photos, Vol. 3, No. 4. Out of print.

Alaska's Volcanoes: Northern Link in the Ring of Fire, Vol. 4, No. 1. Scientific overview supplemented with eyewitness accounts of Alaska's historic volcano eruptions. Includes color and black- and-white photos and a schematic description of the effects of plate movement upon volcanic activity. 88 pages, $7.95

The Brooks Range: Environmental Watershed, Vol. 4, No. 2. Out of print.

Kodiak: Island of Change, Vol. 4, No. 3. Out of print.

Wilderness Proposals: Which Way for Alaska's Lands?, Vol. 4, No. 4. Out of print.

Cook Inlet Country, Vol. 5, No. 1. A visual tour of the region — its communities, big and small, and its countryside. Begins at the southern tip of the Kenai Peninsula, circles Turnagain Arm and Knik Arm for a close-up view of Anchorage, and visits the Matanuska and Susitna valleys and the wild, west side of the inlet. 230 color photos, separate map. 144 pages, $9.95

Southeast: Alaska's Panhandle, Vol. 5, No. 2. Explores Southeastern Alaska's maze of fjords and islands, mossy forests and glacier-draped mountains — from Dixon Entrance to Icy Bay, including all of the state's fabled Inside Passage. Along the way are profiles of every town, together with a look at the region's history, economy, people, attractions and future. Includes large fold-out map and seven area maps. 192 pages, $12.95.

Bristol Bay Basin, Vol. 5, No. 3. Explores the land and the people of the region known to many as the commercial salmon-fishing capital of Alaska. Illustrated with contemporary color and historic black-and-white photos. Includes a large fold-out map of the region. 96 pages, $9.95.

Alaska Whales and Whaling, Vol. 5, No. 4. The wonders of whales in Alaska — their life cycles, travels and travails — are examined, with an authoritative history of commercial and subsistence whaling in the North. Includes a fold-out poster of 14 major whale species in Alaska in perspective, color photos and illustrations, with historical photos and line drawings. 144 pages, $9.95.

Yukon-Kuskokwim Delta, Vol. 6, No. 1. Out of print.

Aurora Borealis: The Amazing Northern Lights, Vol. 6, No. 2. The northern lights — in ancient times seen as a dreadful forecast of doom, in modern days an inspiration to countless poets. Here one of the world's leading experts — Dr. S.-I. Akasofu of the University of Alaska — explains in an easily understood manner, aided by many diagrams and spectacular color and black-and-white photos, what causes the aurora, how it works, how and why scientists are studying it today and its implications for our future. 96 pages, $7.95.

Alaska's Native People, Vol. 6, No. 3. In the largest edition to date — result of several years of research — the editors examine the varied worlds of the Inupiat Eskimo, Yup'ik Eskimo, Athabascan, Aleut, Tlingit, Haida and Tsimshian. Most photos are by Lael Morgan, *ALASKA* magazine's roving editor, who since 1974 has been gathering impressions and images from virtually every Native village in Alaska. Included are sensitive, informative articles by Native writers, plus a large, four-color map detailing the Native villages and defining the language areas. 304 pages, $19.95.

The Stikine, Vol. 6, No 4. River route to three Canadian gold strikes in the 1800s, the Stikine is the largest and most navigable of several rivers that flow from northwestern Canada through Southeastern Alaska on their way to the sea. This edition explores 400 miles of Stikine wilderness, recounts the river's paddlewheel past and looks into the future, wondering if the Stikine will survive as one of the North's great free-flowing rivers. Illustrated with contemporary color photos and historic black-and-white; includes a large fold-out map. 96 pages, $9.95.

Alaska's Great Interior, Vol. 7, No. 1. Alaska's rich Interior country, west from the Alaska-Yukon Territory border and including the huge drainage between the Alaska Range and the Brooks Range, is covered thoroughly. Included are the region's people, communities, history, economy, wilderness areas and wildlife. Illustrated with contemporary color and black-and-white photos. Includes a large fold-out map. 128 pages, $9.95.

A Photographic Geography of Alaska, Vol. 7, No. 2. An overview of the entire state — a visual tour through the six regions of Alaska: Southeast, Southcentral/Gulf Coast, Alaska Peninsula and Aleutians, Bering Sea Coast, Arctic and Interior. Plus a handy appendix of valuable information — "Facts About Alaska." Approximately 160 color and black-and-white photos and 35 maps. 192 pages, $14.95.

The Aleutians, Vol. 7, No. 3. The fog-shrouded Aleutians are many things — home of the Aleut, a tremendous wildlife spectacle, a major World War II battleground and now the heart of a thriving new commercial fishing industry. Roving editor Lael Morgan contributes most of the text; also included are contemporary color and black-and-white photographs, and a large fold-out map. 224 pages, $14.95.

Klondike Lost: A Decade of Photographs by Kinsey & Kinsey, Vol. 7, No. 4. An album of rare photographs and all-new text about the lost Klondike boom town of Grand Forks, second in size only to Dawson during the gold rush. Introduction by noted historian Pierre Berton: 138 pages, area maps and more than 100 historical photos, most never before published. $12.95.

Wrangell-Saint Elias, Vol. 8, No. 1. Mountains, including the continent's second- and fourth-highest peaks, dominate this international wilderness that sweeps from the Wrangell Mountains in Alaska to the southern Saint Elias range in Canada. The region draws backpackers, mountain climbers, and miners, and is home for a few hardy, year-round inhabitants. Illustrated with contemporary color and historical black-and-white photographs. Includes a large fold-out map. $9.95.

Alaska Mammals, Vol. 8, No. 2. From tiny ground squirrels to the powerful polar bear, and from the tundra hare to the magnificent whales inhabiting Alaska's waters, this volume includes 80 species of mammals found in Alaska. Included are beautiful color photographs and personal accounts of wildlife encounters. *The* book on Alaska's mammals — from Southeast to the Arctic, and beyond! $12.95.

COMING ATTRACTION

Alaska National Interest Lands, Vol. 8, No. 4. Following passage of the bill formalizing Alaska's national interest land selections (d-2 lands), longtime Alaskans Celia Hunter and Ginny Wood review each selection, outlining location, size, access, and briefly describing the region's special attractions. Illustrated with contemporary color photographs depicting as no other medium can the grandeur of Alaska's national interest lands. To members November 1981. Price to be announced.

Your $30.00 membership in The Alaska Geographic Society includes 4 subsequent issues of *ALASKA GEOGRAPHIC*, the Society's official quarterly. Please add $4 for non-U.S. membership.

Additional membership information available upon request. Single copies of the *ALASKA GEOGRAPHIC* back issues available, per listing here. When ordering please add $1 postage/handling per copy. To order back issues send your check or money order and volumes desired to:

The Alaska Geographic Society

Box 4-EEE, Anchorage, Alaska 99509